A Single Desperate Prayer

a memoir

LUDMILA RITZ

A Single Desperate Prayer
Copyright © 2019 Ludmila Ritz
All Rights Reserved.
This book or any portion thereof may not be reproduced or used in any manner without written permission of the copyright owner except for the use of brief quotations in a book review.
First Edition, 2019
ISBN: 9781070781853

Book Design by Jane Dixon-Smith
Edited by Melissa J. Hayes
Printed in United States of America
www.ludmilaritz.com

I would like to dedicate this book to all of the kind and loving souls who have helped me along the way to become the person I am today.

If it weren't for your kindness, compassion, and light, I would have known only darkness.

Keep paying it forward, for one day, another soul will be saved.

Furthermore, I would like to dedicate this book to Jesus Christ, and The Divine Source, for helping me to recognize and follow the light amid all the darkness.

Thank you, all.
Peace and blessings to you!

Chapter 1

Just the Two of Us

I spent a lot of time constantly wondering why I was here, in this hell of a place—at least, that's how it felt for a while. I was pretty much vulnerable and exposed, with nothing to grip on to. It was like living in a black hole with no options or possibilities, just fear, hunger, and emptiness.

It was just the two of us—Mom and I—but most of the time it was just me, myself, and I. Everyone else was gone. They'd either died, or left. Like my grandparents, who passed away before I could meet them, or my father and older sister, Victoria, who had left and never looked back.

So that left me and Mom.

Mom was young, about twenty-four, and boy, she was trouble. She was wild—a "free spirit," as some might say. But she was not the happiest person. Underneath all of that negativity and depression, though, was a kind, genuine being who once loved, had a family, a job, and a stable home.

After Mom lost her parents, she also lost a daughter and a husband, while I lost a father and a sister, who left us for good. I was too young to give a damn, but Mom was very much aware of the pain, betrayal, and loneliness she felt. I was about two when they left, so

I only cared about three things—food, love, and affection—none of which I got.

Mom was broken before I came into this world, and after I arrived she was even more broken, which made her less interested in me and more interested in trying to remedy her feelings and everything she had to deal with. I was about three years old when I knew I was in trouble.

I hated my life just as much as Mom hated hers; she just didn't know it yet. I was too young to tell her, but I was dealing with my own shit—literally. No changing diapers, no milk, no toys, no comfort, no company! Damn, what was I supposed to do? I spent many days and nights lying in my crib, crying, and in my head demanding that someone please help me out here. Crying helped me to fall asleep fast, and leave this place. Sleeping was the only solution, the only way to feel safe, and far away from the nightmare of being here. This went on for the first three years of my life, where I desperately hoped that what was happening to me would change any day, any moment, any second.

What I learned from my baby years was that the world was a dark, scary place. A place where I couldn't help but feel I was its prey. This led me to believe I needed to hide away as much as possible. I felt that any second my life was going to be over—that something was going to come and get me.

The worst part of the day was when the sun would begin to set. The more it did, the more my entire being felt terrified as the night slowly swallowed the day away. Man, I wish I would have had some sort of defense, you know? Like in nature, where everyone has something going on—a turtle has a shell, a scorpion has its tail filled with poison, an elephant has its giant self for protection. But thankfully, in time, I too got my precious shell; I just didn't know it yet.

By the time I was five, my intuition was so very well developed,

I could tell whether someone had good intentions or bad, whether they were telling the truth or lying. Later on, my intuition saved my life, and helped me to stay away from lying bad people.

I had very little interest in getting in trouble; I had enough bad in my life as it was. Besides, I was more interested in getting to know what the "good" meant. Every year I became stronger and smarter. Mom would leave in the morning for the day, and I would waste no time getting myself ready to roll. I would sneak out of my crib and begin to investigate my surroundings. After a while, I was a strong walker. I could pick heavy things up off the ground, or at least, as heavy as it would be for a four-year-old. Before long, I knew every inch of our apartment.

My favorite spot in the apartment was the kitchen window. This was the place where I spent a lot of time looking outside, like an indoor cat observing the world outside its own. I enjoyed people watching; it was my only way to learn about humanity around me. Truth be told, it was my only activity. I liked that the picture changed constantly outside as people came and went; there was some sort of movement—unlike inside, where I felt trapped and alone.

At some point, though, I got pretty curious about what it would be like to go outside and experience what other folks were experiencing. Part of me felt like I was missing out on something; after all, they were out there, and I was in here. The thought kept circling around as I imagined the world outside. Mostly I wanted to meet the kids I had seen many times playing together on the street. I wanted to know *how* to play, and how to have fun like them. I needed connection, and I was desperate to know what that felt like.

My curiosity kept growing, giving me more and more motivation that I could pull this off one day and find myself outside our walls. Before long I was not only sneaking out of my crib on a daily basis, I was also learning everything I could about the door and the lock system. I wanted to find a way to peek beyond our walls. I wanted to one day be outside, like most kids.

Though as the saying goes, "Be careful what you wish for." As one day, too soon, I would get my chance to be outside for the very first time.

Except it didn't go exactly as planned.

Chapter 2

Little White Lie

Knock, knock, knock.

Holding my breath, I stood next to the door, hoping this neighbor would have what I needed.

It was one in the morning, and I knew the moment I knocked on someone's door they were not going to be happy. Everyone was sleeping, like normal folks do, while at our apartment heroin was being made from scratch by Mom and her friends. They had run into a problem in the middle of the process. They did not have enough vinegar to make the drug, and without the drug, all hell was going to break loose.

I was soundly asleep when I was woken up to go and solve their problem and find some vinegar. My job was to ask around the apartment complex for help. Did I want to go out there to do this for Mom? Absolutely not. If anything, I wanted to go back to sleep and pretend this was all just a terrible dream.

"Why do I have to do this crap I have nothing to do with?" I asked myself.

I was angry at Mom for forcing me to do her dirty work. To be honest, I was very surprised when Mom didn't seem to care that I was scared shitless. I was begging her not to send me out there when

I had never been outside our apartment walls. Sure, I wouldn't have minded some discovery time, but certainly not alone, and not at night!

"You are young, Ludmila. People will help you before they will help me," Mom said as she handed me some clothes to put on.

I got dressed, put on my shoes, and slowly walked over to the door, about to cry, but I didn't. Instead, I did my best to prepare for what was coming next—I was about to step into the night full of terrors. At least, that's how it felt—like I was going to get eaten alive by the black hole of darkness and fear. I remember I was so terrified for my life. I was about five, so my imagination was already running wild in my head.

Mom handed me a small jar with lid. "Don't come back till you got what we need, okay? It's important, very important!"

I took the jar and nodded in agreement. There was no changing Mom's mind about this. She needed her fix, and she would do anything for it.

As the door closed behind me, darkness consumed all surroundings. I found myself blind, not able to see a darn thing. Every inch of my body was working against me. I felt heavy, nauseous and scared. Fear was what I knew most, and best. This was the worst fear I had ever felt, and right now, it grew so big I didn't know if I was going to be able to handle it.

Somehow, though, I did. Somehow I found enough courage within me to walk up to a door and knock on it. I remember my heart beating so fast it felt like it was going to explode out of my chest. After all, I was doing something that to me felt wrong. It felt like breaking and entering, you know? Or stepping into someone else's business where I am not welcomed. But there I was, awaiting someone's response as I stood by the door I had just knocked on, hoping someone would help me with this and not scream and yell.

When I didn't hear anyone coming to the door, I moved on to

another one, and another one—and in doing so, it became a little easier and easier to do this. I was not as afraid to knock on neighbors' doors, though I was overwhelmingly scared of the darkness. There was no lighting around of any sort, and I didn't have a flashlight, making getting around extremely hard.

Finally, after walking around like a blind person and knocking on doors, a nice, middle-aged lady opened the door and helped me out, filling my jar with the vinegar Mom so desperately needed. I told her the story my mom told me to say—that we were making some sort of dish and ran out of the important ingredient. I was so grateful it worked!

"*Spasibo*," I said happily as she closed the door, and I went on my way.

Carefully, holding on to the rail, I walked down two flights of stairs, making sure to count each turn as I didn't want to get lost, or slip and break the jar of vinegar. I held on to that jar for dear life, checking every two seconds to make sure it was still in my hands. *Ahh, I made it!* I thought, as I knocked with the secret knock Mom had taught me, so excited to give her what she wanted. Moments later Mom answered the door, and before I entered, I handed her the jar filled with vinegar.

"You did it!" she exclaimed as she ran into the kitchen.

Although the entire experience lasted about an hour, to me it felt like a lifetime. It was the scariest moment of my life yet. It was the best feeling in the world when I was safely back in my familiar crib, going to sleep. I was back in my element, back home! The nightmare was over, at least for now.

I placed the blanket over my face in an effort to prevent myself from smelling the fumes this drug-making business made. It filled every inch of the place with a smell so bad I could barely breathe. Going to sleep, I thought how strange it was to lie. I had never lied before, and somehow I knew it wouldn't be the last time.

* * *

Our apartment was a small one. We had a tiny kitchen, another slightly bigger room we used as our bedroom and living room, and a bathroom by the hallway leading into the kitchen, where we kept our coats and shoes. There was the one good-size window in the kitchen where I stayed, but it was not openable; only the balcony door in the bedroom could be opened for some fresh air. Mom wouldn't do that, most likely for my safety, as we lived on the fourth floor of a nine-story apartment complex building. Oftentimes, I would see people out on their balconies, enjoying the sun and summer breeze, but they were adults; I had a long way to go before I reached that stage. I had a tough time being a kid; I so much wanted to have the freedom everyone around me had. Though it wouldn't be long before I felt like I was doing things that everyone around me were doing.

That terrifying night spent wandering, asking for vinegar, changed everything for me. While the experience was horrifying, it did give me a brilliant idea that would take care of me, and help me feel like I too was capable of taking care of my business. I told myself that it was time to take matters into my own hands now that I'd been exposed to the environment outside our walls, and met someone other than Mom or her friends. Most often her friends kept their distance from me, since they were there to do shady business, and no kid should be seeing any of that.

Little did they know, I was very much aware of what was taking place, as I snuck up and watched it all. It was definitely a strange thing to watch—especially once the heroin was properly injected into the arm. The person would immediately change, just like Mom, who would become a completely new person—a person I didn't mind seeing, as she was laughing, talking, and having fun. Normally this never happened. Not even alcohol brought Mom this much happiness.

I never really had to worry when Mom was doing heroin. She was much easier to take care of then, compared to when she would come home late at night, so drunk she couldn't even open the door, screaming my name to let her in. It was bad. Mom got out of control so many times, I was afraid I was going to lose her. She got so intoxicated once that she passed out in the elevator for a while. Early in the morning, neighbors were knocking on our door, saying to get her out of the elevator, as she was passed out drunk inside. Other people were not willing to use the elevator that was occupied by Mom's drunken, smelly, and disheveled body.

That's when I started to understand that the neighbors didn't like us very much. No one was willing to help me, and the looks I got sent a very clear message: "Stay away." That was a tough one. I hadn't realized before that we were so disliked, but after that morning, it was crystal clear that the neighbors didn't like us at all. I had to find the strength to drag her back inside, which took a long time. Somehow I managed to get her in and put a pillow under her head to sleep it off. I knew that like most other times, Mom would wake up and be cranky, but all right.

I slept on the floor by her side that day to make sure I could hear her breathing. Deep down inside, I knew Mom had gone too far this time. I just felt it; she was not right.

That was not the hardest part, though; the hardest part was knowing that Mom had been violated. When I saw her spread out unconscious in the elevator, I noticed that her clothes were not on properly. Her panties were partly pulled down, while her blouse was undone and her skirt somewhat twisted. I felt it. I knew it, and I hated whoever did this to my mom. I didn't understand why people did bad things.

That's why I didn't mind when Mom found something that seemed to work better for her—something that actually helped her to be okay and function better. Plus, because of this drug business, I also benefited, since it led to my brilliant idea that would come in very handy!

Chapter 3

Let There Be Food

So what was my so-called brilliant idea?

Well, while it may not seem so brilliant, to me at the time it was the best idea ever. It was the first time I put my brain to real work! Learning to basically beg door to door for ingredients Mom would need once in a while—baking soda was another—taught me that I could also beg for any spare food the neighbors were willing to share with me. After all, being constantly hungry, with only a couple meals per week was not going to fly. I was growing, and I needed food! A piece of bread with some salt wasn't going to cut it—although I did love bread, especially if it was freshly made that day. Most of the time the bread was pretty stale, and even moldy—but cheap.

So, while Mom was out and about, taking care of her business, I was taking care of mine. That was how we operated—Mom doing her thing, and me, doing mine. I got good at sneaking outside to go into other identical buildings surrounding the area to beg for food. Most of the time people would share food with me that I had never eaten before. All I knew were the delicious aromas flying through the hallway and spilling out of other people's homes, making me salivate and imagine what was cooking. But now, I actually got to eat some of those foods! Like borscht, a type of soup; mashed potatoes with *katleti*—a beef patty, nicely crisp. It was all so good; I wished I could always eat like that. Other times I would get to try some sort of pastry, or even a cake! Apples, peaches, pears, and watermelon were some of the fruits I got to try; I didn't know much about the world I was a part of, including nature, and all that it provided us with.

Let me say that by the time I got home, all I wanted to do was take a nice long nap. I was so full! Total food coma, as they say. I didn't complain; I had found a way to get the only thing I cared about—food—and to top it off, I no longer had to wait for Mom to come home empty-handed after waiting the entire day, wishing she would show up with something to eat. Because bread was the only thing I ate most of the time, it didn't last long. Mom wanted me to eat less, but I was like, yeah, right; I wasn't going to stare at the bread, hungry, while it whispered, "Eat me, eat me!"

Problem solved! Life was good; better than good! For once in my life, I was in control. The only trick was to make sure not to mix my thing with Mom's thing. I made sure to only go to people I had never been to before to ask for food. The cherry on top was the opportunity to finally experience beautiful summer days outside of our apartment building.

To be honest, when I first stepped outside into the real world, it felt like I was tripping on mushrooms. That's the only way to explain it. I was in awe, completely mesmerized by how the sun felt on my skin, how the breeze brushed against me, how loudly the birds were singing, how clear and detailed the leaves appeared on the trees and flowers, the smell in the air so sweet and fresh. There was a new feeling inside myself, a feeling of hope, a feeling that not all was lost, that this big beautiful world was here for me to explore—and *big* meant *endless!* I felt lighter, and I knew that everything was about to change. I was no longer helpless, with nothing to do. My heart was filled with wonder and liberation, maybe even happiness. This was one of the most memorable moments in my life. I had less fear of the world around me than I used to, lying in the crib, crying, scared. Now that I had had a taste of the world, my heart was filled with a sparkle of hope, and a tiniest sliver of knowing that not all was against me.

Once in a while my mom would get deep and spill the beans about my father—how she despised him. She would talk about my grandma, who had loved me to death when she took care of me after I was born. That's when I started to learn little bits and pieces about our family. Once, when I was about six, I found a photo album filled with pictures of Mom and the entire family on the day of my parents' wedding. When I first approached the subject, asking her who these people were, well, let's just say she wasn't very happy about it. She wouldn't talk about them other than to tell me angrily not to ask her about any of them.

I took advantage of the rare moments when she was in a good mood to ask questions. I wanted to know about our family! Of course, I think she didn't want to tell me anything because she knew I would jump the gun and start picturing the perfect, happily-ever-after movie in my head; where my dad would return with my supposed sister Victoria, and we would live like the normal people who have families. Like most imaginary stories that don't come true, neither did mine, making me more upset than I wanted to be.

Before long I started thinking two things: First, I blamed myself for my dad's absence. Maybe I wasn't good enough—not worthy. Second, I started feeling anger toward him, because he left us behind and never looked back. I hated his guts. Even if he wanted to meet me one day, it was too late. I wanted nothing to do with him, and it was obvious to me that he was, after all, not a person I wanted in my life. I was done making him out to be a "good dad" who comes to the rescue. I made it my business to rely on no one but myself. I kept my whereabouts clandestine, as technically, I wasn't allowed to go outside alone.

"You're too young, Ludmila; six is too young," Mom would say—not that I had any clue what that meant, nor was I going to believe this after she'd sent me out to fetch her stuff in the middle of the night. Come on! Too young? More like too bothersome. I knew exactly what Mom meant—not that she was ever truthful about it.

The important thing was that she loved me, and I loved her. We might not have said it out loud, but it was always there, underneath the cloak of suffering, hurt, and anger. Like with everything in life—we do the best we can with what we got.

Chapter 4

New Order

Mom showed up at home one day with a boyfriend I had never heard of till the day he arrived to live with us. Say what? Live with us—this stranger I didn't know? The guy was probably in his early thirties. He looked like every other guy who had come through here, but this was a first, as he wasn't going anywhere.

The moment I met him I knew he was not a good guy, and that he didn't have good intentions. I remember he smiled at me as he said "Hey, kid, how's it going?" He tried his best to pretend he was a nice guy, but he wasn't fooling me. I let him know that I knew exactly who he was when I didn't smile back. Instead, I took a step back, giving him a look that said something like "You're full of shit, and I know it." I knew in that moment he was aware that his game was not going to work on me. His "I'm a nice guy" act was not going to last, and because he couldn't get me in his pocket, I became his punching bag. Mom didn't know this for about a year. I never told her; I was too afraid he would kill me the next time.

It became a usual occurrence: The moment he got back, he would come over to the crib and start saying terrible things, putting words in my mouth and completely believing this fake story he was saying about me as he started to get more and more angry toward me. I prepared myself, as I knew what was coming next. I braced myself for the pain that was about to be traveling through my body like a bolt of lightning. My head would hurt for days from my hair being pulled while thrown across the room. I would fold up on the floor, trying to protect myself as much as I could—not that it was any help. He was huge and strong compared to my tiny body. I had no choice but to take it.

I remember holding my breath, so tense and in pain that I didn't feel anything after a couple of minutes. No blood, but many bruises decorated my body. He was smart; he didn't hurt my face, so there was little proof, as I made sure to wear clothes that didn't expose the bruises. Since Mom rarely checked up on me, I knew I would be safe. It was not my idea to wear long-sleeved shirts and pants; he was the one who ordered me to do so, which I did. "Cover yourself up—you're embarrassing," he would say when he was done. Moments later he would be passed out on the couch, snoring. All was well again.

Mom would come home from doing whatever she was doing and the two of them would either go out together or lock themselves in the bathroom to have sex. Didn't like that a bit, obviously; not something I wanted to be around for. I remember closing my ears as much as I could, not hearing anything but the ringing in my ears.

I became angry and confused. I felt betrayed by my mom, who was always more interested in her piece-of-shit boyfriend or the drug buddy friends she liked to party with. Mostly I couldn't stand him being near her—this monster, this ugly son-of-a-bitch who had Mom in his pocket. Maybe this was because she really loved him, which was very hard for me to make sense of, but as they say, you can't help who you love.

I just hoped she would never find out about his monster side.

Chapter 5

Breaking Down the House

One day, sitting on the table by the kitchen window, staring outside as usual, I heard arguing in the other room. I kept looking outside, pretending all was quiet. The sky looked angry; it was so dark and gray out, and the wind was picking up. A storm was coming, and not just outside, but in here, too. Mom was still yelling at him, and he was swearing and yelling at her. The honeymoon was over, and his true nature had started to shine through.

I folded my legs against my chest and rested my head on my knees, trying to imagine being fed by strangers with yummy foods. I was very much missing this, as I couldn't sneak outside anymore. Everything was pretty unpredictable with him here. It had been the only good thing I'd had going for me, and now that I couldn't sneak out anymore, it was even worse than before—when I used to be so hungry, without any food. At least then, I had had no clue as to what I was missing . . . but now I did.

I won't lie; I was scared. I knew what he was capable of, while Mom had no idea. She was strong, like a bull. She wasn't going to give up. She had a strong will, and would do anything in order to stand by her beliefs and desires. That's what I was afraid of; she was going to make him so mad one of these days. It was only a matter of time before the two of them would tear the place apart. Mom had just as much of a temper as he did, and just like him, she didn't hold back.

At that moment, I heard the door slam, and someone stormed out of the place. I really hoped it was him who had left, but instead, it was Mom who left me alone with him—angry. I got a really good beating that day. Even though I was used to it, this time was worse: I was getting hit for both of us, Mom and myself.

When she got home later on that night, I didn't waste any time telling her about what had happened. I just showed her my body. I came clean and explained that this had been happening for a long time, and that he was going to do the same to her if she didn't tell him to leave. Now that they were fighting verbally, I knew Mom would be on my side. I remember her being very upset; she was crying and saying how sorry she was, which completely surprised me. I had never seen her this upset before. I was a hundred percent certain Mom was going to throw him out the moment he came walking through that door. I was pretty excited; I was ready to go back to just the two of us again, where I had the freedom to do what I needed to do.

* * *

"You son of a bitch!" I heard Mom yelling from the kitchen. It was the middle of the night when I was abruptly woken up to violence.

I got myself out of the crib and rushed into the kitchen to make sure Mom was all right.

"Shut your filthy mouth!" he shouted.

Mom was now screaming from pain as he grabbed her hair and forced her head against the wall, full force. I could hear the bang her head made as it met the wall.

I was standing in the hallway, screaming at him to stop, to leave her alone.

"Please, stop it—stop it, please!" Tears ran down my face. My heart was pounding, and I felt sick to my stomach. Mom was unrecognizable, her face twice as big as usual, and covered in red.

"Ludmila, go in the other room, please," Mom cried out, doing her best to look at me. I could tell she was terrified he might beat me too. "Go!" she yelled, pleading for me to leave the room.

I ran into the bedroom, climbed back into my crib, and closed my ears. As much as I didn't want to hear another cry, another scream, or his ugly voice yelling at Mom, it was no use. It seemed like I couldn't squeeze my hands over my ears hard enough to stop the dreadful sounds from coming into the room.

I don't remember how long it was before everything went silent again, although to me it felt like eternity. I heard the door slam. At last he was gone—at least for now.

I got out of the crib and rushed to Mom, who was still lying on the floor, trying to recover. It took hours to clean her up, as she was in so much pain, the slightest touch would make her scream.

* * *

I never thought I would be so happy to be alone in the apartment with nothing but distant echoes coming from outside our walls. No fighting, no screaming for your life. No throwing up.

I folded the blanket closer around me and climbed on the table to watch the snow fall. By now the ground had been transformed from a gray gloomy landscape into an angelic bright white. It was like I was the ground being covered up with snow, transformed in some way. Somehow it felt good to think, it was a good escape from being myself. I was depressed, I didn't want to be here, not with him still in the picture.

Nothing changed other than now Mom and I were both getting beat up. She would try to throw him out and break up with him, but he was very good at apologizing and making it up to her. I couldn't believe it; I couldn't believe that after everything he had done, she still kept taking him back.

When their fights were over and both of them would storm out of the place, I would sit there alone, hoping they wouldn't be back for a long time. The two of them were like a tornado; their fighting had reached new levels, where whatever was around got thrown across the room, directed at each other. The apartment was destroyed, with so many things lying around everywhere. The worst part was that the neighbors heard it all from start to finish. As much as I wished they didn't know our business, they knew exactly what was going on. It made our lives even more complicated when some of them picked up a phone and called the police.

Of course Mom told the officers everything was fine, though that was a big fat lie. She didn't have much choice but to lie since she was in the drug-making business, and having the police involved was driving the customers away. Mom relied on the money she got as a cut from the sales. It was the only job she had, and she couldn't take any risks of losing it. Plus she had gotten her monster boyfriend hooked on heroin as well, so now he was also involved. Luckily the cops left without much investigation while he hid in the bathroom. I was so happy the cops didn't come inside, as there was a lot of proof that drugs were being made here. This was bad; I didn't like knowing that Mom could go to jail if caught, or worse—her monster boyfriend could betray her by blackmailing her. Looked like Mom couldn't get rid of him. Somehow she still loved him, which made it easier for her to keep him around.

It was around this time—when I realized he was not going anywhere—that I started my new hobby of cleaning our apartment. I couldn't stand it anymore, as it constantly reminded me of what happened here when they fought. I found the act of cleaning to be awesome; it was something I could do myself, and on top of that, I was completely transforming something that was ugly into something that was pretty, orderly, and right. I liked the feeling of erasing him from our apartment and making it ours again, with nothing to indicate he was ever here. I would pour the dark red water down the toilet and rinse the bucket one more time, making sure all the evidence of blood was gone, returning the floors, walls, and belongings back to their natural state.

At least for a while.

Chapter 6

The Big News

About five months later, sometime in the spring, Mom told me the big news: She was pregnant with his child. I remember she was so damn happy and excited; I had never seen her this happy before. This wasn't like when Mom was on heroin. This was a new type of happiness I saw in her. She was glowing, with a smile up to her ears. She told me she felt this might bring them closer together. I think she hoped things would change somehow, and we'd all magically turn into a happy family, which was very unlikely in my eyes. Mom was always optimistic that she'd get her way; even if it was never going to happen, she still fought for it. She really wanted to make it work with him, and now, in her mind, there was a way—through this baby.

Don't get me wrong—I was pretty damn excited as well to hear the news. This meant that maybe I'd never be alone again. I was going to have a sister or a brother! It made me feel better—bigger somehow, like my skin got a lot thicker. I couldn't help but notice that this baby was changing me, too.

Mom seemed to be on cloud nine with him most of the time. Things were going very well, probably better than ever before. The fighting stopped; they kept themselves happy-drunk with baby fever. Who knew that having a baby together would have this effect? It was like all was forgiven—like he was suddenly a very nice guy.

It lasted a couple of months, and then the fighting started up again. This time he would put Mom in the hospital, and I wouldn't see her again till she came home months later, with my baby sister in her arms.

This fight left Mom unconscious, lying on the floor, her head bleeding and the rest of her looking like she'd been in a horrible car wreck. I will never forget the smell of blood that filled the room. Not a big fan. It smelled like death itself to me. I don't know how surgeons do it.

He was just about out the door when he realized how seriously he'd beaten her. He didn't even check up on her—just left in a hurry, like it was Mom's fault this happened to her. "Look at what you made me do!" he yelled, slamming the door behind him. No remorse, though I could feel he was scared this time. He knew he had gone too far. I was so happy to watch him leave as I made my way out of the crib to help Mom.

I stayed with her, cleaning up her face with a wet rag, calling for her to wake up. When she did, it was like she'd just woken up from a nightmare. She was confused, and terrified for the baby.

"The baby—I have to go!" she said.

Moments later she stumbled out the door and disappeared.

When a couple days passed and Mom still hadn't come home, he left the apartment, dropping by every so often to check and see whether she had returned. I allowed him back inside because I didn't want to instigate any more trouble, especially because I didn't know where Mom was. I would just look down when he came inside the apartment and hide in my crib till he left. I was happy he never stuck around too long.

At this point I think we were both worried. No one knew where she had gone.

Come to find out, she had gone to the hospital to make sure the baby was okay, and they'd kept her there till she had safely delivered the baby, away from him.

As for me, I was left to my own devices once more, and I didn't waste any time, leaving the apartment to go explore the outdoors, and while I was at it, knocking on some doors for a meal. As usual, food was pretty scarce at home. I was so happy to have food again; I didn't know it at the time, but the food was bringing me comfort I really needed. I was worried sick about Mom.

I never disliked her after she came back. All the things I had felt about Mom in the past were gone. I didn't care anymore that she had left me alone with him, or that she had chosen him over me, or that she didn't take care of me. In that moment, none of it mattered. That was quite the test, you know? Not knowing if your mother will ever return—and wondering how she could have left, knowing *he* was here to hurt me.

While she was gone I had made plans to run away, but I never did, always hoping that Mom hadn't left me here forever with him. Hoping every day that she would come back to us. I just missed her so damn much; it was the first time we'd been separated, and not for a day, but for months.

I felt like all was well again when Mom returned in one piece, healthy, and with my baby sister in her arms. What a feeling! I was so relieved that we were once again a family.

Chapter 7

Bundle of Joy

Wow—she's so tiny, I thought, as I looked at my baby sister. She was sleeping peacefully next to me in the crib we shared.

I had never seen a baby before, and part of me was scared to even touch her. I didn't want to break her or something. I will never forget the feeling I had going to bed every night, hoping I wouldn't hurt her in my sleep. After all, I was much bigger than her. I wondered what her life was going to be like here with us. The more I thought about it, the more it dawned on me that I was going to have to protect her and look after her, if Mom wouldn't. She hadn't looked after me, so I wasn't going to think otherwise when it came to my sister.

Mom was back to doing and selling heroin again. It seemed to be the only thing available to her. It wasn't easy to get a job—it seemed like they were all taken—and it's not like in America, where you can collect unemployment or apply for food stamps. This is Ukraine we are talking about: a beautiful place, but not without its thorns. It was up to Mom to find a way to survive. Since it wasn't easy and she seemed to hit a dead end with everything she tried, Mom turned to what was easier, and possible. While she tried to do it "right" after my sister was born, she couldn't find a way, so she went back to what she knew.

Her boyfriend was also back in the picture. He wasn't going anywhere now that he had a daughter—his first child, I believe. I bet none of his other relationships had lasted this long. No one in their right mind would settle for a life with him. But Mom was not like other women; she had too much compassion, and she forgave others easily. She never held anything against anyone. She just did the best she could, being herself.

I was glad he was back; at least this time around, he cared for my sister. There was always baby formula and milk for her in the fridge that he would bring over. I watched him like a hawk when he was with my sister. Part of me didn't want him to touch her at all; every time I looked at him, all I could see was a monster.

My sister, on the other hand—Mom had named her Alyona—was a little bundle of pure joy. I felt like I didn't want her to go through what I had with him. I felt overprotective. Every time he touched her I was ready to jump in and take her away. I didn't trust him—not now, not ever. He was so violent. I didn't think he knew how to handle something as small and delicate as Alyona. I was paranoid he would drop her or squeeze her little body too hard.

Eventually, after all of his successful visits with Alyona, he found his way back to living with us. Alyona became an excuse for him to stick around and continue to boss Mom around, or worse, beat her up. He never touched me again after Mom threatened him to the point where somehow, he finally got the memo. I always wondered what she said to him, for him to actually stop.

Surprisingly, he didn't beat her all the time, as they were both preoccupied with doing heroin and partying, getting home at the crack of dawn. Luckily, Mom had taught me how to mix the formula for Alyona, so at least I was able to feed her.

But when it came to everything else, I lacked the skills. We didn't have many clean sheets, and while I was used to sleeping on them when they were wet and smelly, my sister wasn't. Like myself many years ago, she was demanding something that I knew she needed, but I had no way to get it done. She wasn't the only one to wet the bed; I was still having accidents at night, so it wasn't pleasant to lay in it. I remember taking some clothes out of the dresser and putting them on top of the wet sheets to make her feel better.

We didn't have any disposable diapers, so I had to wash the cloth diapers Mom made for her. I will never forget having to do this in our creepy-looking bathroom. I would gag every time from the smell of baby poop, by far the worst thing I had ever smelled. I did my best to get the job done as soon as possible, surrounded by exposed pipes, burned wallpaper, and an ancient dirty tub, along with the weird noises coming from the pipes. The mirror was cracked so you couldn't see much, and the toilet scared me. I always felt like I was going to fall in and never get out—that there was a monster living in the pipes, and if I sat on the toilet it would get me. Sometimes the lights would flicker a little, sending me right out of there. I never went inside unless the lights were on!

Despite my fears, I was more than happy to help my baby sister. I really thought I had this—that I would be very good at taking care of her.

Unfortunately, it didn't quite turn out that way.

Chapter 8

Helpless and Annoyed

I dragged my weak, tired body to the kitchen and grabbed the last piece of bread we had left. Tiptoeing around so as not to wake Alyona, I got on the table to enjoy the view. The sun was getting stronger again. I could feel the warmth coming from the window, making me feel calm and relaxed. I knew I had limited time to enjoy this peace, so I didn't waste any time taking it all in. I didn't even care that my stomach was still gurgling, giving me a hard time.

I was pretty stressed out, being alone with my sister all the time. She didn't need me; she needed a mother's magic touch. It was no crime to need your mother, the one who gave you life. Alyona needed her mother!

I felt so guilty. I knew exactly what my sister was feeling. I had no choice but to sit there helplessly, listening to her cry with rage. I couldn't do a damn thing about it. Nothing was working out the way I thought it would, when I'd promised myself I'd always watch over her and make sure she was happy—or at least happier than I was. What I was able to do for her didn't even make a dent, and I felt like giving up. Everything was becoming too overwhelming.

I won't lie. I was very glad when she finally fell asleep, and stopped crying bloody murder. Every day became more and more difficult.

For me to be okay, I really needed time to myself; I really needed some freedom. It felt like it would be easier to be dead than living without any freedom at all! Part of me felt guilty about feeling this way; after all, I'd promised to take care of my baby sister, and here I was, failing at it—failing myself.

I was angry at Mom for giving me all of this responsibility; yet when I wanted to go outside by myself, she wouldn't let me, saying I was too young. I was pretty sick and tired of hearing the same old story, because I knew she didn't care about my safety as much as she needed me there to keep an eye on my sister. I was not a little girl anymore who didn't know anything. I had figured it all out. I knew Mom's game at this point, and I was no longer naive about her bullshit.

I looked forward to sneaking out the moment it was hot and sunny outside once more. I had to get away, even if it was just for an hour or two. I loved spring and summer, and fall wasn't so bad, but I didn't like winter a bit, and right now it was winter. I couldn't take the cold all that well—it made me shiver, and my breathing shallow. Plus, the snow got so high I could barely make my way around; there were no plows here other than our feet, so I stayed inside during the winter months.

Sometimes I imagined what it would be like to go far away from where we lived. As of yet, I had covered very little distance—I'd been too afraid of getting lost—but things didn't seem as frightening to me anymore. If anything, my desire to investigate and explore kept getting stronger by the day.

What would I see if I went farther? I thought.

I had no idea what existed out there, beyond the quarter-mile radius that extended in each direction from our building.

Before I was able to get too far in my imaginary adventures, I heard a cry from the bedroom. Alyona was awake again, ready to torture me some more.

I got up and went to check on her, grabbing the bottle of formula I'd prepared earlier. She was very demanding, and if I didn't make it over to her in time, she would let me know with a sound I really didn't feel like hearing right now.

I went into the bedroom to feed my sister, wishing Mom would get home and take over so I could get some sleep.

Chapter 9

Free at Last

"Ludmila, I need you to take your sister and go outside to play for a while," Mom said, taking out some warm clothes for me and my sister to put on, as it was cold and snowing outside.

I didn't argue; the only thing running through my head was the thought of going outside. How could that be? I felt like I was dreaming. I couldn't believe those words had come out of her mouth!

I put the second pair of socks over my feet and finished getting dressed. Alyona was all bundled up as well, ready to meet winter for the very first time. I was so excited because I realized Mom was allowing me to go out by myself with my sister, which meant I didn't have to sneak out anymore. I was free at last!

That day I didn't even care that it was cold, or that Mom had sent us outside so she could have some alone time with *him*. It wasn't just during the night that they were suddenly madly in love, doing the cha cha, if you know what I mean; now it was during the day, too! It's like they made up after every fight with sex.

I put my sister down on the floor in the hallway and sat down for a minute to catch my breath and give my arms a break. Alyona was getting heavy fast, and we didn't have a stroller. I had to carry her around, and I was getting hot. I had a fur coat on that was bigger than me, and so did my sister, making both of us heavier. We looked like two furry Oompa Loompas walking around.

After getting the rest I needed, I picked my sister back up and walked down some more stairs, moving to a new location. I didn't want anyone asking questions as to why we were still sitting there. I couldn't bring myself to go *outside*-outside, so I decided to walk up and down the stairs, throughout the building. As I mentioned, I wasn't a big fan of the cold. I also avoided the elevator as much as possible after what had happened to Mom; plus, it was always breaking down, meaning you might not get out for hours.

We made it all the way up the ninth floor that day. Going down was much easier, but scary, as I didn't want to drop Alyona. I am pretty sure I gained some serious muscle after that workout, but I didn't complain, as I would rather be hot than freezing.

We got home just in time, as two hours had passed, and we were allowed back inside. They were done with their business, and all was well again.

That day, I got my mojo back. It was like the life force was getting more and more alive inside me. After a long wait, my dream was finally coming true: I was going to be able to have some freedom and time to myself—well, sort of, as I had Alyona with me most of the time. Nevertheless, it was better than nothing. We could both explore the neighborhood and meet the kids who lived around here, and we could both score some yummy foods! I was determined, and pretty damn happy; say good-bye to hunger and hello to food! This was the first thing on my to-do list, as it had been a while since I'd really eaten a good meal. Once in a while I would take a couple spoonfuls of my sister's formula, but it just wasn't enough. I knew I couldn't eat as much as I needed because Alyona needed it much more than I did.

After that first outing, I sat down by the stereo system in the corner of the bedroom and looked at it for a while. Alyona was with Mom and her father in the kitchen, spending time together. The stereo used to be my toy station just a couple of years earlier. I will never forget how cool I found it to be. I used to sit around and play with its knobs, buttons, and switches, totally lost in my own little world.

Now, though, I barely noticed it. I remembered how small my world was back then, and how much bigger it was now. So much had changed since then. Part of me couldn't believe how far I had come—that only two years ago, I was just learning how to walk, talk, and function.

I was six now. I'd finally reached the age where I could take matters into my own hands. I would never again feel as helpless as I did back then. I wasn't fragile and scared anymore. I'd had two years of learning and preparing, and now I could influence my own life in my own way, without breaking Mom's rules, and without fear of being punished for sneaking out.

I was officially set free, like a bird from its cage. I had been cooped up inside for way too long, and now I looked forward to spreading my wings high, going everywhere I possibly could!

Life was about to get a whole lot better.

Chapter 10

The Chocolate Bar

As I made my way into an adjoining apartment building one day, not long afterward, I thought about which floor I was going to start with—which door I was going to knock on first. I tried to knock on different ones each time around, the ones that felt friendlier, somehow. I'd learned that not everyone took so well to me knocking on their door. A couple of times I'd had to run away. Most often I found that men were angry, while most of the women were kind, usually giving me something to eat.

And then there were those precious times, when a woman would invite me inside and feed me a hot meal right there in their kitchen. That was when I first learned that many people lived quite differently than we did. I will never forget the feeling I got when I was inside a nice safe home. There was this smell that each of these places had—their own "home" smell that somehow made me feel better inside. Like there was liveliness here, not dread.

Most of the kitchens I saw were filled with all sorts of foods, herbs, fruit, plates and silverware, books, and a lot more. I was mesmerized, looking around at everything for the first time, getting to see something different from one apartment to the next. That was always my wish: to get invited inside—not just for the food, but for the surroundings as well. I loved seeing how differently each person lived. To me it was like traveling, except instead of other countries, I was visiting other people's homes.

I was looking forward to scoring something yummy today, something that made me feel better inside, and of course, satisfy my hunger. I needed to feel kindness and comfort. It was nice to be out of our apartment; even though I had more freedom these days, it didn't come around all too often. Today I was more than relieved to be alone, doing my own thing. It helped me to feel less angry about what had happened.

Just the day before, I'd had to watch Alyona eat a chocolate bar in front of me. It wasn't about me not getting a piece of chocolate; it was more about how it all went down that really bothered me. Her father had brought home a chocolate bar, making sure to dangle it in front of my face. "Come into the kitchen," he said, "and bring Alyona with you. I've got something for you."

I got Alyona and went into the kitchen like he asked. He took Alyona from my arms and placed her on his lap. As I stood there, I felt confused, thinking "Was he going to give me a piece?" He'd never done anything nice for me before; this would be a first, which only made me even more suspicious. That's when I realized what was happening. He broke off a piece and offered it to Alyona, who was not going to argue with that.

As she munched on the chocolate I saw him looking at me with a look that said "Did you really think I was going to give you a damn thing?" I could tell he was hoping I would beg for some. I'd never had chocolate before. It smelled good, but I was not going to take anything from him, even if he had offered some. And I sure as hell was not going to beg, either. I hated his guts and he hated mine; there was no fixing that.

Long story short, Alyona pretty much ate the entire thing. He also ate couple of pieces with her, chewing like a cow, saying just how delicious it was.

My blood was boiling. I was so angry that he was using my sister against me, this innocent being who had nothing to do with the hatred between the two of us. I was also pretty damn angry that he was still playing these stupid games with me. I thought we were over this. At least he knows how to handle and provide for Alyona, I thought, as I did my best not to express with my face what I was feeling.

In my mind I was laughing at him; if anything, he wasn't doing much other than feeding my sister, which was fine with me. She deserved it! Besides, I enjoyed watching her attempt to eat it. Her face was completely covered in chocolate, as well as her hands, and most of her, really. It was cute. I was glad she got to try something new and yummy.

He crunched the wrapper and put it in his pocket. "Well, that's it. That was pretty damn good, right?!" He looked at my sister and then at me, as if I'd actually had a piece. He smirked and handed my sister back to me, saying, "Clean her up." Moments later he was out the door.

All I could think about was my next opportunity to go out and get some food to eat. Little did he know that I was no longer starving, like before; I had solved the problem, and was in fact eating plenty. Maybe it wasn't chocolate, but I had plenty of other foods I loved. Sometimes I would bring something back for Alyona to try, too—not that she liked much of what I brought back, as it was often too hard for her teeth still.

Those weren't my proudest moments, when I left Alyona alone while she napped. When I was really hungry, though, sometimes I had no choice but to leave her alone for a while, an hour at the most, sometimes less—just long enough to knock on sufficient doors to get a little bit to eat. I kept it short, and most of the time she was still sleeping by the time I got back. This made me so happy, that she didn't even know I'd been gone. It broke my heart, as part of me felt like I was doing the same thing to her that Mom had done to me for many years. I looked forward to the day she could fully walk on her own; then I could take her with me everywhere!

Chapter 11

Kids on the Block

It was time to get to know the kids who lived around the neighborhood. I had seen them many times, playing together, and while part of me felt like I already knew them, I never approached any of them because I had other priorities—mainly, to get food in my stomach. In the old days, I hadn't had a minute to spare. It had been important to get to know my surroundings and return home before I got busted for sneaking out of the apartment. Now, however, I didn't have to sneak around anymore, and I had plenty of time on my hands to do both.

It was around this time, when I was seven, that I first tried to make friends. It was during a rare moment when Mom and Alyona's father were both at home in the middle of the day, so I didn't have to watch Alyona. I went outside and approached some of the kids, thinking it was going to go well—that we'd all play together . . . you know, just some innocent kid fun, nothing to worry about but the game at hand.

Most days when I saw them playing together they were smiling, laughing—I wanted a slice of that heavenly fun. Little did I know that trying to make friends would blow up in my face. Come to find out, kids were not like adults. They were a different breed, and I had no idea how to handle them. Watching them through my window was much easier, and made them look way nicer than they really were. Adults, I got along with just fine, but when it came to kids, I was missing something. Every time I tried to talk to them, or play with them, suddenly everyone would scatter, then cluster back together again somewhere that wasn't near me.

I could tell they were whispering about me, and I knew it wasn't good; their faces and laughter said it all. I felt it: I was not welcome here. At some point along the way I got sick and tired of kids talking behind my back. I was pretty angry and ready to blow up. Like a ticking bomb, it was just matter of time. I was getting fed up with all the drama. I demanded that they tell me what it was they were saying about me—what was so wrong and terrible about me?

Big mistake.

Maybe I didn't know it then, but I was about to find out. The truth hurts, as the saying goes. I had no clue what was coming. There were at least five of them, and every one of them had something to say to me. Worst part was, I had nothing to say back. They were right: I was dirty and stinky; I was wearing the same clothes a lot; I didn't have a nice hairdo. I didn't know what school was, my mom was a druggie, and I did beg for food.

I felt ashamed—guilty, somehow—hurt by their feelings toward me. I'd had no idea that's who I was in their eyes, and it wasn't long before I started to believe it. I became that kid they described. I realized I had nothing to offer, nothing in common with any of them other than being the same age.

I remember asking my mom if I could go to school, but she said we didn't have the money to pay for it. I won't lie; I was disappointed. I really wanted to go to school and be a part of something. Every morning all the kids would line up outside, dressed up, with what I learned were backpacks on their backs, getting ready to go to school. All the kids looked happy and excited.

Once I snuck up to the school, about a quarter-mile away, maybe more, to see what all the fuss was about. I had watched where everyone went in the morning, so I was able to figure out the way. I remember that no one was around, so I went inside the building. I will never forget how strange it felt, seeing a long hallway with many doors on each side. It looked so endless. I had never seen anything like it. Not that I knew what to expect, but this place didn't make me feel welcome, nor did it feel inviting. I found myself feeling nervous.

There was a sudden noise that scared the crap out of me. All the doors swung open and a herd of people started to walk toward me. I later learned it was the school bell. I will never forget how fast I ran out of there! I thought I was going to get run over, everyone was in such a big hurry. I don't think anyone noticed me—they were all much bigger and taller than me. Luckily the door was right there, so I ran out, and away.

Being outside was much better—less noise and fewer people. I was glad I didn't have to go to school after that day. Still, the feelings inside me didn't change. While I was dealing with accepting the fact that I wasn't like the rest of the kids on the block, it wasn't easy to swallow the idea that everyone knew what was going on in our lives. I couldn't hide it or deny it; it was too late for that.

It wasn't long before every well was poisoned, so to speak. We just didn't belong around here, and adults and kids alike made sure we knew that's how they felt when they would say how much they wished we didn't live in the apartment complex. Who knew we were that much trouble? I'd certainly had no idea. But the fact remained: We *did* live here, and as far as I knew, we weren't going anywhere, so I had to find a way to exist without being seen. I didn't want to deal with it. I was still raw from all the things people were saying about us.

Somehow, not long afterward, I discovered a hatch door up on the top floor of the building. I don't know how I'd never noticed it before, but lo and behold, there was an extra staircase tucked in the corner that led up to a small door leading to the roof.

I will never forget how excited I felt. It was like that scene with the wardrobe in the Narnia movie. I felt like I'd just stepped into a different world. A world with no people, just peace. I remember thinking how small everyone appeared, and how different the world looked from all the way up there. The trees, the people, the roads—everything changed its appearance in a way. I just stood there and enjoyed looking down on everyone and seeing everything while no one could see me—or pick on me. The best part was that the buildings were connected under this same roof, so I could cover a lot of distance without being outside at all. I just hopped from one roof to the next till there were none left, and by then I was far enough away so that none of the kids in the neighborhood could bother me. I had never seen anyone else up on the roof. It was awesome, as kids weren't allowed to wander or go up on the roof. I was happy to have something that was just mine—my own secret.

It took some time to get over myself, but eventually, I did. I soon realized that my life was just fine the way it was: I had freedom, I could go anywhere I pleased, and I didn't have a curfew. I'll never forget the moment I understood that part of the reason the other kids didn't like me was because they were jealous of my freedom.

I recall one time when some of the kids were being called back inside when it was getting dark. I could tell they didn't want to go in for the night. While they slowly walked back into their building with pouty faces, I got to walk away and keep playing, using the slide and the swings, doing whatever I wanted. I was not shackled. I had the freedom to wonder, think, dream, imagine, all on my own. Mom didn't teach me anything, but neither did she discipline me or tell me how to be, or how to think.

I quickly learned that the kids were just acting out based on what their parents told them, and I didn't hold it against them anymore. Because I gave up fighting and caring about what they were saying, I got a chance to meet a nice girl who wanted to spend time with me. She was very interested in talking to me about her Barbie doll named Ariel. I'll never forget the look on her face when she learned I had no clue what she was talking about. She ended up taking me to her apartment to show me her Barbies, because, as she said, "It wasn't right that I didn't know."

I laughed and followed her up the stairs to the fifth floor. We walked inside, straight to her bedroom. "Come on, it's this way," she said, holding my hand. When she opened the door and we walked in, my jaw dropped. The entire room was filled with Barbies, toys of all sorts, and even dollhouses! I didn't know what to do. I was in total shock. I had never seen that many toys before; it was like an entire toy store had been placed in her bedroom.

"Well, don't just stand there," she said, waving me over to play with her. "This is Ariel." She showed me a doll with red hair and a fish tail. "She's a mermaid," the girl said. "She lives in the sea. Didn't you see the movie?"

"No," I replied. "We don't have TV."

"That's okay. Here, you can play with this one," she said, handing me another one of her dolls, this one with blonde hair and blue eyes. She wore a beautiful dress, and her knees and arms could bend. This meant she was the better kind of Barbie, my new friend told me. I had a great time, and if I hadn't stolen one of her Barbies, we might still be friends today.

I don't know what I was thinking. Well, I guess I do; I was thinking that she couldn't possibly notice that I'd taken one of her dolls, since she had so many. I knew I really wanted a doll, so I took one of her newest and prettiest ones and somehow managed to walk away with it stuffed in my clothes.

I had one day to play with the Barbie before the girl and her parents showed up at our door, demanding it back. Mom wasn't happy. She told me to apologize to the girl and her parents. I gave them the doll back and said I was sorry.

"Stealing is wrong," the girl's mother said, looking at me with complete disgust.

I felt horrible. I'd learned my lesson—not to steal from people. Mostly, I was just relieved I wasn't going to get punished. After all, I'm sure my mom's boyfriend wouldn't have minded getting his hands on me one more time. It hadn't been easy for him to stop hitting me, I could tell. If only he knew how much I despised him. My hatred for him had grown bigger than all the oceans and seas combined. He was the worst person I had ever known in my life, thus far!

The news spread like wildfire, and before long, all the kids had something new to talk about. They were mean little shits. No one ever forgave or forgot a damn thing that involved me or my family. No matter what I did, or didn't do, we were never going to get along with others in the neighborhood.

So I stayed away, minding my own business, doing my own thing. I didn't trust anyone at this point; anything I said to anyone was used against me. Kids would pretend to like me just to get information out of me, to spread more rumors. This really did a number on me. I wondered why people were so ugly and mean—why they had to make others feel terrible about themselves. I just didn't understand.

What I did understand loud and clear was that no matter how nice someone was being, I was not to trust them with any information about myself or my family. I was to keep quiet and not say a word. It's not like I was a big talker to begin with, but it seemed like the little I did say managed to ruin our reputation.

Chapter 12

Puppy

Alyona had received a gift from her father. Even though she was only around two years old, he thought it was a good idea to get her a puppy. At this point, I was eight, and knew better. There was no way we'd be able to take care of him. We barely had enough food for ourselves. How was this little fella going to survive here with us? Even though he was the most adorable puppy I'd ever seen—soft fur, the cutest puppy eyes, and a tiny wagging tail—we just couldn't keep him.

Trust me—I wanted to keep him all to myself. It was love at first sight. The puppy instantly put a smile on my face and made me feel good inside—like everything was okay, like the world wasn't all that bad. I took him away from Alyona, who was pulling on his fur and his ears. I could tell the puppy needed a break, so I picked him up and held him close to my heart for a while, crying. I felt so bad that I had to let him go. I had to find a way to make sure he'd survive and have a good, happy life—just not here with us.

I thought long and hard, trying to come up with a plan to make sure the puppy would have a real chance. There were many stray dogs all over the place; most likely Alyona's father had gotten this little pup from someone whose dog had gotten pregnant. Or he'd seen the pup on the street and assumed he was okay, since he didn't smell or look too dirty.

That day I came up with a plan. It was not my first choice, but it was the only way.

I unlocked the door to the balcony and pushed it open. I felt the cold wind brushing against my face. The snow covered the ground once more, making everything a beautiful white. I had never been out on our balcony before. I wasn't scared, as we only lived on the fourth floor, and I was used to wandering around the rooftops, higher than the ninth floor. This felt the same as being on the roof, only easier.

I tiptoed out to see if anyone was around and saw plenty of people outside. All was going according to plan. I went back inside and put on my mean, angry face, a face that wasn't messing around. After all, every step had to be believable; otherwise it was all for nothing. I wiped the tears off my face, picked up the little guy, and gave him one last kiss and hug.

"It's okay, little fella; it's almost over," I said. "I promise you will have a good life."

I took a deep breath and let out a sigh. "Here we go," I said, as I walked out on the balcony. I gathered some junk that was lying around to stand on, to make myself higher so that everyone could see me and the puppy. Holding him tightly, I put him over the rail so everyone could see. I was the laughing stock of the neighborhood—the weird one, the messed-up one. You get the point. I knew that the way people felt about me was going to save the puppy's life.

I noticed that a lot of people had started to gather around. The kids left their snowmen and sleds behind as they rushed to the scene. I could tell by the looks on their faces that everyone was worried about the pup.

Great, I thought. *Almost there.*

People started shouting up at me.

"Don't do it!"

"You're crazy!"

By now they were yelling and screaming at me not to drop him. Some kids were crying, afraid the puppy was going to die. Everyone was believing my story. I made sure to give them all a couple of scares, just to make sure they were paying attention, and when the moment was right, I dropped him carefully, so that he would land on his feet. I will never forget the feeling I had as he was going down—so afraid for his life, but somehow knowing deep down he was going to make it, that he was going to be loved and cared for.

That moment felt like forever, even though it was just seconds. I heard a yelp, and everyone held their breath as a couple kids who were ready to claim the puppy circled around to check on him.

"He's alive! He's alive!" I heard one of the girls say. She had the puppy in her hands, and I could tell he was all right. I didn't see any blood; he was moving and licking the girl's face, the girl who was going to give him a chance to have a good life.

While this was one of the hardest experiences of my life, I knew it was something I could live with; having the puppy starve to death or become a punching bag was not. That would have broken my heart to pieces, and I couldn't have handled it. I wouldn't allow such an outcome—not if I could help it.

That night, just as I knew would happen, Alyona's father got home and found out the puppy was gone. I don't know if I told him what happened, or if I lied and said I'd let him out the door by accident. It didn't matter; I got a good beating for losing my sister's gift.

I didn't mind; I could take it. I was used to it. I was used to my life. I just felt bad for Alyona, having to hear me scream and cry. She was crying too; she knew something was wrong. Going to bed later, I calmed her down, letting her know that everything was okay now; it was safe to go to sleep.

She was out within seconds. It took me a while, though. My body was still on fire, pulsing with pain. What kept me up the most was thinking about the puppy.

A couple of weeks later I found out that the puppy was doing great—that he had been adopted by the girl's family. I was told that he was the girl's dog, that they were the best of friends and she loved him very much. I don't remember who told me the news, but I do remember how happy I was to hear it—how it lifted my spirits. This was the best news I could ever wish for!

That night did haunt me for a while. I would wake up sweating from the nightmare of that moment, when I had to drop him. I had never had nightmares really, till that day. I couldn't help but wonder if I'd done the right thing, or if I, too, was a monster for throwing him off the balcony. I hoped the nightmare would go away, and in time, it finally did—although shortly afterward, it was replaced by another.

Chapter 13

Pay It Forward

One day while skipping down the stairs in our building, which I loved doing, I stumbled upon a lady who had a bucket in her hands full of trash, mostly compost. She looked frail and was having a hard time with the bucket, which was clearly too heavy for her.

I didn't waste any time.

"I'll take your garbage out for you," I said, taking the bucket from her. I could tell she wasn't well. I didn't know what was wrong, but something definitely was.

"You would do that for me?" she asked. She was smiling, and I could tell she was relieved.

"Of course—it's no problem," I said. I told her I'd be right back.

This was my first time taking out trash, as we usually didn't have much to throw away. It made me feel normal for a moment.

I was back within minutes, as the bucket wasn't that heavy for me, and the dumpsters were just up the hill from the building. When I returned, the lady was standing in the doorway.

"Here you go," I said, as I handed her bucket back.

I was just about to leave when the lady said, "Hang on—I have something for you." She took my hand and placed some coins in my palm. "Go get yourself a little something." The frail lady smiled and thanked me again.

I was soon on my way to the kiosk, thinking about how I'd had no idea this was going to happen. Without really knowing what I was doing, I had paid it forward, and in the end, all was well. I had a good feeling inside. It sure beat the bad feelings. I understood then and there that when I did good things that felt right, there were no bad feelings, and no one was in trouble, which told me that this was the right way to be.

This was not the only thing I learned that day. I also learned what it felt like to have to choose something that I wanted. Of course, I wanted everything at the kiosk, especially the big chocolate bar. Since I had no idea what the coins were worth, I thought I could get anything. Come to find out, I had enough for three pieces of bubble gum—which was just as exciting, as I'd never had gum before!

I handed the man behind the kiosk window all the coins I had and chose three pieces from the many kinds of gum on display. I stuffed every piece in my mouth; it was so delicious, I couldn't help myself.

Making my way back home, I thought about what I was going to do about the gum. I didn't want Mom or Alyona's father to know about it, as I felt like I'd get in trouble. So I hid the chewed wad of gum in the corner of the stairs and went back inside, hoping to chew it some more the next day, as there was plenty of flavor left.

To my dismay, when I went back for the gum the next day, it was gone. I was so disappointed. I wondered if someone else was chewing it. Let's be real—most likely someone just tossed it out.

What a waste, I thought. I could have chewed it forever!

Chapter 14

Strange Day

One day, out of the blue, two strangers showed up at our apartment. Mom was home, and she welcomed them with open arms. All I could think was, *You know these people?*

It was a middle-aged woman and her teenage son. Apparently, we were related! I remember thinking how Mom and this woman looked nothing alike. Mom had blue eyes, blonde hair, and fair skin, and was a little over five feet tall. The woman, on the other hand, was much taller, with long black hair, brown eyes, and very defined black eyebrows. I realized she looked just like my grandma. We had one photograph in the apartment—a portrait of Grandma, hanging on one of the bedroom walls.

I noticed that the woman at the door had a walking cane, and I could tell something had happened to one of her legs, as it looked like she couldn't move it freely.

"Ludmila, this is your aunt Ludmila, and her son, Victor," Mom said.

I was dumbfounded. I couldn't believe the words that had just come out of her mouth. I had never heard of them in all my eight years of life, and had a hard time coming to terms with this news. This woman even had the same name as me and Grandma; we definitely were related.

"Hello," I said, doing my best to appear friendly.

"I hear you have a sister now," said the woman. I could tell she was excited to meet Alyona, although she was clearly out of touch. She must have heard about my sister only recently, since it had been two years since she was born. It seemed like she would have shown up earlier if she'd known. At least I knew why they were here; at first, I thought something must have been wrong.

They were here to stay with us for couple of days, so we made a bed on the floor for Mom and me, so my aunt could sleep on the bed. Alyona was happy in her crib, while the son slept in the kitchen, on a single bed against the wall. Mom had gotten it from someone who didn't want it a short while ago. It came in handy. We never had company sleep over, so I was glad everyone was set.

The next morning, I woke up to find that Mom was gone. Alyona and I had been left with our supposed family. It was very awkward. All I wanted to know was when Mom was going to be back. Honestly, I would have preferred to be left alone with my sister than to stay in the apartment with estranged relatives.

I went to the kitchen to ask my aunt if she knew when Mom was coming home. I was getting nervous staying here with them. I wasn't happy that Mom had left us here with them.

"Sometime tonight," my aunt said. Victor was sitting with her at the kitchen table. They were both smoking cigarettes and talking about stuff that was none of my business.

I wasn't going to spill the beans about how we lived, so I went back to the bed on the floor and pretended I was napping, so I didn't have to talk. I ended up falling back asleep for a little while, and when I woke up, I found Victor sitting by me on the floor. I could tell he was staring at me, and I didn't know why. *Was I still dreaming?* This was very strange. I kept lying there, looking back at him as if to say "Why are you staring at me like that?" Something was very wrong.

"Victor!" I heard his mother yell from the kitchen. "Come here—I need you to run out to get more cigarettes."

"All right," he said. He got up and gave me one more creepy smile.

What's up with this guy? I thought. All I knew was that I should stay away from him. I was ready for Mom to come home, and soon.

Mom ended up being gone all day. I really couldn't sleep when she was gone—I didn't feel comfortable—so I had stayed up, waiting for her return. Suddenly I heard a knock on the door. At first, I thought it was Mom, but then I realized it wasn't, as the knocking turned into banging, with male voices demanding we open up.

I was nervous. This didn't usually happen, and somehow I knew it had to do with my mom.

Don't open it, I thought, but my aunt, having no idea what was about to happen, opened the door, probably thinking it was Mom's boyfriend, or an angry neighbor.

Moments later five men I had never seen before barged inside our apartment.

"Get on the fucking ground!" I heard one of them yell at my aunt.

She tried to explain that she couldn't, due to her leg, but the men didn't seem to care. I heard my aunt scream from the pain of them forcing her to the floor.

"Victor, don't," she screamed, as her son tried to intervene. He was also pushed to the floor, and I knew he was unconscious. His mother screamed, "Please don't hurt him, please—he was just trying to protect me!" She was pleading for his life.

"Stay down, and we won't do anything to him," a deep voice said. "Where's Natasha? Where is that bitch?" He was pretty angry to find that my mother wasn't there.

"I don't know," my aunt said. "She went out for the day and asked me to babysit her kids." I could hear the fear in her voice as she tried to answer truthfully. "We are just visiting for a couple of days. I really don't know where she is!" My aunt was crying, down on the floor, hugging her son and calling his name.

I went to check on Alyona, who was still sleeping. I climbed into the crib to be close to her. I didn't want her to be scared.

The men looked pretty damn terrifying to me. They wore masks, and had several tattoos that seemed to say "Stay away, or else." I mainly remember the ugly skull tattoo one of the men had on his arm.

One of the guys came up to the crib and threw the sheets over my face so I couldn't see anything. I pretended like I was sleeping, but when he went on to destroy our apartment, inch by inch, I carefully peeked out to see what was going on. He was obviously searching for something.

"Come on! There's nothing here, man."

The man with the skull tattoo was disappointed. "Let's take this rug—looks like it might be worth something."

I watched the five scary men take the big Persian rug off the wall, folding it up to take with them. Mom had just bought it recently.

At that moment, Mom and Alyona's father walked in. I will never forget it. It was just like that movie, *Catch Me If You Can*, where the main character realizes what's coming for him and books it, a million miles an hour, so as not to get caught.

That's exactly how it went down.

I could see Mom's eyes get really wide. She froze for a split second, and no one knew what to do. Suddenly I heard a voice shout "Get her, get her!" Mom was out the door like a shot, along with her boyfriend, also running for his life.

That's when I knew Mom was in some big shit. These men were bad news. They had huge shiny knives, and maybe even guns; I didn't see any, but that didn't mean they didn't have them.

None of us slept that night. Aunt Ludmila and Victor kept watch by the window, smoking cigarette after cigarette. I could tell Victor was still scared, confused as to what the hell had just happened. He missed the entire thing, waking up when it was all over.

We made sure to keep the lights off so that we could see better what was outside, just in case we spotted Mom. Hours went by where we saw and heard nothing.

I went back to the bedroom and crawled into the crib again. Hugging Alyona, I quietly cried, thinking horrible thoughts. *What if they got Mom? What if they caught her and they're doing something bad to her?* I couldn't breathe. I was so scared I would never see Mom again.

Next morning, Mom was still missing. We were all exhausted from barely sleeping, worried sick about Mom. Alyona was now in the kitchen with my aunt. She was adorable, and I'm sure she made my aunt feel better just by being her adorable self.

I went back to the bedroom and returned to the floor bed. I was so tired, and at this point couldn't help but fall asleep. I woke up a couple hours later to Victor sitting on the floor, watching me again. I didn't move—just tried to figure out what he was up to. His mother was in the kitchen as usual, smoking cigarettes, and Alyona was down for a nap.

"You want to feel better?" he asked, moving closer to me. "I can do something that will make all this go away for a while," he said, a weird look on his face.

I knew how to read people, but this was something else entirely—something I hadn't come across before. I had no clue, other than realizing that what happened next was wrong—seriously wrong.

My heart was beating faster, and I could feel that something bad was going to happen to me. I saw his hand go under the sheets. Before I knew it, his hand was wandering around where it didn't belong. I was eight, and had no idea what was happening to me, I wouldn't understand until weeks later.

"Doesn't that feel good?" he asked, smiling. I could feel that he was doing something inside me with his hand, and no, it didn't feel good; it felt horrible. I was completely frozen, with feelings of disgust and shock. It only lasted a minute, but it felt like forever, and it sure as hell changed me forever.

I didn't know what was wrong with me—just that I wasn't feeling well. I felt like I didn't want my body anymore. Whatever had happened was not right, not right at all. I tried not to think about it too much, as I felt guilty thinking about myself when Mom was still missing. I was missing her, especially now, after what had happened. I just desperately needed my mom to hold me. *Please come home*, I thought.

Afterward, Victor got up and left as if nothing had happened. I didn't know what to do, so I kept it to myself, not saying a word to his mother, who was just in the other room when it happened.

It was the most amazing feeling when Mom finally showed up a few hours later, not a scratch on her. I could tell she was scared, and that this wasn't over yet. Alyona's father didn't come back; I think he got really scared this time, and decided not to show his face around here ever again.

Years later, he was on the news for nearly beating a woman to death. Luckily, she survived. She made sure he was arrested for it, and he got life in prison. He'd messed with the wrong woman. I was happy he was behind bars, where he belonged.

Chapter 15

The Big Shift

After what happened, Mom didn't want Alyona and me to stay in the apartment with her any longer. She was afraid that the next time those men showed up, looking for her, the outcome might be much worse. She didn't want to "risk our lives." She'd decided that it would be best for us to go and live with my aunt and her family while she stayed behind to fix the problem she had created.

"When it's all over, I will come and get you, okay?" Mom said, as she continued packing our bag.

Even though I knew she was right, I still didn't want to leave her there all alone, without anyone to protect her. I felt like it was much worse to be so far away from Mom during this time. If anything, I felt like we should all stick together. Not that I said any of this out loud. There was no talking to Mom about this, and I knew it. It was the worst conversation ever. I couldn't believe this was happening. Things couldn't get any worse.

My mom had been dealing heroin for these men, and after a couple of years, she'd gotten greedy. She had started to use their heroin instead of selling it. I heard her telling my aunt everything—from her alcoholism, to being abused by Alyona's father, to the heroin addiction. Now the men were after Mom to collect what she owed them, which was a lot of money she didn't have.

I was surprised to hear that Alyona's father was the innocent one this time. He'd been caught in the middle of Mom's mess, and had no clue about what she'd been doing. He'd barely been living with us at the time, so he didn't really know what she was up to. I think the two of them had become nothing but drug business buddies, and in the end, there was very little love left.

I was crying as we walked to the bus station to go to Aunt Ludmila's home. I tried to take in as much as possible of my neighborhood as we walked. I wanted to make sure I remembered how things looked so I'd never forget. I had no idea when I would see Mom again, or if she was going to be okay at the end of this thing. Nor did I know when we would be coming home. For a split second, my entire life flashed before my eyes, and I realized just how much I was going to miss my home and our neighborhood. Suddenly everything I felt about everyone giving me a hard time was gone, replaced with nostalgia and regret for not appreciating everything I had while I'd lived here.

What a strange day, I thought. I was learning so much, so fast. I couldn't keep up. And while this day felt like my last one on Earth, because of all the overwhelming feelings going through my head, on the outside, the world was just as it always was. The sky was blue, the sun was shining, the kids jumping rope, having a good time. All was as usual; nothing was different in the world.

To me, however, everything was different. Everything had changed. I was walking past all the neighbors, wondering if any of them would even notice that we were gone. I kept wondering if anyone could see what was happening to me—that deep down inside, I felt like the world was ending, and I needed someone to tell me that it wasn't— that everything would turn out okay.

I had never taken the bus before, and neither had Alyona.

"First time for both of us," I told my sister as I sat down and made sure she was comfortable.

Victor and his mother sat across from us, talking and laughing. It wasn't like their lives were being completely destroyed.

I turned around and concentrated on looking out the window. I was feeling nauseous, and didn't feel like throwing up inside the bus, which was full of people. The heat was not helping; it was really hot outside. Looking out the window helped, and while the bus drove farther and farther away from my home, I drifted off, lost inside memory lane.

I had no desire to think of what was going to happen once we got off this bus. I was scared shitless, especially knowing that I was going to live under the same roof with Victor. I promised myself that if he ever tried to touch my sister, I would do everything in my power to stop it. *I need a knife*, I thought.

Finally, the bus came to a stop, and my aunt signaled me to get up. We were here—wherever *here* was.

Chapter 16

Summer in the Suburbs

I will admit, living with my aunt's family didn't turn out to be so bad; in fact, I found myself enjoying summer in the suburbs. There was so much to do! Here, rules were a little different than back at home. My aunt didn't rely on me to take care of Alyona; if anything, I realized she wanted to spend time with my sister, which was so nice to see. She was a mother to two boys, and two daughters who lived far away.

Her oldest son was in his early twenties, and much nicer than Victor. He never did anything to me, and I was grateful. He was very tall, and looked a lot like his mother. My aunt's husband was much older than her, maybe in his fifties, but he looked even older. A long time alcoholic, he couldn't function well at all if he didn't drink. Most of the time he was either sleeping it off or away getting drunk somewhere. My aunt was the responsible adult who took care of us all. Her oldest son had some kind of shady job, so he was able to help out financially, helping to put food on the table. He wasn't around all that much, and neither was Victor. There were times when I wouldn't see any of the men in the family for days. That left Alyona, my aunt, and me.

I did a lot of observing when we first arrived. I needed to know what kind of people we were living with. My goal was to assess the situation, learn their rules, and blend in. I didn't want any trouble. Who knew what that would be like? I wasn't going to take any chances. It had been a couple of weeks, and so far, so good. I could leave the courtyard area to wander around, and as long as I was back for my curfew—something new for me—I was in the clear. "Be back by eight p.m.," my aunt would say, every time I left.

Some things were easy to adjust to, while others proved to be very hard. The first thing I had to get used to was living in the suburbs, where there were no tall buildings—not one! Every single house was tiny, most just one floor, all lined up, one after another, stretching for miles and miles. Every place had a gate to walk through with big locks; inside the gate stood three to four tiny houses around their own little courtyard. It was the same for us: three tiny houses, all bunched together. We had a big courtyard, and the neighbors who lived the next section over were visible due to the poor handmade fence.

My aunt's place was all the way at the end, by the corner. My first reaction when we entered her house was *Wow*. While I might have thought our apartment wasn't that great, this place was much worse. There was one small room right when you entered that served as a kitchen/living room. There were no kitchen cabinets, no stovetop or oven, not even a fridge. The walls appeared cracked, and their color made the place look gloomy. There was one small table, two flimsy chairs, and a big stone object against the wall in the corner, on the opposite side of the room. I'd never seen anything like it before. Later on I learned it was a stove used for both heating and cooking. I didn't mess around with this thing. It would get very loud when the coals were burning inside, and while my aunt warmed up some water to make pea soup, some of the big flames would come through the bottom. You had to know how to handle this beast to be anywhere near it.

In the middle of the room stood another door that led into the bedroom, much smaller than the main room. The walls were identical, with the same gloomy paint color and cracked texture where some of the paint or plaster was peeling off. There were two single beds on each side of the wall, along with a chair that served as a table, where ashtrays held several cigarette butts. At the end of the room was enough space to fit a mattress for Alyona and me to sleep on. It wasn't the cleanest or thickest of mattresses, but it was better than nothing. We got one pillow and one blanket to share.

I remember the first night we slept there, I was so afraid to fall asleep because I didn't want to wet the bed. I knew I was too old for this, but it still happened at home now and then. Amazingly enough, I didn't wet the bed that night, or any other night after that. For whatever reason it had stopped, which was a huge relief.

There was a small window right above where we slept. It was strange, because I couldn't see the outdoors—only people's feet were visible as they walked by on the sidewalk. It was pretty dirty, since this side of the house was literally underground.

I remember thinking, *Where is the bathroom—and the shower?* It was surprising to me, as I'd had no idea people lived this way. There was an outhouse, but it was a dreadful, scary, and smelly place, with nothing but four terribly built walls made of wood and a big hole in the middle to get the business done. I couldn't get used to it. The first time I went into one, I was so grossed out, just from the smell alone; even my eyes were watering. Flies were everywhere, and there was nothing to wipe with, not even a newspaper! Aside from that, the hole was so damn big I was afraid I might fall in. Shit and piss everywhere—it was pretty disgusting, if you ask me. I couldn't believe that was how people went to the bathroom! I found other ways to go, but not in this thing; I just couldn't do it. I was glad Alyona was too young to go inside one of these things. She had a metal bucket-like thing to do her business; my aunt was "potty training" her, which I had never heard of before. It was pretty fun, learning stuff from my aunt.

As for showering, well, no one showered or bathed much around here, which was fine with me, as we didn't do much of it back home, either. If we needed to bathe or wipe ourselves clean at my aunt's house, we would fill up the metal buckets with water from the pump down the street and pour all the water into a big metal tub outside. We had a piece of cloth to wash ourselves with and a brown bar of soap. I remember my aunt would shave bits of the soap into the tub and let it sit in the sun for a while. Later in the afternoon we would take our baths, as it would begin to get cooler outside, while the water was still warm.

Alyona loved the tub. She never wanted to get out, playing and splashing for hours and having a great time. I would take a bath, too, but with my clothes on. There was no privacy—not that my aunt cared. She'd sit buck naked in that tub with her eyes closed, saying it was her way "to get some peace."

Chapter 17

Apricot Tree

While it was fun to be somewhere different and learn about my aunt's family's way of life, I was constantly thinking of Mom and her well-being. An entire month went by, and still, no word from Mom—not that she would have had much to go on, as we didn't have a phone or spare change to buy a stamp, to write to her. The only option was to wait for her to show up.

Just down the street by the corner, across from a hair salon, stood an apricot tree. At this point it had completely transformed; it looked orange rather than green, filled with more apricots than leaves. I had tried an apricot before, but never knew that this was what it looked like, growing on the tree. I learned that in order to eat the fruit you had to wait for it to grow. I found it so cool! I loved that tree, and not just because of the delicious, sweet, and juicy apricots, but also because the tree had very welcoming branches that allowed me to climb up in them and rest.

I will never forget the aroma of that tree, nor just how many apricots were on it. I loved spending time in its branches, munching on apricots, watching people change as they got their hair done. I had never seen a hair salon before, and I found it fascinating—how different people looked afterward, like it wasn't even the same person.

I never knew you could change your hair color from brown to blond to black. I remember thinking, *Wow, that's too cool!* I liked the fact that the windows were big enough for me to see in; the apricot tree supplied the perfect vantage point from which to enjoy the show.

As I sat there, eating apricots, I kept wondering what Mom was up to, and if she'd made any progress in taking care of the mess we were in. I couldn't get rid of this feeling inside, in the pit of my stomach. I felt like part of me was missing; no matter what I did, I couldn't help but feel this storm cloud above my head, following me everywhere, all the time.

Maybe Mom needs to change her hair, I thought. Maybe then the bad guys wouldn't be able to find her, since she wouldn't look the same. I wondered if Mom thought of this too.

I wished for her to come back every day. Some days I would sit in the courtyard just watching the gate, hoping Mom would be the next to walk through. Every time I heard a woman's voice I would jump up with excitement, only to be crushed back down with disappointment. I hated that feeling. It was like sinking back down all over again; every time felt deeper and deeper. I was slipping into the abyss. I had spent many days by myself before, but this time, the alone feeling felt completely different—like I'd never really known what *alone* felt like till now.

When I needed to take a break and get out of my head, I would visit the apricot tree for some comfort. She was so good to me, embracing me with her branches, feeding me with her fruit, making me feel better inside—even if just for a short while. It was better than nothing, and better than being around people. I was so happy to have this tree, and I was happy that no one else cared to climb her. It was like she was there just for me. I remember how shocked I felt seeing other people walk by without even stopping to look at the tree, or take an apricot. It was like they didn't even notice the tree was there at all. As the saying goes, "One person's penny is someone else's gold," and to me, this tree was just that—it was like I'd hit the jackpot, and won. Now it wasn't the roof of my old apartment complex that gave me comfort, but rather trees.

I wondered what other fruit trees I might be missing. I was very curious to see what apple trees were like, or cherry trees, and how their fruit might taste straight off the tree. I was looking forward to climbing other trees and trying the fruit. For a short while, I was able to wonder and think about something other than Mom. I couldn't stop thinking that she might be dead; after all, those men were pretty crazy dangerous, and anything was possible, as laws were rarely enforced. There was only corruption, and crimes that went unpunished, which is why I couldn't help but imagine the worst. The police officers were just as involved in corruption. The only thing that could help was a lot of money to pay people off, which we had no chance of having; no one had a real job around here.

I did my best to believe she was still alive. Part of me refused to believe she might never come back. *What would happen to us?* I thought, as I slowly made my way back down to the ground. I took some apricots to take back with me, to share, thinking maybe it would make them feel better too. My aunt was just as worried about Mom as I was; I could feel it. She seemed worried and sad. Everyone was on the edge of their seats, waiting for Mom to return. I especially looked forward to going back home. Aside from missing Mom, I missed our home just as much—maybe not the other people in the neighborhood, but definitely our home.

Chapter 18

Friends

While I'd had a hard time making friends back at home, here, I had no problems. Making friends with the kids in my aunt's neighborhood was as easy as breathing. I didn't even have to try very hard, or prove myself in any way. None of them made fun of me, or said bad things, which was a first. Part of me felt like in some ways, Alyona and I belonged here more than we did back at home. It seemed like everyone who lived around my aunt faced the same challenges my family had endured.

There was one family who lived a couple doors down from us. They had two boys—one about my age, named Vanya, and the other, around thirteen. I figured the older one was probably a friend of Victor's, so I stayed away from him. There was one more family with kids—two boys—who lived in the next section over, across the fence. One of them was also my age, so we could play together, while his younger brother was about five.

Sometimes we'd set fires for fun—safe fires, of course. We didn't like starting grass fires, as we'd learned they were too dangerous. Someone had tried it once, burning an entire field, and nearly setting a building on fire. I was glad it wasn't any of us. We'd also chase each other with fake guns, pretending to be good cops killing bad guys. We took turns switching roles, from bad guys to good cops, and vice versa. I had never played with guns before, but I found myself enjoying the game nevertheless. It was like, for a minute, while in character, we were able to feel powerful—like we mattered and were important, so others had to follow and listen to us. It was our way to feel better about all the fucked-up shit going on in our lives.

I was so happy to be included for once. Sometimes the boys would show up at our door, asking if I was around to play, which blew my mind. I had friends, and it felt good not to be alone in life. We were all in the same boat around here, and that made me feel secure and comfortable. We had each other's backs.

It was early in the morning one day: The sun was just coming up, and the birds were starting to get louder. There was some fog in the air, and the light looked so pretty shining through the fog. I loved this time of day, when there was nothing but silence, and stillness. Everyone was still sleeping—well, almost everyone—and the world wasn't busy yet. This time of day was one of the things I really loved about being here—that I could be outside in one step, no need for windows or stairs, or for the elevator or the balcony. I liked the simplicity in that. I also liked that the boys were willing to share their lives with me.

Like the two boys on the other side of the fence: They had a baby brother on the way, and their parents didn't work. They were barely scraping by. Their father was just like Alyona's father. I felt so bad for them; I knew exactly what that felt like. When it came to the boys on our side, Vanya and his older brother, well, their living situation was even worse. Their parents were alcoholics who were so hooked on booze that they forced the boys to leave the house and go find a way to bring them liquor, or else, which meant a good beating if they weren't successful. There were times when I heard them scream.

I will never forget the time Vanya was so scared for his brother's life that he took the blame to spare him.

"We take turns," he said. "That way we both get some time to heal a little before the next time comes around."

"Is that why you guys burn the rubber—to sell it, in order to get your parents booze?" I asked.

Many times I'd seen the boys burning stuff at the back of the courtyard, collecting copper wires to sell. It was pretty cool. I'd had no idea that's what cables looked like underneath all the rubber.

"Yeah, that helps," Vanya replied.

Before long, I knew my way around as well as the people who lived here. Vanya took me on trips to different places in the neighborhood, showing me where one of the elementary schools was located. I remember we would sneak in through a hole in the fence and go up to the playground area. All of the kids and adults were inside the building, so we were okay for a while. We were trespassing, and if caught, we would have gotten in trouble with the police. I wasn't scared. I knew I was a fast runner, and so was Vanya; plus, we would see them coming, which meant we'd have plenty of time to run away.

I loved the swing the most, so we stayed there, swinging for a while. It was like meditation for us; no talking, just swinging, lost in thought. We got each other, and it wasn't long before he told me that he liked me. I will never forget that day, when I found out a boy actually liked me. It felt so weird. Part of me couldn't believe it; what was it about me he liked? Of course, we were just kids, so it was harmless, and it never went anywhere other than us being friends. I wasn't ready for that stuff. I was too young, and had no idea what *girlfriend* and *boyfriend* meant. And after what had happened with Victor . . . well, there was no way in hell I was going to go through that again.

So we remained good friends, wandering and discovering new places together, having a blast, as any eight-year-old would. I remember thinking how excited I was to tell the other kids back home about my friends here and how tough they were. Vanya carried a knife, and smoked cigarettes—a total badass. He was street-smart, and knew how to take care of himself in case of danger. I trusted him with my life, as I was pretty clueless about what lurked in the shadows.

Chapter 19

What a Feeling

"Do you want to try it?" Vanya asked me, waving his cigarette around.

It was early morning, and I was up and ready to go out for the day. As usual everyone was still sleeping off their hangovers. All was nice and quiet for the moment.

As Vanya continued smoking, I thought about it and figured, How bad could it be? If Vanya could do it, so could I.

"I'm going to try it," I said, looking at Vanya, who by now appeared pretty excited.

He looked at me with big eyes and smiled. "Here." He passed me the cigarette.

"Now what?" I asked. While it may have looked easy, I realized it wasn't once the cigarette was in my hands.

"Put it next to your lips, like this, and pull the air toward your mouth," he said. "Once you feel smoke in your mouth, inhale it into your lungs—like this." Vanya demonstrated. "Ready?" he asked.

"Ready." I did just what Vanya said, and seconds later I was coughing my brains out. My throat felt like it was on fire.

"Shit, you didn't tell me about this part!" I said, handing back the cigarette.

Vanya was laughing. He knew exactly what was going to happen, and to him, it was something to look forward to. I guess it's not every day you teach someone how to smoke. I wasn't mad or anything; I trusted him. We were best friends.

"I know—my bad," he said, still laughing. "It's just how it goes at first, but it'll get better every time you smoke."

I giggled. "Wow, this feels crazy," I said.

By now I had a head rush; my muscles felt relaxed, and my entire body felt lighter. I was impressed. "Now I get why you smoke," I said, as I lay down on the shed roof, looking up at the sky.

"My brother taught me," he said, as he lay back down next to me. "I was five," he added, exhaling. I loved it when he puffed out perfect smoke rings.

"Can I take another drag?" I asked. I wanted to test his theory. He passed me the cigarette and I took another drag, and then another. Every time, it became easier and easier. Vanya was right! I felt like a pro already. It felt so good to have something to calm my nerves. I had no idea how much smoking would help me; it was a relief I'd never felt before. In the days to come, I wouldn't smoke every day like Vanya did—only once in a while, or when I was hanging out with him. I knew that what I was doing was wrong, as I was too young, but I didn't care. In my eyes, I wasn't young. I needed to feel better just as much as all the adults around here did; after all, I was going through shit just as much as they were, and I felt I deserved to feel better.

"Make sure no one sees you smoking," Vanya said that first time, as he put out the little bit of the cigarette that was left and threw it in the bushes. "If your parents find out, you will be in big trouble, most likely; you're a girl."

"So? What does that have to do with it?" I asked, puzzled.

"Rules are different for girls; you should watch your back," he replied. "Bad things happen to girls and women sometimes, but not men." He showed me the knife he had in his pocket, and another one in his boots, as if to prove he could take care of himself.

"We are leaving soon, anyway, I'm sure. I don't have to worry about that," I said, putting on a confident face.

But deep down inside, he got to me. I understood that there were many Victors around here, and that I had to learn how to recognize if I was in danger.

* * *

Two months had passed, and Mom was still missing. We hadn't heard a word from her. I had to start thinking more like the kids around the neighborhood and adapt to their way of life, before it was too late. I knew what people were capable of, and it was time to make a choice—no more dual realities, no more thinking about going back home. I needed to put that behind me for a while; otherwise, I'd never be able to adjust or feel like I was part of *this* reality, which was now. Home was part of the past, and perhaps my future—but who knew when that might be. I told myself that *this* was my life now, and I was going to live it fully, as if it was my home.

All I really cared about was for my mom, wherever she was, to be okay, and come back to us, whenever that might be. I had to keep going. I had to keep living the best way I could, with what I had, because if I didn't, it felt like parts of me would slowly die. I was falling apart, always thinking about going home—but not anymore. I was tired of dying a little bit every day for the past two months. I knew I had to do something, and this was the only thing I could think of: I would give it all up—the daydreaming, the longing to return home—as if it was nothing but a distant dream.

Every time I smoked a cigarette, it served as a reminder that my life was different now. Although I would never forget Mom or our life together back home, I was different now. I was no longer the same girl I'd been just two short months ago. I was no longer an innocent child. Now I was a street kid—one of the boys—swearing up a storm, smoking cigarettes, and scavenging for cables to burn for copper, to sell for some spare change. I was ready to make some money if I could. We'd all go out together and bring back a whole bunch of crap to burn. I will never forget the nasty smoke from that rubber. I was not a big fan of that part—the smell was horrible—but it was worth it. With the money we earned, we could buy some cigarettes and gum, two new favorites that I'd developed a taste for.

And so my new life had begun.

Chapter 20

She's Alive!

One day, about a month later, I was making my way back to the house after wandering the neighborhood and visiting the apricot tree. I heard a familiar voice as I came through the gate. *Could it be?* I couldn't believe I was hearing my mom's voice! It was like I was dreaming!

I ran into the house as fast as I could and saw Mom sitting at the table, Alyona in her lap.

"Mom! You're back!" I cried. I had butterflies in my stomach. All I felt was happiness and relief. This wasn't a dream—it was really happening.

"Come here," Mom said, passing my sister over to my aunt to give me a hug.

"I missed you so much!" I said, as I hugged her tight. I didn't want to let go. It was like suddenly, I was exactly where I belonged—next to Mom, the only parent I had. She was everything to me, and despite our history, I couldn't imagine the world without her. She was my mom, and without her, what would we be?

I was glad to see that she looked all right; there wasn't a scratch on her. I wondered what she could have been up to this entire time. I wanted to know what had happened.

That same day, after Mom had caught up with my aunt, our belongings were packed and we were ready to go back home. I didn't even have time to say good-bye to any of my friends, which really sucked. They would have to find out through my aunt when they showed up, looking for me. I knew Vanya was going to be the most upset, as I'd promised him I'd say good-bye before I left.

From what I'd gathered while listening to Mom's every word, she "had taken care of it." No one was after us anymore. Apparently, she'd met a nice man who had been helping her stay clear of the bad guys by letting her stay at his place. She said he was a businessman, and that he knew how to help her.

"He really cares," she said. "He didn't give up. He's always finding ways to help me." She seemed pretty confident in this man—like she really confided in him, and trusted him implicitly. "He didn't try to get in my pants," Mom said, laughing. "I couldn't believe it. He really cares about helping us out. I can't believe it's all over, and we can go home!"

I was surprised to see Mom so excited about going home. I'd thought all this time that she'd been home, or somewhere near it, at least. After all, she'd said she would be taking care of the mess. Come to find out, her new friend had wanted her to stay away from the apartment until he'd had a chance to take care of things for her, and it was safe for her to go back. She'd been staying at his house for free all this time, while he took care of business. Now he'd told her that it was finally safe to go back, so we weren't wasting any time.

There was an old truck waiting for us outside the gate, its engine rumbling. It had a wooden bed and two rusted doors, a nice blue color showing through the rust. Mom got in first, saying "Help Alyona up." She stretched out her hands to grab her. I placed our belongings on the floor of the truck and jumped in, closing the rusty door behind me.

I had never been inside a car before, never mind riding in one. As far as I was concerned, only rich people had that luxury. Plus, in my experience, women didn't drive; it was like an unspoken rule or something. I'd never seen a woman driving any type of vehicle. I was beside myself with excitement to be riding in a truck. The windows were open, which was nice, as it was August and pretty hot outside this time of day.

Mom was busy chatting with the driver, who seemed pretty nice, even though he had a serious expression. His bushy eyebrows and mustache made him look scary, like he was going to yell or something, like he was bothered somehow, but he was actually a good man who'd had a hard life working in the fields. Every summer people had the opportunity to work the fields, harvesting fruits and vegetables for the state to sell. It was a big operation, from what I'd heard, but the pay was terrible, according to our driver. This made me angry; all of these terrible stories about people being taken advantage of made me sick to my stomach—especially when I heard that if anything was stolen and someone found out, the accused would be shot.

About an hour had gone by, and I was finally seeing some familiar streets and buildings. We were almost there! I realized the closer we got, the faster my heart was beating. I was so nervous all of a sudden, freaking out about everyone seeing our return. It was like my past life in this neighborhood suddenly flooded back into existence. I realized that being back here made me feel strange. After all, a lot had happened in the past three months. Nevertheless, I was very excited to say hello to our home and see all of our belongings again. This home was what made our lives real, what made us feel like we had roots—that we were a family.

The truck came to a halt and the driver announced we had arrived. One by one we all got out of the truck and Mom handed the man some money for the ride.

"Thank you, sir," Mom said as she closed the truck door.

We all stood there for a second, watching the truck drive away, filling the air with smoke.

"Are we ready?" Mom asked. She was just as excited to finally be home.

I followed her inside, helping Alyona walk into the building, and then the elevator, which luckily didn't break as we made our way to the fourth floor.

Almost there, I thought.

Moments later, we were all standing outside the door to our apartment, overjoyed, ready to go inside and remind ourselves what our home looked like.

Chapter 21

Big Fat Lie

Turns out, Mom's so-called friend, the one supposedly helping her, ended up being someone completely different. He was able to convince Mom that he was honorable—probably pretty easy to do, since Mom was desperate, alone and vulnerable. This guy knew exactly what he was doing. I learned later that this nice "friend" told Mom to give him all of our important documents for safekeeping, just in case the bad guys came back. Mom trusted him, and did as he asked. No wonder he wasn't interested in "getting in her pants"; he'd had quite a different agenda in mind. Everything he said and did had been a big fat lie.

When we showed up at our apartment, we noticed that the neighbors looked surprised to see us back, as if to say "You still live here?" They looked confused, but we figured that wasn't surprising, as no one around here liked us very much.

What *was* surprising was the fact that we couldn't get inside our home. Mom's keys didn't work, like someone had changed the locks.

"That's strange," Mom said, as she tried over and over again to open the door, hoping the lock would just turn and let us inside.

Nothing happened; we were still locked out.

At this point, Mom and I were freaking out. Something was

wrong; this didn't make any sense. Why would her friend tell her it was safe to return, only to find we weren't able to get inside? Our only option was to knock on our neighbors' doors to see if anyone might know something. After all, someone had to know *something*; if there was one thing I was certain of, it was that everyone knew everything around here. I stayed behind with Alyona while Mom went to find out what was going on.

Shortly afterward, Mom showed up with a man she said would let us inside. I don't know who he was—maybe the landlord, maybe the new owner; I had no idea—just that Mom was mad at him. She kept saying, "Open the damn door," and "I don't believe you." She was upset, demanding to be let inside.

I just stood there with Alyona, watching, totally oblivious as to what was really going on. I saw the man finally opening the door, and seconds later, we all burst inside. I will never forget what I saw next, one of the most horrible nightmares I had yet to experience. I found myself totally frozen in the hallway, unable to take another step. Everything went silent—I couldn't hear anything around me, and my heart felt like it just hit the floor and shattered into a million tiny pieces.

The entire place we once called home was now entirely empty—nothing but white walls and ceilings. Even the flooring wasn't the same. There was nothing inside to indicate that we'd ever lived here. Everything we'd ever owned—furniture, clothing, photographs, sentimental belongings, other stuff—was all gone. Not a trace had been left behind.

For a second, I felt like my entire life force left me. I just couldn't freaking believe it; it felt like my brain exploded. A couple minutes later, I was running full speed toward the dumpsters up the hill, hoping I might be able to find some of our belongings there. I was so hopeful, I dove right in, but the little spark I had left inside me soon burned out. I had no luck finding anything—not one damn thing. No matter how hard I sorted through the trash—section by section, layer by layer—nothing was there, not even a single photograph. That's all I wanted, to find just one picture of our family, just one picture to remind us that we'd had a life here, that we existed, that we were a family once.

I sat inside the dumpster, trying to catch my breath, tears flowing down my face. I knew what this meant for us, and I knew who was responsible. This made me feel angrier with Mom than with the con artist she'd thought was her friend. Here we were—officially homeless, with no money, nothing of value or anyone to help.

I've blocked out what happened after I got out of the dumpster to make my way back to Mom, who was standing outside, watching me. After that, everything was a blur. I don't even know how we ended up in another town, in another apartment. Maybe Mom knew of this neighborhood, and had come up with this plan for the time being. My guess was she'd chosen this place because it was brand-new, and no one knew Mom or her reputation here. Whatever lies she'd sold the landlord were believed. For now, it was a safe place to stay until the rest of the plan could be carried out, which was to leave without paying a dime for the month's rent. We had thirty days to get our shit together and figure out where we were going to live, for real this time.

Most days after what had happened, I was pretty out of it. I didn't want to do anything other than lie in bed. I was grateful the new place had a bed; it was part of the package. Other than that, it was entirely empty, with white walls, and a small furnished kitchen and bathroom. Everything was brand-new, including the building itself, built just a year earlier, from what Mom told me when she was trying to make small talk. Maybe if the circumstances had been different I would have appreciated this place, but despite its shiny clean tub, polished windows, and perfect white walls, I didn't care about it. This wasn't at all home to me, but rather a strange place, devoid of any memories, of any part of the life I once knew.

She knew I was fuming with anger, and I knew she was too. It made it awkward, as neither of us wanted to talk, or do anything, really. I could tell she was hurting as she looked out the window, puffing away on cigarette after cigarette. I really could have used one myself, thinking that Mom would have killed me if she'd ever found out.

I laid back in bed and closed my eyes, imagining our lost home and what it used to look like, before they erased us. I never wanted to forget any details of our old home; the memories were the only thing I had left to confirm that it was real once, and that I wasn't crazy.

I thought about Vanya and the rest of the crew back at my aunt's place. Part of me wished we'd just go back and live with them. I was pretty used to being there, I had friends, and we were accepted just as we were.

As it turned out, a month later, before the rent was due, we did return to live with my aunt and her family. It was our only option, other than sleeping on a corner somewhere and hoping no one would kill us in our sleep. Vanya had told me plenty of such stories, where bad things happened to people like us.

Chapter 22

New Reality

When we moved back in with my aunt and her family, my feelings about losing our home began to subside a bit each day. I did my best to shove them somewhere deep down inside, and move on. This was our reality, our new way of life. I didn't miss the neighborhood or the people back home, just our apartment and our belongings. Being somewhere familiar helped me deal with big changes; in some ways, it was like we'd never left. Well, at least for Alyona and me; it felt like we'd always been here, and that what had happened back at our old place was just a bad dream.

Mom, on the other hand, was swearing up a storm on a daily basis, getting heated while talking about what she was going to do to the big fat liar when she found him. Not that she ever did anything; I think just talking about it made her feel better. After all, this son-of-a-bitch had all of our important papers, including the apartment documents; somehow he'd been able to forge Mom's signature in order to sell our place. Makes sense why he didn't want Mom there at the apartment; who knows, maybe that was his plan all along. How can you trust anyone after that? Mom was especially angry because she couldn't do a damn thing about it; he was long gone, on to the next con, the next desperate soul looking to trust and confide in someone.

I was a kid, so I had an easier time adapting to whatever life threw our way, and I didn't hold grudges. I only cared about surviving. I had more important matters to worry about at this point, and wanted to find a way to put my time to good use. No one worked around here, so money was scarce; everyone in the family was dreaming about something. Mom wanted a dose of heroin, my aunt wished she had some cigarettes, Alyona and I wished we had some food to eat, and my aunt's husband—well, he wasn't there anymore, but if he had been, I'm sure he would have wanted booze. I think my aunt got tired of him doing nothing around the place, so she'd thrown him out.

Mom did manage to earn some income working side by side with my aunt's oldest son, who was a thief, and a good one. This was his new business venture. Every day, Mom would leave to meet Oleg somewhere in the city to steal stuff, whatever they could, and resell it on the streets for some cash. They were pretty successful, but still, it wasn't much money. Even the little bit Mom walked away with after splitting their shares was spent on cigarettes, alcohol, and eventually, heroin too. It didn't take long before Mom, my aunt, and Oleg were all making and shooting heroin, putting together every little bit of money they had to purchase all the ingredients to make it.

Mom was the worst. Her addiction was ruthless, and if she didn't get a dose, it was like she became a zombie, lying in bed, whining, yelling, delusional. It was terrible. I felt so bad for her. I had no idea how to help her, and she really needed help. She hadn't been herself lately. Some days were better than others, but I knew Mom was at her lowest. I knew she was dealing with the pain of losing our home, being taken advantage of over and over. Her heart was more than broken. She felt so far away most of the time, lost somewhere in her memories, refusing to accept what had happened to us—that this was our life. I think she blamed herself for everything, even when my aunt told her that she'd had no choice, or that it wasn't her fault. It didn't seem to matter much. Although things were pretty dreadful, I was glad Alyona had no idea what was going on, as she was still too young.

I, on the other hand, was glad I could leave the house the moment I got up. I couldn't deal with being inside for too long, so I made sure to wander around, spending all day outdoors. Watching Mom earn money and then do whatever she wanted with it made me want to do the same. I decided I was going to find a way to make my own money somehow, for me; I also wanted to have some to bring back to help feed the family. I came up with a plan to do what other kids in the city many miles away were doing—begging on the streets for money. It was the only thing I could think of; plus, I'd observed that many kids who begged at restaurants around here got handouts not just from one table, but from several—especially outside of nice fancy restaurants.

Vanya used to bring me to the city sometimes, teaching me how to be street-smart. Because of him I knew the city pretty well, including good places to score a smoke, or where I could snatch some food without anyone noticing. I loved the outdoor food markets during the summer; they were as big as football fields, and filled with people—so different from wintertime, when the entire place looked like a ghost town. The markets were full of anything you'd possibly want, from clothes, shoes, and hair accessories to fish, meats, fruits and vegetables—even dogs; yes, I mean everything! Many slightly damaged or spoiled foods were thrown out, and I'd be right there, filling my T-shirt with as much stuff as I could carry.

Chapter 23

Life in Crimea

Finally, I had a daily routine; life made sense, and I had a purpose. I didn't play as much with the boys anymore; Vanya was gone most of the time with his brother, probably making money somehow, and I'd become more interested in making money than playing, too.

My day started early. The moment I was up and dressed, I would cut myself a piece of bread for breakfast. Since I usually fell asleep before any dinner was made, by morning, I was ready to eat something. It was definitely "You snooze, you lose"; there wasn't much left over after the adults ate. Oleg was living with us again, and so was my aunt's other son. One pot of soup provided one meal per day, per person, and whatever was left for me and Alyona was often eaten up, most likely by the boys. They were nice enough to leave us some bread.

It was insanely crowded in the house, but at least we all had enough beds to sleep on. Mom shared one of the beds with my aunt, while the brothers shared the other one. My sister and I continued sleeping on the mattress on the floor. The entire place always smelled like cigarettes and leftover vinegar from making heroin. At this point, I knew how to make heroin from scratch; if anyone asked me today how to make it, I'd be able to tell them exactly what they needed.

It was important to make it to the city early before all the other kids started swarming the streets. We were all competing, trying to hit the right places at the right times that would guarantee some cash. I liked finding new places, as I was still pretty new at this, learning "the ways." I wanted to be good at my job; after all, this was it. This job was going to give me a sense of freedom and control over my life!

Having an early start was the way to go. Otherwise, I might come across one of the rebel groups of kids. They were older, in their teens, and their job was terrorizing those of us who were young and new to the game. I made the mistake of trusting a girl I met who played me. It was all fun and games till the gang showed up, and she told them exactly how much I had. How was I to know she was playing me by asking all these questions? Man, that day I learned my lesson, and did my best not to hang around that part of the city anymore. It was their turf, and if you were caught, well, better start emptying your pockets and obeying their commands. They were a mean, crazy bunch, capable of anything. Most of the time I was successful at keeping far away from them; other times, I wasn't so lucky. The good news is, I wasn't hurt. I could always make more money.

It was crazy in the city, especially when the sun would start to set. A different breed would come out then. This was one of the first rules I learned from one of the nicer kids on the block. "Don't stay around here after nine," she said. She was no older than me, yet knew enough to warn me that bad things happened around here at night. I didn't know what she meant, but I listened. I could tell she was scared, telling me about the nighttime, so when I asked her to tell me more, she said, "Little girls go missing around here sometimes. Once, they found a dead body right over there, by that restaurant." She pointed toward the corner, where dumpsters were placed in an alley. I couldn't believe it; I was really freaked out.

Life was different in the city compared to the suburbs, where we lived. The city was about an hour's walk by foot, but only twenty minutes by trolley. I didn't care to ride one unless it was winter, or I was going somewhere really far. I loved walking. It was my chance to be alone for a little while. I was around people all the time, so walking the suburban streets to get to the city early in the morning was bliss. While on my way I could smoke a cigarette in peace, without anyone giving me dirty looks. I could grab fruit that hung over the fences, like apples, pears, and sometimes plums, or I could make a pit stop at the playground before school was in session, to use the swings. Sometimes I'd find coins on the ground, which was pretty awesome!

I knew I was getting closer to the city when I heard music. There was always music playing, which I enjoyed. Some songs made me feel better, and not so alone. Eventually I knew all the lyrics of my favorites, and would sing along; sometimes I danced, too. It was something I looked forward to, that brought me happiness. My favorite group was Ruki Vverh!; they had great techno beats and pleasant voices. I will never forget the time I was dancing by the outdoor patio of a restaurant—the music was loudest right there—and the song was one of my favorites, so I broke it down, dancing. I didn't realize people on the patio were watching.

When the song was over, a man approached me. He was a kind black man I had never seen before; in fact, I'd never seen a person of color before. He smiled at me and said, "Never stop dancing, little girl." He handed me a large bill, enough earnings for an entire day's work! I thanked the kind man and went on, skipping my way to the next place. It was the first time in my life someone had complimented me, never mind noticed me. It made me feel uncomfortable, but at the same time, it felt nice to be noticed for something other than being a kid begging on the street. It made my day! While everyone else may have seen me as a street kid, not the nice black man. I could tell he didn't feel sorry for me. He looked at me like he'd look at a normal person.

This moment has always stayed very close to my heart, alongside all of my other happy experiences. It was like getting revived, you know? Like a reminder that I was alive, and I was not invisible to the world. Normally that's how it was; people pretended I wasn't there as they walked by, making sure to have some distance between us, like I was a filthy rat with diseases. I didn't care; all I cared about was begging for money to feed the family who was relying on me. The worse I looked, the better my chances. I knew where I stood, and where other people stood; it's like we were on totally different planets.

Nevertheless, life was good. It was exciting, and I was happy. I had money to buy cigarettes, gum, candy, and, once in a while, I would splurge if I'd made more that day. When I hit the jackpot with the amount I needed to bring home, I would pocket—or spend—the rest.

My favorite snack was pierogi—deep-fried pastry with potato or meat inside. It was so delicious, and cooked right there on the spot, making the entire block smell like a potato pie. Other times I got something sweet, like a pastry or a chocolate bar—Bounty was one of my favorites, filled with coconut on the inside, along with other candy bars with different fillings, like strawberry or banana. There was so much to do and so much to see every day. I will never forget how excited I was to explore, wondering what the next day was going to be like. As long as I watched my back, I was good.

About six months into it, I finally told my family what I was doing. Before this point, I'd been able to come up with lies as to where I got the money, saying it was from selling copper, iron, and other metals with the boys. Other times I would say I'd found a bill on the ground—basically, whatever story I could come up with, I did. Because we were all desperate for cash, no one doubted me, or cared to ask whether or not I was telling the truth.

By now, though, I was running out of excuses, so I had to come clean. I didn't know whether the reaction would be good or bad. I was ready to get punished or beat up or something, but when I put all the money on the table and told everyone that I'd been earning money by begging, everybody looked at one another, surprised that I'd earned so much, and that was it. I was helping out the family, bringing home money every day.

The deal was that my aunt would be in charge of the money. I was very happy about that, because she was responsible, unlike Mom, who would have spent the money on heroin. Mom liked to live in the moment—she wasn't as logical about things—but my aunt wasn't like that. She knew how to make things last longer, and how to be smart with money. Plus, my aunt wasn't as hooked on heroin as Mom was; she cared more about having food to eat. My aunt would go to the market every afternoon to get enough ingredients to make soup or something, as well as cigarettes for her and mom. That was my aunt's job, to shop and make food.

Meanwhile, Mom and Oleg had to look for another job. They couldn't go out to steal anymore, as they'd been noticed. They were on the cops' radar now, with officers now trying to catch them in the act. Luckily they'd been able to get out in time, with the help of a tip from someone they knew on the streets. It was time to lay low and not show their faces for a while, till things calmed down again.

Mom never did find any work after that, and we couldn't rely on Oleg, either, as he was now living with some girl he'd recently met. Victor was also never really around after his brother left; he was more like his lazy father, who didn't work or do anything to help anyone, other than himself. My job became crucial, as there was no other income coming in. Mom and my aunt and my sister relied on me to bring home money to feed us all. I felt so happy to be able to help in a big way; it sure beat feeling hopeless and helpless. Now I had choices, options; I was in control. This was what made me so dedicated to earning money. It was all I had to make me feel alive, to make me feel like I was part of something.

Not all days were as good as others, especially in the wintertime, when there were fewer people on the streets, and all the restaurant patios were closed for the season. I had to work extra hard to earn enough without all of those outdoor tables. Inside the restaurants was off limits; no one was allowed to go inside to beg. There was always someone standing inside the doors to make sure we didn't come in. Also, I couldn't stay outside all day long, since I didn't have warm clothes. They were more appropriate for fall than winter. I remember my toes and fingertips were so cold, it hurt like hell. I could barely walk or talk, pretty much a Popsicle after several hours. I had to get home by five or six o'clock, before it got too icy and freezing cold.

At least during the day there was sunshine. I was glad there were a few safe places to hide for a couple of minutes, to warm up before someone saw me and asked me to leave. Most of the time I would sneak into the toy store, where I would soon get busted. "Get out! You're scaring off the customers" was what I heard over and over, even when I wasn't begging. Still, two minutes indoors were better than nothing.

I really disliked winter, and not just because of the cold; it was also because everyone was so miserable, unlike in the summertime, when people were happy and generous, and less irritated and angry. The only time people weren't that angry in the winter was when the holidays came around. I learned about New Year's Eve—how people celebrated every December 31st with fireworks, music, and lots of drinking and eating. This was a very handy time of year for all of us street kids. People were happy, the entire city was decorated and brightly lit; it was amazing!

I remember I wouldn't get home till ten p.m. during the holiday season; between eight and ten p.m. were the magic hours. That's when most people were out and about, celebrating, which meant they had money! They gave more at this time of year, too. I remember kids sharing their stories with each other: "This guy gave me five *hryvni!*" "That woman gave me ten!" These amounts were usually unheard of, but around the holidays, some people knew how to share. It was like a nice, big feast!

Chapter 24

Secrets and Lies

It had been a couple of years since we'd moved back in with my aunt. At some point my aunt's husband came to the door, pleading with her to take him back, and she did. I think it made my aunt feel a bit better to have a familiar face around. She was having a tough time being with my mom all the time, taking care of her. It was mostly just the two of them, along with Alyona.

Mom wasn't doing great. I think she was depressed, more so than ever before. We didn't have any extra money to spare for heroin, and my aunt made it clear that it was time for Mom to stop before it was too late. Mom's veins were shot—not just in her arms, but also her legs, and pretty much the rest of her body. I will never forget the infection she had on one of her butt cheeks. My aunt would squeeze the area while a giant tube of pretty solid white stuff came out; it was so gross. I couldn't believe so much could come out of her. Mom weighed no more than 110 pounds, and this thing just looked way too large to come out of anyone. The hole from which the stuff came out never closed up, either, remaining a tunnel. I remember Mom was sick as a dog for a while, with a fever, and throwing up. After this illness she seemed to have fewer cravings for heroin, giving it up completely. Drinking became more common around the house.

I would get home at night and find everyone singing, laughing, and drinking vodka. I was just glad to see some boiled potatoes, salted fish, and bread sharing the table with the empty bottles.

I was around eight at this time, going on nine, when Mom found out my secret. At least one of them. She caught me smoking in the courtyard by the gate one day. I don't know what I was thinking. Maybe part of me felt like I wanted Mom to find out; I guess I didn't want to keep it a secret anymore. I will never forget the moment she came out of the house and we locked eyes. I knew I was in big trouble. Man, she was mad.

Without saying a word, Mom raced over to where I was standing. I was trying to hide the cigarette behind me as I blew out the smoke real fast. She grabbed the cigarette out of my hand and put it out by forcing it against my lips. I don't remember what she was saying at that point, as my lips were on fire! It burned; man, it burned bad. I wasn't able to eat for days, as I couldn't open my mouth till the skin grew back.

I was extremely furious with Mom. It was the first time she'd ever put her hands on me, or punished me like this. I was so angry. It felt like I was betrayed or something. Maybe because the last time anyone really laid their hands on me, it was her long-lost boyfriend and father of my sister, who was rotting in jail, where he belonged. I couldn't shake that feeling for a while, so I told myself that after I healed I would continue smoking, no matter what she did to me. At one point or another she'd have to stop punishing me, unless she planned to kill me.

Mom continued to do her best to prevent me from smoking. The next time she caught me with a pack of cigarettes in my pocket, she fed me the entire pack. She was screaming, holding my mouth open and shoving them down my throat. I felt like I was going to die. I'd never felt so sick in my life. I puked bad, to the point where I was coughing up little bits of blood. I was unable to sleep; I felt like I'd never get that bitter, disgusting, harsh taste out of my mouth.

Honestly, Mom's punishments only made me more motivated to continue smoking. I guess Mom and I were more alike than we'd thought. I was just as stubborn, and didn't give up easily. When I got over feeling sick from her last punishment, I went back to smoking again. This time when Mom saw me, she didn't do anything other than to say "Just do it where I can't see you." She wasn't happy about it, but that was it; the secret was out, and I was safe again for a while.

Until I had a new secret.

But this time, I would keep it from the whole world, never mind just Mom. I knew that if she ever found out, she would kill me—and possibly for real this time. And if anyone else found out, I would lose whatever dignity I had left. What I was up to was not good, and very dangerous too—not that I knew this at the time.

By now I was nine. I was getting older, and begging wasn't as easy as it once was. There was a shift, and I realized I was too old to beg for money. People just wouldn't give as much to kids my age, and it became very hard to earn enough money to feed the family. I earned half as much as I had just the year before. So when a new opportunity came along, I couldn't say no. I needed the money badly; I couldn't let my family starve. As much as I hated myself for it, I had to go through with it—no matter how horrible, offended, and disgusted I felt afterward.

It all started one spring, when a man started to come around our street. At first I was clueless; I was just doing my thing, visiting the apricot tree, or playing on the newly built area for university students just up the road. I would play there on weekends, or when no one was around for classes. I would pretend I lived there, claiming one of the pretty doorways with nice steps and railing as my own. I remember I would play with one of the neighbor kids sometimes; she was a couple years younger than me, and we would talk and pretend that were all proper and educated. We would have imaginary phones that would ring and we'd talk about our "classes," pretending we were all grown up, going to college. It was fun.

On my way home, I would see this guy on our street, day after day. He was in his forties or fifties, with dark black hair and a mustache. He was wearing a hat and a nice coat. His shoes looked barely worn and he smelled of cologne, as I would get a whiff once in a while, passing him on the street. I was feeling pretty fed up with seeing this man, wandering around where he didn't belong. No one looked that nice around here. What did this guy want?

Being a tomboy, not afraid of much, I ended up confronting the guy. I walked right up to him, all up in his business, just like Vanya would do when he had beef with someone. I didn't know how girls handled themselves in situations like this, as I barely hung out with girls—we just didn't seem to get along—but I had no problems when I hung out with my guy friends.

So, there I was, facing this man, ready to fight. I wasn't scared; if anything, I just wanted to know why he was lurking around here all the time.

"What do you want?" I asked. Maybe he was looking for someone.

"You want to make some good money?" the man said quietly. He took a pile of cash from his coat pocket and continued. "Follow me if you want to earn some cash—but keep your distance, as if you don't know me." He put the cash back in his pocket and started to walk away.

I don't know you, I thought—but I was curious now, so I followed him around the corner, a couple streets down, where an abandoned school building stood. I knew this area, although typically didn't come by here, as I didn't go to school. All the school people were snobby and mean. Besides, we didn't have the money for me to go to school and be like the normal folk; that just wasn't in the cards for us. Part of me was relieved I didn't have to deal with any of the teachers and students, not to mention all the rules. I heard from other kids who went to school how much they didn't like it, and from what they had to say, I felt like I wasn't missing much, although of course I was.

Finally, I saw the man walk inside the building, and I did the same, finding myself in a large, creepy, abandoned room. I noticed he was by the wall on the other side, where it was dark.

"Come over here," he said. "No one will see us this way."

"What do you want me to do?" I asked. At this point I was feeling scared that this guy was going to kill me and dispose of my body in a dumpster somewhere.

"Don't worry, I won't hurt you—I promise," he said, waving me over.

I hesitated at first, but then slowly made my way over to where he was standing. I stopped where I felt I was a safe distance away, in case I had to take off. "Now what?" I asked.

"Now, I show you what I want you to do if you want to make some money," the guy said.

"What is it??" I asked, suddenly weary.

"It's up to you," he said. "You can make more or less depending on what you are willing to do."

"Like what?" I asked.

"Have you ever seen a penis before?" the man asked, as he began to unzip his pants.

I didn't say anything—just stood there, not sure what to do. *Should I run?* While I was busy trying to come up with a plan, he was busy playing with his thing.

"I want you to watch me do it," the man said. "Just stand next to me and let me touch you a little."

He was really going at it now, and I didn't see any harm in just standing there. I felt like I could handle it; after all, to me it was a lot of money—enough for an entire day's work—and I couldn't let the opportunity pass me by, especially when I knew this money was guaranteed, and it wouldn't take me all day to earn it.

I stood there, watching him get hard, feeling his nasty hands on my chest and butt. I was pretty much screaming with agony inside, wishing it was all over, wishing I'd never agreed in the first place. I had no idea what I'd just done. Five minutes later I saw white stuff come out and the man exhaled with relief. He was done.

"Now my money," I said to the man, desperate to get the hell out of there. This was not something I wanted to be around for. I was so ashamed of myself, I was shaking, and getting nauseous.

He put his thing back where it belonged and pulled up his zipper. Taking out the stack of cash, the man said, "Next time I can pay you more if you do other stuff. I can teach you."

I did my best not to listen, concentrating on the money and all it was going to do for my family. I grabbed the cash and ran off as fast as I could.

There was a small store just a street over, so I ran inside to feel safe for a moment. There were other people inside, so I knew he wouldn't bother me there.

I wasn't sure if I would ever do such a thing again, but at the same time, it didn't feel as horrible as eating an innocent dog. Our neighbors, the ones with the two boys, were so hungry that the father had ended up killing their old dog, a longtime pet, because they were starving. The man was a monster; he didn't give a shit. I happened to be over there that day because they'd invited me to have dinner with them. The boys wanted me to meet their newborn baby sister. I had no idea what had happened till I ate a couple pieces of the stew he'd made. Although the meat was tough, it tasted like any other meat, I suppose. I didn't eat much of it, as I assumed it was really expensive.

After everyone had had some, the father burst out laughing, telling us that we were eating the dog, whose name I don't recall. This was horrific for all of us kids, as we'd all loved that dog. We'd played with him often. He was an old fella with black-and-white coloring and a kind soul. I cried for months; we all did. The boys were so angry with their father; they had it even worse, as it was their dog—their only companion. It broke my heart. Even though I understood why he did it—many people were literally starving in the neighborhood—it didn't make it any easier.

From that moment on, there was no way I would ever say no to money—especially if it meant I would never have to resort to eating dogs or cats, or rats. I was not going to find myself or my family in those shoes. I would do everything in my power to make sure we had money to feed ourselves.

But it didn't come without a price.

I was breaking every rule in the book, keeping a heavy, dark secret from my family and the world. It wasn't long before I was meeting up with this man and giving him hand jobs, letting him touch my body to touch; sometimes I would give him a blow job, which was rare, and depending on how much money I needed. He taught me all of the things he wanted me to do, and how he wanted it done. Sometimes I saw the man in the late afternoon, and other times, in the morning, if it was a weekend. The guy had a ring on his finger, and most likely had a wife and kids. Man, I hated him. And at the same time, I needed him for the money. At one point, there was another man in the picture; he stopped in a car as I was walking on the sidewalk, and asked me if I wanted to make money by giving him a hand job. I hopped in the car and we drove to an empty street down the road where I did what he asked, and got paid.

I don't know what it was about me; I had no idea how they knew to approach me. But somehow they knew. It was like they had some secret lens that could read into my soul. Every day after those jobs, I had to deal with feeling like everyone around me knew—like I was getting judged. I was pretty paranoid, and afraid someone would find out—that I'd feel more ashamed than I already felt. I knew how it would look to others, and hoped nobody would ever find out, as they would never understand my position.

So I kept my secret and lied to Mom and everyone else, saying I was still earning the money by begging.

Chapter 25

Alyona

The time was finally here: I was allowed to take Alyona to the city with me.

Mom had decided that Alyona needed some fun and interaction in her life, since she was mostly stuck at the house with nothing to do, just like I'd been, years ago. Since I was gone most of every day, I had no idea what she was dealing with, but I knew she was fed up with Mom.

"Hold her hand and keep a close eye on her," Mom said as we left the house.

I was so excited to take her with me, although it proved difficult at first. Four-year-old Alyona was not used to walking long distances, so we would take the trolley part of the distance and then walk the rest of the way to the city. She was ecstatic—always curious, and ready to get her hands on everything she saw, jumping around and pointing at things like cotton candy and stuffed toys. I did my best to calm her down, which she did, but I could tell she was sad.

It was tough to work when I had Alyona with me. It took time to explain to her that we were here to work, and that she was going to work alongside with me.

"We're going to go over to that table and ask those nice people for some money, okay?" I would say. Before long, I was making way more money than ever before! My sister seemed to do the trick. She was much more profitable, as an adorable kid, and a smart one too! I was amazed; I couldn't believe how much we were making. It made me so happy, because I knew it meant I wouldn't have to do any more side jobs for men. I was so relieved! And making it even better was the fact that Alyona was enjoying herself while we worked. She wanted to try it on her own, so I let her. I think she wanted to earn her own money.

I'll never forget this one time when I sent her into a restaurant and ended up waiting for her for over an hour. Come to find out, she was inside sitting at a table with a man and a woman, eating food, having a great time. She didn't want to leave, getting the attention and love she needed. I let her enjoy herself, but when she came out and I asked her for the money, she told me she didn't get any. I figured she was telling the truth, so on we went. Suddenly I heard jingling sounds coming from her shoes. Turns out she *did* get some money, and plenty of it, which she'd carefully stashed in her shoes! I couldn't believe my little sister had hidden money from me, even though she had no idea how to spend it. She was too smart for her own good. I did take the money, telling her it wasn't okay. I asked her to never lie to me again. Of course she was upset, but I made it up to her with an ice-cream cone. She liked the chocolate kind, while I liked vanilla.

I loved Alyona, and wanted to give her everything I could as her big sister. I would take her to the playground and push her on the swings, which she loved as much as I did. Other times, we would visit the lake I'd found where several kids gathered together to swim. It was free, and anyone could swim there. It was a couple miles away from one of the cities I visited, where they held an outside market during the summer. I'd gone there many times before, but had never actually gone swimming. I was pretty shy, and there were a lot of kids there. At some point I made some friends, and before long I was getting my toes wet, checking out the scene and imagining what it would be like to swim. "Next time I'll have a bathing suit," I told myself. I didn't have one yet, and neither did Alyona, so it was the perfect time to get suits for both of us.

I found a small store that sold secondhand clothing, and luckily I found an adorable bathing suit for Alyona. It was pink with polka dots and ruffles, the best one there! I purchased it and put it on her before we left. It was the first thing I'd ever bought her. I got one for myself, too, although I don't remember mine as well as hers.

Alyona was so excited to get in the water, running right up to the edge, ready to jump in. I had to watch her like a hawk, teaching her the right way. "You have to walk in, okay? Like this—see?" I showed her the safe way to be in the water, staying near the edge in case she needed to grab my hand. Neither of us were strong swimmers, so we stayed in the shallow end. I wished I was in the deep end where all the older kids were, jumping off a pier. It looked like so much fun, and I wanted to try it, so I did.

It didn't end well. I almost drowned.

I jumped off the pier and swam underwater—in the wrong direction. When I tried to come up for air and stand on my feet, it was still too deep to touch the bottom. I kept swimming even further till I was able to get above water and see where I was. I ended up being halfway across the lake with no idea how I'd swim back, as I was exhausted, fighting for my life. I will never forget how it felt to let go and stop fighting, knowing it was over. I was going down when I felt a hand grab me and pull me out. It was a young girl who was half my age and an amazing swimmer. She grabbed my ponytail and got me safely back to shore. At that moment I believed I would never swim again, it was so scary. I just lay there, kissing the ground. Learning this swimming business was no easy task.

Same thing happened to Alyona once when she got too far away from the shallow end; luckily I was watching her, but she still swallowed some water and was coughing, very scared. It was a dangerous scene. I don't know how many kids drowned there each year, but I bet the number was pretty high. There were never any adults around, never mind a lifeguard. If something happened, you just had to hope there was someone there who knew how to swim, and would save you.

We took a long break from the lake when a dead body was discovered floating around, right near where we swam. I will never forget this blue-skinned man. I had no idea it was a dead body till someone screamed. It was terrifying to see a corpse. Some kids decided to poke the body with a stick to get it away from where we were swimming. The body was as hard as rock. Thankfully Alyona never saw it; she was with some of the younger kids, swimming in the shallow end. I was at the pier by then, as I'd finally learned how to stay above water when I swam. I felt so liberated and accomplished, very proud of myself for sticking with it. Jumping off the pier at full speed was the best thing ever! Nevertheless, after that, we stayed in the city and on land for a while.

Like me, Alyona loved music. She would stop on the sidewalk or wherever we were to boogie. It was so much fun to be with her; it was like part of my innocence was brought back to life when I was with her. Everyone she ever came in contact with loved her; there was just something about her spirit. She was a special little girl. Because of Alyona, my life improved a lot. I remember a nice lady who worked in one of the restaurants in the city; she brought us inside to feed us a meal, even though she wasn't supposed to. She brought us downstairs where no one else was seated and served us warm borscht with bread. She was a nice young woman, probably in her late twenties, with kind blue eyes and brown hair that fell on her shoulders, shiny and clean.

She was well dressed and smelled nice. I couldn't believe the effect my sister had on people. Here we were, eating inside a restaurant! I had never eaten inside one before; it was pretty awesome. Once in a while she'd invite us back in if it wasn't busy, the only one who ever did this for us. She was a kind lady.

Alyona and I spent every day together, from early morning to late at night. We often didn't return home till eight p.m. I got her ready for bed, and Mom and my aunt were happy to have some freedom. Alyona wasn't always an easy little kid, and my aunt's injury made it difficult for her to run after Alyona. Mom was too wrapped up in her feelings to handle the stress. It was easy for me—I was tough, because I was young—and it was a blast having her by my side.

Don't get me wrong; there were plenty of times when she would throw fits and cry to get her way, like any kid. Sometimes she would stop walking and cross her arms, with a face that said "I'm not moving." Man, she could be a pain in the ass sometimes; she sure knew how to make a scene. The worst was when I saw her pick up a cigarette butt she found on the street and put it in her mouth, pretending she was smoking, like me. She copied everything I did! I stopped that real fast, telling her to never do that again or I wouldn't bring her with me anymore.

Alyona loved city life; there was always plenty to do. To her it was endless fun, food, attention, and music. She loved some songs more than others. One time when we were in the city, she somehow managed to sneak off, and I couldn't find her. One moment she was next to me, and the next, she was gone! I will never forget the feeling I had inside. It was like someone had stabbed me in the heart and I was bleeding to death. So many thoughts ran through my head; I was so afraid for her life. What if someone had taken her?

It took about ten dreadful minutes to find her, the longest of my life, but somehow I went to the right place. She was one block over, by the circus area, where the music was blaring. Man, I was so angry at her! I did scream at her that time, crying and telling her to never leave my side again. "I wanted to dance" was her response. She had no idea how horrible I was feeling, or that what she'd done was wrong. She was a handful, I won't lie, but what four-year-old isn't? I was just glad she was okay, and unharmed.

Chapter 26

Unexpected Move

We were renting the house we lived in from a little old lady who owned all of the houses in the courtyard. Normally, she was barely around, dropping by here and there to collect rent, which I am pretty sure we rarely had. This time, however, the old lady never left, moving in right next to us, into a house I'd never been inside of, but always wondered about. It was never occupied, and had dark curtains, making it tough to see inside. It all made sense when the old lady didn't move anything in; it was like everything she needed was already inside, which made me think she'd lived there before.

I didn't like this lady; I was scared of her, maybe because she was really old. I'd never seen a person this old before. Her skin was so wrinkly, and she didn't smile. She reminded me of a witch or something, always wearing black clothes, with a shawl over her head. She didn't appear to be poor or lacking in any way, other than being alone.

My aunt and mom were not happy that the old lady had returned to live next door. I think they knew she was not like the rest of us living here, and it wasn't going to be as easy to drink and party, or to sing the songs people sang when they got drunk. Nevertheless, my aunt and mom continued to do what they always did. That didn't help us at all; the old lady wasn't happy, and after barely keeping up with rent and receiving several warnings from her, the old lady told us she'd had it with us. We had to move out immediately, or she would bring her sons over to make sure we did.

I wasn't there when it happened, but Mom told me the news when Alyona and I got home that night. She skipped the part about why we were being forced to move out, but I already knew. There was no way we could live side by side with someone who didn't share our lifestyle; it had just been a matter of time. The lady hadn't liked us to begin with, always giving Alyona and me unkind looks when she saw us playing outside. Man, that lady gave me the creeps. I was totally okay with moving far away from her. It felt like she'd been watching us through the wall with magic eyes, like there was someone else in the room, listening to our every move.

I was glad to learn we were moving just a couple streets up the road. It made it so much easier to carry all the stuff we owned; although it wasn't much, it was still enough when you had to carry it all by hand the entire way. The old lady gave us a day to gather our stuff and clean up the place—mostly the enormous pile of dirty clothes we had piled up over the winter. Most of the clothing was Alyona's and mine; we were kids, so nothing stayed clean for long, and we didn't have enough money to get the soap to wash everything by hand, especially during the winter. And we didn't have the time or energy to walk in the freezing cold to get several buckets of water.

It wasn't fun cleaning it up. There was mold entwined with some of Alyona's clothes, from when she'd have an accident. It smelled so awful. I'm not going to go into details, but let's just say that no one expected to find so many bugs, worms, or mold in the midst of the pile. The horrific smell brewing in the middle of this giant pile reached all the way up to the ceiling.

We never did that again; we attempted to wash them with water, and if that didn't work, we just threw them away. Alyona and I had gotten pretty good at begging for everything these days—money, food, clothes. Before long, I'd found plenty of tall buildings where we could beg for a meal, and some clean clothes. It was pretty exciting, wondering what people were going to give away. A nice jacket? A beautiful dress—maybe even a pair of shoes? I will never forget how normal Alyona and I looked when we had nice clothes to wear; if it wasn't for us scratching our heads, hunting for lice, or spitting, we totally would have gotten away with it! (Since I was a smoker, I had developed a spitting habit.) Sometimes we had to adjust what we wore when we went to work; if we looked too nice, people wouldn't give us as much money, if any at all, saying "You don't look homeless." It was so weird; I couldn't believe that what you wore could so easily change someone's mind about you, in an instant.

After a dreadful, tiring day of cleaning and moving, we finally made our way to our new place. It was one room the size of an average living room, just big enough for us to squeeze in the two single beds we had, and the table and a couple chairs. We placed one of the beds against the wall at the end of the room, where Alyona and I would sleep, and the other bed next to the side wall, where mom and my aunt would sleep. (Her husband had bounced again; it was like he had a double life or something, as he would show up every six months or so, as if out of nowhere.)

The other wall was for kitchen stuff, like the hot plate we plugged into the wall for cooking, a general knife for cutting, a cooking pot, a couple of soup bowls and spoons, and last but not least, the thing we used to roll out dough with. My aunt was really good at making and rolling the dough when we made pierogis from scratch, once in a blue moon. They were my favorite! The only thing I didn't like was that our room was pretty dark inside, with no windows; it made the place seem like a vampire den. Still, it was better than being on the streets.

No one gave us a hard time, but I do remember everyone looking at us like we had three eyes. I could tell people didn't want us here; the energy was creepy, like there was a secret no one wanted us to know—like only certain people were supposed to live here, and that didn't include us. I suppose no one trusted anyone around here, including these people, to whom we were absolute strangers. I was such a detective as a kid; it was like I wanted to solve the mystery of why everyone in this courtyard felt so strange. I was like a dog sniffing its new surroundings, making sure everything checked out. If not, I'd be able to declare "I was right!" It was something I liked to do when I was by myself, wandering around, trying to find something to do for a while. I did find several photos under puddles of water once. It was fun to find random belongings that people had left behind as my evidence. My friends had taught me these detective skills years ago—just like being a cop with a gun, but better.

I thought about the boys often, wondering how they were holding up, especially the brothers, with whom I had shared that awful stew, made from the remains of their pet. I was still recovering myself; I wasn't sure I'd ever be able to forgive myself for eating a few bites of it. They must have felt the same, missing their dear pup friend. I went to visit them a couple of times, but had no luck finding them around. They were both older now, and probably on to the next stage of their lives, somewhere out there, where they could forget. Vanya was hardly ever around. I was sure he'd moved out for good with his brother. I didn't blame him. I wouldn't have wanted to live with raging, abusive alcoholics who enslaved their kids to bring them booze.

Times were changing. Nothing felt the same anymore. I just had distant memories of us kids from a couple years ago, playing with our fake guns and starting fires to burn for fun. So much had changed since then. I hoped they were all doing okay, wherever they were.

Chapter 27

Hospital Visit

We didn't end up staying at the new place for more than a month. Turns out, Mom had once again met some guy who she described as "nice," who was willing to help us out by letting us live in a house he owned in a better neighborhood. Mom said it wasn't going to be much longer before we went to check out the house. She was so excited. I, on the other hand, was a bit nervous, especially after her last "nice" friend ended up being a con artist who sold our home.

I hadn't met this new friend yet, but I already knew I didn't like or trust him. Besides, this place wasn't that bad, other than the giant rats that came out to play at night. I will never forget how scared I was when they announced themselves by jumping down from the ceiling onto the table to hunt for leftover food. I was lying in our bed, which was pretty low to the ground, holding my breath and hoping they wouldn't come up and try to eat us, too. They were the size of cats and fought each other for scraps. They had no trouble getting up on things, like the bed we were sleeping in. Alyona was against the wall, while I was on the outside, making sure she didn't fall off the bed. I was really terrified for my life. I wanted to yell for Mom to wake up, but I was too afraid the rats would hear me and come running.

Finally, the giant rats made enough noise to wake my aunt, and then my mom. I will never forget the moment they turned on the lights and saw these rats everywhere. Not an inch of the floor was visible. They were angry now, trying to get out; some of them were about to jump on the bed where Mom and my aunt were sleeping. "Oh hell no!" my aunt screamed, grabbing a broom.

Somehow they managed to get rid of the rats without any of us getting hurt. Alyona slept through the entire thing. I couldn't believe how deeply she could sleep! I was happy she'd missed it; I had nightmares for days!

Living in this place was much less sanitary, as one of the outside toilets we used, the kind with the big hole in the ground, was leaking with urine and poop when it rained a lot. To top it off, Alyona broke out in hives from some illness that I had no clue about. It started near her mouth and then spread all over her face and body. I was a kid, so I didn't think much of it; I figured it would just go away on its own. She was feeling okay, not complaining, so I thought she was fine.

But one day when we went to visit our nice restaurant lady to see if we could get a hot meal, she saw Alyona and immediately had a worried look on her face.

"How long has she had this?" the lady asked, while checking Alyona's body.

"Not long," I replied, wondering what was going on here.

"She needs to be checked out at the hospital," the lady said. "This is serious."

I could tell the woman was worried about Alyona, but there was no way I was going to let her be taken by strangers into a hospital, whatever that was.

"I won't let her go there," I told the lady. I was getting nervous and was ready to leave.

Suddenly the woman changed her tune.

"That's okay . . . Come on in and I'll give you something to eat," she said, taking Alyona's hand. We walked downstairs, where we normally ate. I didn't think much of it—just that she was cool with it, now that I'd made it clear I did not want Alyona going to a hospital.

We sat at our usual table and the lady told us she would be right back with something to eat. She returned with two plates filled with mashed potatoes and *katleti*.

"Wow," I said. "This looks amazing!" I could smell the *katleti*, and so could Alyona. She had a big smile on her face as the lady put the full plates in front of us.

"You eat—I'll be right back," the woman said. She'd usually leave us to eat while she went upstairs to make sure those customers were taken care of.

We were halfway through our meal when two people in white came downstairs with the lady. I knew what she had done.

"No!" I yelled, getting out of the chair to grab Alyona to leave. I was freaking out now. I didn't know what it was about those people in white, but I was not a big fan. I felt like I would never see my sister again if they took her from me.

"Please, hang on—your sister needs help," the lady yelled as I started to run as fast as I could, gripping Alyona by the hand. I turned around to see the two men in white chasing after us, and ran even faster. Alyona was tripping; she couldn't run as fast as I could, so I picked her up and kept running.

Thinking to fool them, I ran inside a food court where people were buying and eating food. It had two entrances, so I figured I could run in one door and then back out the other, in hopes of losing the men in white. I should have kept running, because they totally cornered me, one on each side of the door, gaining on me now.

"It's okay," one of the men said. "Just give her to us. She's sick, and needs to get better." He swept in and held my hands while the other man picked up Alyona. The restaurant lady took over, holding me tightly as the men carried my sister away. I was crying, pleading with them to leave us alone. Alyona was also scared, crying and screaming for me.

I pulled away from the lady and chased after the men to see where they were going. By the time I'd caught up to them, they were driving away in a hospital van.

I made my way back to the restaurant to have a chat with the lady. I was so mad; why would she do this? I walked inside to find the place packed with people, but no lady in sight. I waited around outside, peeking through the window. When I finally spotted her, I ran inside, angry and ready to tell her that she had no business sticking her nose in where it didn't belong.

"You're not my mother!" I screamed. "You had no right!"

The lady approached me. "Outside!" she said, nudging me toward the door. "Your sister is staying in the city, okay?" I could tell she was mad at me for scaring her customers. "You can go see her any time you want, and when she gets better, she'll come back home."

"Really?" I asked, relieved.

"Really," the lady replied. "Now go on—I have to go back to work."

That was the last time I saw that lady or ate at that restaurant. I felt betrayed, and I'd made a big scene. I'm pretty sure we wouldn't have been allowed anywhere near that place.

I made my way back home to inform my mom and my aunt about what happened.

Mom was angry. "How could you let this happen?" she said. "You know I can't go see her, right?"

"Why not?" I asked. "The lady told me we can go see her any time."

"Look at me! Look at where we are. Do you think anyone is going to see me as a fit mother?!"

Mom was too ashamed of herself; she was afraid to be seen by those people in the hospital. She was afraid that once they saw her, they would turn her away, and worse, not allow her to see Alyona.

"I can't take that chance," Mom said. "We will have to wait till they discharge her, and then bring her back."

"I will go see her then!" I said. "I am her sister, not her mother. They will have to let me see her."

I walked over to Mom to give her a hug. She was crying, missing Alyona already. We had no idea how long it would take before they brought her back, but we all hoped it would be very soon.

* * *

A month went by, and still no Alyona. At this point I decided it was time to suck it up and go visit her at the hospital the lady had told me they'd taken her to. It was far away. I had to take different trolleys to get there, and it took about an hour. I was so excited to see her! I'd saved up some money to purchase a gift for her: a big box of assorted cookies, the kind she loved.

The last trolley stopped and I was finally there. Everyone was getting off to visit their loved ones. The hospital was huge, with many floors; it felt like it took forever to walk to the building. I really didn't want to go inside. I saw a lady walking in, so I followed her. I found myself standing in the lobby, where everyone was heading toward the counter to check in.

I had no idea what to do, so I did what everyone else was doing. I stood in line, waiting for my turn to announce that I was here to visit my sister.

When it was finally my turn, the lady behind the counter asked, "Can I help you?"

"I'm here to see my sister, Alyona," I said. "She is four years old, and arrived a month ago, with hives all over her body."

"Yes, of course—Alyona!" the lady said, smiling. "What a cute kid she is; your sister, you said?"

"Yes, ma'am. These are for her." I showed her the box of cookies, and told her how excited I was to see my little sister.

"Wait here; we'll bring her out. But you can't touch her, okay? She is still sick and it's contagious," the lady said.

"Okay, but I can still give her the cookies, right?" I asked. I was disappointed I was going to have to visit my sister from a distance.

"Sure. Here, we will give them to her," the lady said, reaching out for the cookies. I handed the box to her. "Wait over there, okay?" She walked away to go and get my sister.

Moments later I saw her. She was completely unrecognizable. They had cut off all her hair, due to lice, and she was covered in green spots—some sort of medicine to treat her rash.

I felt so far away from her. They made me stand all the way at the other end of the room, so I could barely see her.

"Alyona, *privet!*" I said loudly, to make sure she could hear me. I was smiling at her, so happy to see my little sister. I saw her wave at me. She was also smiling as she held the big box of cookies in her hands.

"You doing good?" I asked. She nodded "yes." She seemed totally happy, like she didn't mind being there at all. It was the sweetest thing when she tried to run toward me to give me a hug—not that she made it very far, but it still made me feel better. She missed me after all!

I saw the lady take her hand to walk her back to her room. I felt so sad. The entire visit had lasted no more than five minutes!

"Bye! I will see you soon, okay?" I yelled as she walked away, waving good-bye.

She looked just as sad as I did. We all missed her terribly, and were eagerly awaiting her return to us.

Chapter 28

Flames

While Alyona was still in the hospital, healing, I had to beg for money on my own. To be honest, I was pretty rusty, and even when I did my best, I was making shit. People were done with me. Nevertheless, I still went to the city to watch the world come alive. I refused to go back to doing favors for men; I'd had enough of that for a lifetime. I found myself wandering around more than working. I was missing Alyona, and nothing felt the same without her by my side. I ended up coming home early each day, just waiting for Alyona's return.

It was time for me to go see this new house we were about to move into. Mom was so excited. "You'll see, Ludmila—this place is perfect!" It had been a while since I'd seen Mom this happy about anything. I was glad she was feeling better, and more excited about life again.

We took the trolley since my aunt was with us, and couldn't walk very far. The house was located off the main road, and only about five minutes from the city. I remember thinking that I'd walked past this gate many times on my way home. I couldn't believe it; this house was a perfect distance from the city, which made me really happy.

We walked through the main gate that led into a large courtyard with several pretty houses and big beautiful trees. There was much more privacy here; the place we were going to occupy was all the way at the end of the dirt path. It was a small white house, one floor, with good windows. Despite its good appearance, standing next to this house, I had a funny feeling in my stomach that told me to stay away. Something was seriously off here.

I'll never forget what happened next.

While my aunt and mom went inside to see the house, I stayed outside, unable to take another step. At that moment, I envisioned the entire house on fire—nothing but flames swallowing the house. It felt so real; I could feel the heat of the flames as they spread through the windows and doors, smoke coming out of the roof as the house roared with fire.

I screamed for Mom and my aunt to get out of there. "The house is on fire—it's burning! Get out now!" I yelled.

By the time they walked back outside to see why I was yelling, the flames were gone, as if nothing had happened. But the feeling from the vision remained. The message was clear: We should not move here. I felt like something bad was going to happen to us in this house. I begged Mom to believe me.

"Please don't make us live here—let's go back to the other place. It's not that bad!" I pleaded. I was terrified of this house, refusing to live there. Not that it mattered; no one listened to me.

A couple days later we were living there, at this place where I didn't feel like we were welcome, especially after what had happened.

I wondered why I had been the only one to see the house in flames. I just hoped that whatever this vision meant, it wouldn't come true. Maybe nothing bad would happen here. I remember I didn't know how to feel about this; part of me felt like I should pay attention to the warning, while another part of me felt like I was going crazy. A year later, however, something horrible *would* happen—something that would change all of our lives forever.

* * *

Mom's friend stopped by to check on us, to make sure we had settled in. I remember I was surprised when I met him. He was actually a nice guy, well dressed, nice hair, shiny shoes, well mannered; he didn't even swear. I didn't feel threatened by him, so I was able to put my nightmare aside and live like everything was fine. "Fake it till you make it," as they say. So I did just that, baffled for a while as to what that vision was all about.

Truth be told, this was the best house we had ever lived in. There was a tiny kitchen area with a table, a bathroom with a real toilet, and a nice-size living room that had a big window overlooking the yard. There was even some extra furniture, like a dresser and a coffee table. I was impressed, and more so, grateful that Mom had someone nice in her life for a change. I did wonder sometimes if they were more than friends—not that I saw anything go down, but I felt like he liked Mom as more than just a friend. I think my mother had a way with men. I don't know how she met this guy, or what she told him, but here we were, living in his spooky house that he just happened to have available.

I do remember feeling like we had upgraded big-time: We had our own water source, where we could pump water just feet away. The yard was full of nice healthy trees and bushes, providing perfect shade and some privacy. It was always peaceful and quiet; we never had to worry about something bad happening, since it was a good neighborhood. Everyone who lived around us had jobs and stuff.

My favorite thing was the toilet! I was so happy to be able to take a break from bushes and isolated areas to do my business. Sometimes I wished I could bring the toilet with me; being in the city all day, it was often difficult to find a bathroom when I needed one. There were no public restrooms, and no one would allow me to use one inside a restaurant or store. They thought I was just making it up to get inside so I could beg for money, when in fact I desperately had to go!

I remember once in a while I had to go so bad that my kidneys would seize and I would find myself wet and in lots of pain. I could barely stand, let alone walk. It was awful. Afterward, when my kidneys finally released, I would get a terribly high fever that made me feel even worse. I would sit in place or sometimes just lie there, wherever it happened, crumpled over and waiting for the pain to subside so I could walk again.

It was so embarrassing to walk around with wet pants on. I was just glad there were a couple of large fountains by the parliament building, big and deep enough for me to swim in—one way for me to wash off real quick, as well as collect some of the coins that people threw in.

Man, I loved that place; when I first saw the bottom of the fountain sparkling in perfectly clear water, I couldn't believe my eyes. The entire bottom looked like it was made of coins, shining in all directions, just waiting to be collected. I felt like a pirate discovering treasure! I dove right in without hesitation, before someone else did and took all that money! If it was cold outside, however, well, then, I was shit out of luck. I was forced to hide somewhere and wait it out till my pants or whatever I was wearing had completely dried.

As I sat on the toilet at the house to do my business before I left for the day, I wondered why Alyona was still not back. I was so excited for her to see our new home!

Chapter 29

Tick, Tock, Tick, Tock

It was now August. About three months had gone by, and Alyona was still not home.

At this point we were all worried, not sure why this would be, so I told Mom I would go visit the hospital again to see what was taking so long. I got there with no problem, got off the trolley, and found myself next to the enormous building once again. I realized how much easier this was the second time around; I knew exactly which door to go through, and who to see. I went up to the counter where a different lady was sitting this time, and asked her if she could help me find out about my sister's whereabouts. Luckily no one else was there, so I had the lobby all to myself, which made it easier. I didn't like to be inside public places; too many eyes.

"What did you say her name was?" the lady asked, flipping through some book.

"Alyona," I said.

"What's her last name?" the lady asked.

"I don't know," I said, thinking, *What's a last name?*

"Got it," the lady said, closing the book. "Did you move recently?" she asked.

"Yes, actually, we did—how did you know that?" I asked. It was like she was a magician!

"I ask because the hospital did bring your sister back, but they couldn't locate the family, and were told you had all moved somewhere else, but no one knew where," the lady said, taking off her glasses. "The hospital had no choice but to bring her to an orphanage. Here, you can go visit her there." She handed me the name of the orphanage she had on file.

I didn't say a word, just took the piece of paper with something written on it, put it in my pocket, and walked out, feeling like my lungs had left my body, leaving me to gasp for air. *Orphanage* was all I'd heard. This was the worst news possible. Alyona being placed in an orphanage meant we might never get her back.

I got home as fast as I could to share the terrible news. That's when I learned about my aunt's two daughters who were far away—in an orphanage! One of her daughters was about fourteen, and the other, around seventeen. After all this time, I'd had no idea that her daughters were also in an orphanage. *But not her sons?* I wondered. I never asked, however; I was more worried about how we were going to get Alyona out.

"I'm going to go and try to get her out," Mom said.

"We'll do what we can, but I don't know, Ludmila," my aunt said. She knew it was a slim chance at best, especially because we had no documents to even prove she was ours—that Mom had given birth to Alyona, that she was, in fact, my little sister. I stayed positive, trying to hope for the best and believe we'd get Alyona out, but part of me felt terrified.

* * *

The orphanage was pretty far away from where we lived, a small two-story building surrounded by a fence and some woods. It was located about a quarter-mile from the bus stop. Outside the fenced-in area were average suburban homes.

We walked through the gate and went inside, where a woman showed us the way to the director's office. "Whatever reason you are here, she'll be able to help you," the lady said, pointing us toward the office door. "Wait here, please."

We all stood there, doing our best to look normal, but inside I'm pretty sure we were all freaking out, nervous about how this was going to go.

"You may go in now," the lady said a few minutes later, holding the door open for us.

Another woman was sitting behind the desk. She looked serious, and out of our league—like there was no way we were going to win against this lady.

"Sit," the woman said. "How can I help?" she asked, looking around the room, waiting for someone to take charge and say something.

"We are here because my youngest daughter was placed here by accident not long ago," Mom answered. "We moved a while back, and when the hospital tried to bring her to our old address, we weren't there anymore."

"I see," the woman said, looking down at some papers and then back at Mom. "Do you have her birth certificate?"

"No. Unfortunately, we lost all of our documents," Mom said.

"I see. Well, you understand that without the proper documentation, we can't give her back to you. We would also need to inspect where you live now, and where you work. Would this be possible?"

I looked at Mom, who was still sitting there, frozen, not sure what to say or not to say. This was the type of news we were all afraid of. I was a bit nervous as to what Mom might do; any moment now there was the potential of her exploding, and then we would definitely never see Alyona again.

We were in trouble. Mom's face was red, and she was about to go off.

"So what are you saying?" she asked, clearly furious.

My aunt came to the rescue, putting her arm around Mom, trying to calm her down.

"I am saying we won't discharge Alyona because you have none of the proper documents, nor the right tools to raise this child. Kids don't end up here for no reason," the woman said. "I am very sorry, but the law is the law."

I could tell she truly was sorry, but what good was that going to do any of us?

"Thank you for your time," my aunt said, nudging Mom toward the door.

I could tell this wasn't easy for Mom; it was obvious she wanted to snap this woman's neck and go and get Alyona. Mom had a real temper. The good news was, she was sober, and more in control than usual.

On our way home, I thought about how strict this orphanage place was—that they wouldn't even let us see Alyona, even for a moment—like she was theirs and not ours. This was incredibly upsetting for all of us.

I didn't know much about orphanages, though sometimes, especially around the New Year's holiday, I would see group after group of kids in the city headed somewhere. Sometimes they would gather around the circus area waiting to get in to watch the show. I always wondered what that was like, although I wouldn't have traded places with any of them. None of the kids looked happy, nor did they seem to say much. They just looked down at the ground as they walked, holding hands with whomever they were paired with. It felt like a funeral more than a holiday celebration, watching them pass by. There was an adult at the front and back of the group. I remember thinking how awful it was that all the girls had boys' haircuts, and how their clothing was way out of style or way too big.

There were some kids around the city who had said that orphanages were the most horrible places, though not many would really explain why. I suppose they had their reasons. I didn't want to end up in one because I didn't want that life, nor did I want to lose all my hair, or my friends. I didn't want someone telling me what to do all day long, either. I think that was the biggest issue for most kids who feared orphanages: We couldn't imagine being stuck someplace like that. We were free, and we didn't have the ability to handle being told how to be and what to do, all day long, in the same place.

Mom was never the same after that day. Years ago she had lost my older sister, Victoria; now, she'd lost another daughter. She blamed herself for how our lives had turned out. She believed that if it wasn't for her, we would be better off. Mom couldn't stand the thought of never seeing her little girl again—none of us could—and we didn't know of any way to get our documents back.

It was an impossible situation. On the one hand, Mom must have known that Alyona was in fact better off in the orphanage, as she would be well provided for and taken care of. On the other, she must have felt like a piece of her was being chopped off—like she had just lost a big part of who she was. While she had every right to be upset, she also felt guilty for wanting her little one back, as she knew that we couldn't provide for her like they could. I knew it, my aunt knew it, and so did the people at the orphanage. Despite our nice clothes, fake smiles, and best behavior, we didn't have what it took to get Alyona back. It really hurt us. We all lost a little piece of ourselves that day.

It was heartbreaking, and very depressing. I couldn't believe that just like that, in the blink of an eye, my sister was no longer with us. She was living with strangers who were now raising her and watching out for her. It made me sick to my stomach. This wasn't right! There had to be a way to visit her, a way to tell her how much we missed her, and loved her.

I thought about what it must feel like for Alyona. I hoped that somehow she knew we hadn't abandoned her—that we'd tried to get her back, and that her big sister was going to come up with some sort of plan to get her out of there, back with us, where she belonged.

Chapter 30

The Show Must Go On

As I walked around the city, trying to bring myself to go to work, all I could really think about was Alyona. I missed her so much; so did my mom and my aunt, of course, but they both seemed to have given up trying to find a way to get her out.

I, on the other hand, couldn't give up. Every day I wondered how I was going to find a way to see my sister again, and how in the world I was going to be able to bring her back home. I decided I would ask around, in hopes that some of the street kids might have some more information about orphanages.

I made my way to the busiest and most popular area of the city, where several kids seemed to hang out. After I'd been set up by that girl, I hadn't been as anxious to hang around other kids, but today was different. I was on a mission: to learn everything I possibly could about orphanages. Thus far, all I knew was that my sister was living in one, and that people there had power I didn't.

I was very surprised to find out just how much most of these kids knew about orphanages, and the fact that almost all of them had brothers or sisters living in one.

"There are only two orphanages around here," one of the boys said. He was around my age, and looked like he had been through hell. He was addicted to sniffing glue to get high. His eyes were bloodshot, while his hair was a big mess, all tangled up with glue. I knew exactly what had happened to him. A while back I'd seen some kids being scolded by the cops, who took the glue the kids were sniffing and rubbed it all over their heads, to teach them a lesson. Whatever they'd hoped to teach the kids hadn't worked, as this boy as still breathing glue from a bag, getting high.

This was the strangest thing to me; I didn't get it. What was the big deal? So many kids were doing this, mainly boys, so right then and there, I decided to try it, to see what all the fuss was about.

One of the boys handed me a bag, saying, "Do it like this." He showed me how to get a proper hit. I held the end of the bag tightly, just enough to let some air into my lungs once I'd inflated the bag with my breath.

"Yeah, girl, you got this," the boy said, laughing.

I took a deep breath and exhaled into the bag, then quickly inhaled the air into my lungs. I'll never forget the nasty taste in my mouth, or how harsh the stuff was. I felt like I'd never recover, coughing my brains out. This wasn't something I cared to ever try again. You couldn't pay me to do it! I couldn't believe this was what they were spending every cent on. It didn't make me feel better at all—what a waste of money!

As I stood there, recovering, a girl approached me. "Are you the one asking about orphanages?" she said.

"Yes, I am," I replied.

"Did you just lose someone to an orphanage?"

"Yeah, my younger sister," I said.

"That sucks," she said. "It's really hard at first, but you'll adjust." She continued, in a mysterious voice. "You know, there's one option to consider if you want to see your sister again."

I was intrigued. "Tell me," I said quietly.

"Well, some of us here have tried this. It doesn't always work."

"That's okay; tell me anyway," I said. Anything was better than nothing.

"One of my girlfriends has a little brother in the same orphanage as your sister. They took him away one day while they were wandering the streets. She went to the orphanage and asked to join her brother there. Then one day she took him and they ran away together, when no one was watching." The girl smiled. "They ran through the woods and got on the bus to ride into the city, far away from the orphanage. It worked for a little while, but then they found them again, and took her brother back." The girl paused for a moment, then continued. "Maybe they won't find you and your sister—you never know."

"Thank you so much!" I exclaimed. "This just might work!"

The girl smiled with satisfaction. "Sure, no problem! Good luck!" she yelled, as I took off to run home and tell Mom that I'd come up with a plan to rescue Alyona.

As I raced home I realized this was not going to be as easy as one, two, three. I found myself hesitating. Suddenly I knew I wasn't ready. I had to find a way to prepare myself, so I could actually convince the people at the orphanage I wanted to come and join my sister there. I hoped I would be able to get out and not be stuck there forever!

I turned around and went back to the city. I needed to work, to take my mind off this terrifying plan I was considering. I felt ashamed of myself for not racing straight to the orphanage, to be with Alyona. The feeling I had inside made me feel so small and helpless; I needed to do something I was familiar with—and that was working. Though I didn't make as much money as I used to with Alyona, I did manage to earn something, which was better than nothing. Sometimes I would also find beer bottles left behind on the streets and exchange them for some coins, which added up. Doing something was better than driving myself up the wall.

I kept myself busy. Life had to go on; we still had to eat and have money for other things like soap, cigarettes, and vodka for my mom and my aunt. Although they didn't drink as much as they used to, it was comforting to have a bottle laying around—especially if Mom was having one of her really bad days. Drinking a little helped her anxiety. They relied on me to help out, and I wasn't going to let them down.

Although it was a great distraction, and I was making some money, it didn't change how I felt. Everything in the city reminded me of Alyona and our times together, so I found myself going to other cities, where I hadn't brought Alyona yet. I felt like part of me had died—like I was never going to be the same person without my sister by my side. I was hurting, trying to forget that I was just a small fish in a large sea, powerless to do anything other than beg for money.

I wished I was rich—that I had a good life—so they'd give Alyona back to us. But that wasn't going to happen. Nothing was possible without documentation. It's like we didn't exist without our papers. I realized there was a lot I didn't understand, and that I was playing with fire with this idea of trying to join my sister at the orphanage. But the thought never went away. It haunted me, my longing to save Alyona.

It sure would make Mom happy; she needed Alyona back even more than I did. Alyona was always able to make Mom smile. I was mostly gone all day, so I wasn't there to see how Mom was doing. My aunt had been telling me that Mom was really out of it; she wasn't herself. She'd just sit there and stare at the walls. She was losing weight, as she was eating next to nothing. My aunt was really worried about her. None of us knew how to bring her back, how to snap her out of whatever this was.

Chapter 31

June 20, 1998

It was summer once more, with warm sunny days and blue skies. There were plenty of customers at the outdoor market, and plenty of glorious fruit! I was so excited to go to the busiest and largest market around to gather up some of the slightly old or damaged food that people routinely threw away, including fruit, my favorite. It was like being in paradise. I tried something I'd never had before—I think it was a banana!—and I loved it.

I also looked forward to going swimming at the lake now that a year had gone by. I couldn't believe how fast the year had flown. It was just last spring that Alyona had been taken away from us.

I found that the girl was right: I did adjust, and I was able to go on. Not that I ever recovered, but I went on. I kept on living, knowing that orphanage life wasn't as horrible as I'd thought before. The street kids had told me that there was plenty of food, three meals a day, and that you get presents at Christmas! I guess those were two of the most exciting things these kids could imagine. In some ways, having Alyona at the orphanage gave me a good feeling, because I didn't have to worry about her well-being. She had plenty to eat, and got presents at Christmas. Plus, I was sure that everyone had fallen in love with her by this point; everyone always did. She was safe, and, I hoped, in good hands.

While I figured I could join her at the orphanage any time I wanted, I was getting older, and the thought of trading my freedom to be behind closed walls felt more and more dreadful by the day. It felt like going to prison, to never see the light of day again. Also, I really couldn't imagine leaving Mom behind. I felt like she'd already lost two daughters; she couldn't afford to lose another. I was the last kid left, and I was taking care of her and my aunt financially.

Not that it made much difference. Some days weren't as successful as others, so mom would have to sell some of the nicer belongings she still had left, like her pretty shoes and silk blouses, or her jewelry. I think most of these items were stolen during the time Mom worked with Oleg; nevertheless, it wasn't easy for Mom to part with everything she had left. Except for a pair of white flip-flops and couple of outfits, Mom had nothing.

It didn't seem like she cared very much, although maybe she was just putting on a face, pretending that she didn't. It was tough to tell these days. She was pretty unpredictable; sometimes she made no sense at all, once again lost somewhere, deep within her memories, and an imaginary life where Alyona was still with us, along with my father and older sister, Victoria. I'd never known either of them, so I couldn't really miss something I'd never had. Mom, on the other hand, frequently lost herself in memories of times when everything was great. She would come out of it and realize where she was, only to be disappointed. Nothing was good anymore. I would hold her and rub her shoulders when she cried, missing Alyona.

"I know, Mom. I miss her too—so much—every single day," I'd say, trying to make her feel better, retelling happy stories about Alyona. Sometimes it worked; other times, Mom didn't want me to talk about her at all.

On June 20, I went out to work for the day, leaving later than usual. I'd slept in after taking care of Mom the night before. She had needed comfort and love, and at least I could give her that much.

I decided to hit up some houses for new clothes, as my stuff didn't fit well anymore. I'd grown! I went back to a neighborhood where I knew the people always had something to give away, and knocked on some doors, begging for clothes they no longer needed, or could spare. I remember I got several cute summer dresses, one of which was red velvet with lace-like strings on each side, most likely to tie around the back. I found them useless, so when I got home to show Mom my new clothes, I asked her to cut off the lace strings, as I didn't need them.

I wore the dress that same day when I went back out to work. I probably shouldn't have, as I barely made anything that afternoon—I looked too nice—but I really wanted to wear the dress! I guess it was a trade-off: I could either make more money by not looking pretty, or make less money looking nice. Not really a fair trade, but you know, it's like going to get your nails done, or going to a spa. Wearing the dress (which fit perfectly), I felt like a brand-new person.

I don't know if it was the new dress, or the fact that it was a lovely evening, but that night I was walking home way past my curfew. I knew I was in trouble, as it was already past eleven when I approached the gate. I'd thought it was earlier, but when I'd asked a man with a watch what time it was, he said 10:45. I was still pretty far away at that point. Finally, I made it home, and was closing in toward the gate. I braced myself as I opened it, hoping my punishment wouldn't be as bad as it had been the last time I returned after curfew.

That time I'd gotten lost in one of the cities I wasn't as familiar with, and couldn't find my way home. It was late and all the trolleys were done for the night. The only way I knew how to get home was by trolley. Upon my return home, I got a really good beating—not from Mom, but from my aunt. She had one of those walking canes made of aluminum that blind people use, that fold up into a smaller size. My aunt beat me so hard with her cane that it got completely bent. I was bent over myself, with pain; damn, that hurt. It had been a while since I'd been beaten this badly. My body had forgotten what that kind of pain felt like.

This time as I approached our house, I hoped it wouldn't be a stick beating again, or worse, a belt! I remembered the times Alyona's father would beat me with a belt buckle. "Put your hands out and spread your fingers apart," he'd say, swinging full force down on my hands. This was the most painful experience—much worse than being beaten on any other part of my body. He wanted me to write my name on a piece of paper, and told me to pick up the pencil and do it, which I did. I remember him saying, "That's the wrong hand!" That was it: hands out, fingers spread, and get ready.

I didn't stand a chance. It just so happened that I grabbed the pencil with my left hand. I'd never done anything like this before. I didn't even know how to write a damn thing, but he knew that; it was just another excuse to beat me up. He gave me just one try; I didn't even have time to do anything but grab the damn pencil.

This was the first and last time I would pick up any sort of writing utensil for a long time. It wasn't until three or four years later that I learned why he was yelling at me: Writing with the right hand was the only proper, correct way.

I was so glad he was gone and out of our lives—forever!

As I got to the house, I noticed that the living room window was open, and the door to the house was also completely wide open.

That's strange, I thought, as I slowly made my way inside.

At first I thought that maybe someone had broken in and robbed us—not that we had anything of value—but this wasn't normal. That was the only explanation I could come up with. I saw the clean clothes still hanging on the clothesline; Mom hadn't taken them down yet. Just that morning before I left, Mom had been cleaning the house and doing our laundry. She had washed all of the new clothes I'd scored earlier in the day by hand. She was in such a great mood when I left, like she'd done a "total 180." I was so glad to see her happy; she even gave me a kiss good-bye before I left and told me she loved me, which was the first time she'd done that in a really long time. I couldn't remember the last time I'd seen her like this, if ever.

I walked inside the house to find that no one was there, either sleeping or awake. I stood in the hallway by the door, looking around to see if anything was missing or vandalized. Everything was still where it had been when I'd left this morning, except for the table, which had several empty vodka bottles on it, and more cigarette butts than ever before. Maybe my mom and my aunt had had some company over and then ended up going out or something.

I figured I would jump into bed and pretend I'd been sleeping the whole time when I heard them come back. Till then I was going to smoke a nice new cigarette out of the mostly full pack that had been left on the table. I stood by the open window, smoking the cigarette and keeping an eye out for Mom and my aunt. I knew I'd hear them before I could see them, so I'd have plenty of time to get rid of the cigarette and jump into bed before they came in. I took the last drag, and still nothing; it looked like no one was coming back anytime soon. I closed the window and locked the door, then climbed into bed, keeping the lights on as they'd been when I arrived. I cautiously listened for their voices.

About an hour later, I heard a voice. It was my aunt, and she didn't sound like she'd been having a great time. Instead she was weeping and saying something I couldn't make out. Worried, I closed my eyes and pretended I was asleep. I heard her unlock the door and peeked out to see what was wrong.

My aunt and Mom's guy friend, the one who was letting us live here, walked in. The man was helping my aunt stay on her feet; she looked like she could barely stand, although it didn't look like anything was physically wrong. *What the hell is going on?* I thought, closing my eyes and pulling the blanket over my face, still able to see from a little gap in the covers.

The man helped my aunt take a seat by the table and poured her some vodka. She took a shot while still weeping uncontrollably, and lit a cigarette.

"I am so sorry, Ludmila," he said. "How are you going to tell the kids?" He looked gloomy and sad, trying to keep himself together.

I saw my aunt look over at my bed. "Come here, Ludmila—I know you're not sleeping," she said.

Damn—how did she know that? I took the covers off and stood up against the wall. I didn't say anything—just looked at my aunt, confused, curious to know what she was going to tell me. *What was the man sorry for? What had happened?* Something was very wrong.

"Ludmila, I have to tell you something horrible," my aunt said. "It's about your mom." She could barely talk, still sobbing.

"What is it? Where's Mom?" I said. At this point I was about to cry, too.

"Your mom—she's..." My aunt took a long pause and then blurted out the most dreadful, world-ending news. "Your mom—she's gone. She's gone." She was wiping her face with the bedsheets.

"What do you mean, she's gone?" I asked, puzzled. I thought maybe she'd gotten arrested again, as had happened once before when she'd said the wrong thing to a cop she saw on the street when she and her friend had been out, getting drunk. "She got arrested?" I asked.

My aunt looked at the man sitting beside her and said, "You tell her, please." I could tell my aunt just couldn't find the words; she was messed up, drunk—a big mess.

"Tell me!" I demanded, looking at the man. "Please, someone tell me—where's Mom?"

"Ludmila, your mom has died," the man said slowly. "She took her own life earlier today, when your aunt went to the market to get food." The man wiped at the tears that streamed down his face.

"What?!" I screamed. "I don't believe you! Why would you say that?!" I couldn't believe this; it couldn't be true! I'd just seen my mom this morning. She was happy, doing fine. This made no sense.

I started to cry, looking at my aunt, on her way to hug me. "I am so sorry, Ludmila; I am so very sorry." She held me and swayed me back and forth on the bed, holding my head with one hand and my back with the other.

I couldn't breathe. I was gasping for air like a fish out of water, fighting for a living breath. Every inch of my body felt heavy, as if I weighed a thousand pounds, as if I was getting pulled down into the ocean, deep down, like a thousand-pound rock. Everything got darker around me and I couldn't see, like I needed glasses.

I pushed my aunt away and jumped off the bed to grab the only thing that was left of Mom—her white flip-flops—and held them close to my chest for dear life as I cried and cried and cried. The man had left, and my aunt was on her bed, doing the same. Neither of us knew how we were going to survive this.

I didn't *want* to survive this; I wanted to die too. I felt like I had nothing left to live for in this world. Mom had meant everything to me. I'd never once imagined not having her by my side. I'd never thought she would leave us alone.

I had so many mixed feelings running through my head like a virus. I kept trying to find ways this could have been avoided. Maybe we could have done something differently? Maybe we did something wrong. At some point while I was wailing, crying my eyes out, my heart squeezing as if someone was pressing down on my chest, I fell asleep. I hoped I'd wake up and see Mom again. Part of me couldn't register that this news was true, while another part of me felt like an earthquake was shaking the world to nothingness. A most beautiful summer day, June 20, 1998, had turned into the biggest nightmare of my life, with no point of return.

Mom was only thirty-three years old when she died. I was ten.

Chapter 32

Little Red Dress

"How did it happen?" I asked my aunt.

Mom had been gone for three days, and I found myself wanting to know everything that had happened.

"I'm glad to see you out of bed," she said, as she came over to talk to me. "Since your mom hadn't been herself lately, I'd been trying to stay at home to keep an eye on her. But that day, she was doing well, so I figured I could leave her alone for couple of hours to go to the market." She wiped the tears off her face and continued. "When I got back, I didn't see her, so I called out, but there was no response. I went straight into the kitchen to put the groceries on the table, and that's when I saw her."

"What did you see?" I asked, doing my best not to cry. I needed to hear this; I needed to know every detail, like somehow it would make me feel better or something.

"I found your mom, hanging on the bathroom door. She hung herself, Ludmila. She hung herself."

My aunt got up and walked over to the table to light a cigarette. I could tell that her hands were shaking. She was shattered, just as angry, just as confused.

"I don't understand how those silly laces, the ones she'd cut off your dress, could possibly hold—how they didn't snap. How in the world—"

"You mean, the strings from that little red dress I just got? Those lace strings?!"

"Yes, Ludmila. She tied them together. When I found her, her legs were bent and stiff. She was gone; there was nothing I could do." She was sobbing now.

At this point, all I could do was blame myself. I wished I'd never taken that pretty little dress—like somehow, it was all my fault that this had happened. I felt like I might as well have handed Mom a gun.

I also couldn't help but suddenly recall that dreadful day when I'd seen a vision of the entire place in flames, like a warning for us not to move here. Maybe Mom would still be alive if we had listened to the warning I received and hadn't moved in.

"This is all my fault!" I yelled. "This is all my fault!" I grabbed the red dress and ran outside. Taking some matches, I set the damn dress on fire.

"Burn, you stupid dress!" I screamed, sobbing, wishing I could turn back the clock. It felt so good to watch it go up in flames.

I walked inside and told my aunt I was going out for the day. I couldn't stand being here, at this place where Mom had died, just a few feet away.

While walking to the city it started to pour; everyone scattered, trying to keep dry. I didn't give a shit—just kept walking in the rain. I dragged myself to the exchange building where rich people went to exchange foreign currency to make international calls. It was one of the best places for me to work. The walk normally felt short, but today it felt like a marathon. Today it felt like the world was slowly closing in on me, slowly erasing me from existence. I felt ill, like I'd just taken several different drugs at once. I barely found my way there. All the lights on the cars and trolleys hurt my eyes, the city noises hurt my head, and all the people walking by with family and friends hurt my heart.

Somehow I made it inside and sat down on the stairs, resting against the wall, trying to catch my breath and get comfortable. I needed to be somewhere where I could just sit and do nothing but attempt to breathe. I rested my head on my knees and extended one of my hands out to beg. Here I was safe; no one asked me to leave, and it was always warm inside in winter or cool during the summer, which was usually refreshing. But not today. Today was like being in hell—like at any moment, I too would somehow be gone, like Mom. I considered joining her, thinking I'd reunite with her. I didn't want to live without Mom, and part of me felt like dying more and more every day. It was like every day I felt worse; every day I had more pain than the day before, a never-ending cycle.

I ended up falling asleep for an hour, because when I opened my eyes there was some change in my hand, and I realized the hands on the clock had moved. Having some money, I left to get something sweet and delicious to comfort myself, hoping it would help. But no candy bar, gum, or cigarettes, not even city life, made me feel even slightly better.

Nothing was working; nothing felt right anymore.

* * *

That night I had a dream about Mom. I still remember it perfectly, as if it were yesterday.

In the dream, I found myself underground, in a basement under a building. It was cold there, with a chilly breeze and leaky pipes making small streams everywhere. The lighting was greenish and the ceiling wasn't that high. I saw someone there. It was Mom! In the dream I knew it was her, even though she looked nothing like herself. She was wearing what looked like an old worn-out bathrobe, but not a nice one—more like the ones they hand out at a hospital. I remember she looked very skinny and had no hair—she was completely bald. Her skin looked bluish-purple and her lips very dry, with barely any color. The place felt creepy, but I wasn't scared, because Mom was there. She knew I was there, too. I have no idea what I looked like to her, but we knew of each other's presence.

I only saw her for a moment before she turned around to leave. I yelled after her, "Mom, wait—take me with you! Please, I want to go with you!" I saw her turn around and slowly walk toward me.

When she got close, she paused long enough for me to get a good look at her, and then she bent forward even closer to me and said, "I can't, sweetheart; you have to stay. I love you, but I can't take you with me." She smiled, and moments later, she was gone. I didn't even get to hug her.

I didn't realize I was crying in my sleep, and managed to wake myself up. It was the middle of the night.

"Damn it!" I screamed, waking up my aunt.

She turned on the lights and, half asleep, asked me if I was all right. I told her I wasn't, and shared my dream with her.

"Wow, Ludmila—that's quite a dream," she said, looking worried. "You know that if you'd gone with her in the dream, you would have died?" my aunt said. She got up and lit a cigarette, brushing herself off, saying she felt a chill in the room.

"How do you know that?" I asked.

"I just know," she answered, without giving me an explanation.

I would hold that dream very close to my heart. Night after night, I wished I would dream of Mom again, but I never did. That was the only time.

"You still have that photo of Mom, right?" I asked.

"Yes, I do. It's safely stored away in a book," my aunt said.

"Can I see it?" I asked. I was missing her so much. I needed to see her.

Looking at the picture of her, all dressed up, looking healthy and beautiful, reminded me of how she'd been before she changed. I was so thankful we had this photo—one very precious picture of my mom that I would cherish for the rest of my life.

Chapter 33

Time and Money

It was time to evaluate my life. Where do I go from here? I had no one left except my sister, who was in an orphanage, still without a clue her mom was no longer alive.

I was barely present as summer slipped away right under my nose; the leaves began to fall, and rain took over the sun. I had spent many days trying to piece myself back together, especially after my aunt had shared something with me. My mom had left a note explaining why she'd done what she did. She had said that she couldn't go on anymore, knowing that our lives had turned out this way because of her. She blamed herself for everything that had happened. She felt so ashamed and guilty that she couldn't change anything, except to leave us—like we'd be better off without her.

I hated that note. I barely remember my aunt reading it to me, I was so out of it, but I will never forget the words. I didn't feel that way about our life. I had never blamed Mom for the way things had turned out; I loved her with all my heart, no matter what. I wished she had asked us how we felt first, before she took her own life.

It was still tough to believe she was gone. There had been no funeral; my aunt didn't even allow me to see my mom's body—to say good-bye to her. I didn't have any true closure, other than once going back to revisit our old neighborhood, where I remembered Mom the most, where long ago we once lived together in our own home.

I didn't make it far that day.

On the way there I'd seen a blonde woman, about the same height and weight as Mom. I ran over to her, screaming, "Mom! Mom!" I felt I was seeing her—just how, I don't know. Later I realized I had grabbed onto some woman who may have been blonde, but looked nothing like my mom otherwise. It was the strangest thing; I could have sworn it was Mom.

I had a friend with me that day, a girl about my age who knew what had happened to my mother. She was going back home with me, to help me say good-bye and find some closure.

After seeing the blonde woman, we continued our trip on the trolley. We got off at the next stop and ended up walking a mile or so to the bus stop, planning to take the bus to the neighborhood. I realized I couldn't do it. I couldn't set foot past the station.

"You okay?" my friend asked.

"No," I said. "I feel like I'm going crazy—like Mom is alive and well somewhere. Like she never died, and one day she'll come back to us." I was sobbing. Seeing Mom one minute and then never seeing her again the next was very hard for me to make sense of; it was like my brain was playing tricks on me.

In fact, my memory hadn't been serving me well lately. I ended up leaving my wallet full of the cash I had earned on a bench at the trolley station. Just as I was about to jump out and retrieve it, the doors slammed shut, and I had no choice but to watch as we drove away from my wallet.

I was a mess. At this point I had tried it all, including hanging out with a dangerous crowd of kids who lived in a parking garage, currently under construction. It was huge, at least three floors high. You weren't allowed in unless they considered you "one of them." I had to prove myself in order to join the gang, jumping a tough corner from one side to the other. If I had fallen, I wouldn't have survived.

I will admit, it was good to feel alive, to feel the adrenaline rush. I had been living like a dead fish in the sea, and doing something completely stupid and dangerous made me feel better. I was done being angry, I was done being hurt, I was done being sad. I wanted to feel something I had never felt before, do something I'd never done before. I needed to feel rebellious, and alive. I jumped and made it over, barely missing the edge.

That was definitely the most dangerous thing I had ever done, but I felt like a champion. It felt good to be someone else for a while. Just like that, I was in; I was part of the clan. All the kids were older than me by at least five years, and they were crazy—drinking, sniffing glue, and acting out, doing stupid stuff, like fighting.

"Let the best man win!" the king would say. Yes, they had a king—a master whom they followed around, doing whatever he asked. It got to be too competitive for me personally. There were a couple girls who liked the master, and since I'd joined, it seemed he'd picked me as his next-in-line tough chick, to be by his side. This meant I was safe from anyone harming me, and I got to hang out in the master's den, which consisted of a bed made of fur coats, some sheets, and a lot of other goodies, like pills, cigarettes, snacks, glue, alcohol, and so forth. I was just grateful he didn't put his hands on me; I don't know how well that would have played out. I just knew I wasn't going to have another Victor on my hands.

Everyone worked for the master, either begging or stealing from younger kids, and not just stuff, but also money. It didn't take me long to say enough is enough. I knew that if I stayed, I would turn into someone I didn't want to be, or worse, do something I would really regret later.

I didn't know what I was capable of those days. I was angrier than ever before about a lot of things. Besides, I didn't like following someone around like a puppet, and I didn't like feeling like I belonged to someone else. So after a couple weeks, I left to go do my own thing, one last time. I wanted to enjoy myself and my freedom before I carried out my plan, which was to join my sister at the orphanage. She was the only family I had left, the only one who reminded me that I still had a family—that I was not alone. My aunt was okay, but I didn't feel the same about her. I didn't love her like I loved my mom and my sister.

I ended up back at the exchange building to beg for some money, when something extraordinary happened! As I walked into the building I noticed a foreign bill on the floor. I looked around and saw that no one was going to pick it up, so I grabbed it and went straight to the window to see how much I could get for it.

"Excuse me, miss, I would like to exchange this bill," I said nervously. Part of me felt like what I was doing was wrong, but another part felt like I had every right to do it, since I'd found the bill. I handed it to the lady, thinking I would probably get, like, five bucks' worth of Ukrainian *hryvni*—but no. I got a lot more! I will never forget that moment, when the lady kept going and going and going, handing me large bills. It was a thick pile; I'm pretty sure I walked away with about a thousand Ukrainian *hryvni*. A twenty-dollar bill turned into all that! I couldn't believe it! This was the most money I had ever held in my hands!

Now this is how it's supposed to feel, to be alive! I thought as I walked out. It felt amazing. I was going to blow all of it, doing everything I'd always wanted! My first stop was going to be the toy store. Ever since I'd learned of the Tamagotchi game a while back, when we had lived at the apartment for a month after losing our home, I'd wished I had one.

I remembered meeting a young girl who had just gotten one. She showed me how it worked, and I thought it was so cool, to watch the little fella grow. "The more you take care of him and feed him, the more he will grow," the girl had said, as she fed the crying baby.

Now it was my turn. I was about to have the toy I'd wanted for such a long time! I ended up getting exactly the same one the girl had had, except mine was yellow. I didn't even want to play with it yet; I put it in my pocket for later, so I could continue doing all the things I'd wished I could do during all these years of working in the city. Knowing I was heading to the orphanage soon made me feel like I was enjoying my last days on Earth, so I wasn't going to waste it.

There was a restaurant I'd always wanted to eat at where they made shish kabobs on a charcoal grill. It smelled so damn good every time I walked by; it's like my mouth forgot how to function and my stomach forgot how to be polite. It was expensive to eat there, but not today. I will never forget the waitress, who didn't want to let me onto the outdoor patio. When I took out the pile of cash and showed her I had plenty of money to eat there, it was the best feeling in the world. It was like, for a little while, I got to feel what normal people feel when they have money to get whatever they want. Sure felt nice to be on their side of the fence for once!

After I pigged out, I decided it was time to go sit somewhere to test my new toy, and have a smoke.

On the way I noticed a man I'd seen at the exchange building earlier; he was following me. I started to walk faster, trying to get away, but it was too late. He grabbed my shirt and said, "Don't move." I froze, scared. Why was he after me—what did he want?

"You are coming with me," he said, holding my sleeve.

"What did I do?" I asked, wishing my street friends were around right about now.

"Shut up! No talking," the man said. He was serious. Maybe an undercover cop?

I found myself about a mile away on the same side of street, inside a building I had passed many times before. He took me up to the second floor, to a room where a nicely dressed woman with wavy blonde hair was waiting.

"Empty her pockets," the woman said. She was middle-aged, pretty, with makeup and painted nails. She smelled nice and was wearing a beautiful white coat.

"Don't do anything stupid," the man said as he emptied my pockets. They took everything from me—all the money I had left, and even my Tamagotchi toy! Then they told me to leave, like a dog they didn't want around anymore, like I was nothing.

I ran out of there as fast as I could, to the lake where I came to swim. I was surprised to see so many kids still in the water, even though it had rained on and off, and the wind was a bit chilly. I thought about what had happened—how I should have just gone home with all the money instead of being greedy and spending so much of it right away. *Maybe if I'd kept it in my pocket instead of flashing it around, I'd still have it.* I just couldn't let it go. They had no right—but then again, who would take my side? I was just some useless street kid, powerless when it came to standing up against them.

I hated the world at this point, and all the people in it. It was me against the world. I never thought I could feel so much inside. I was filled with anguish, rage, and pain, lots of pain. I didn't know I could feel this much—I didn't know how to handle myself, or how to turn it off. It just kept hitting and hitting, right where it hurt.

Chapter 34

Day One

Not long afterward, I took the trolley and then the bus to get to the orphanage where Alyona had been living for the past year or so. I was so excited to see her again after all this time. It felt like it had been forever. Now that I had nothing to lose, I was going to put my plan into action. I would join my sister in the orphanage, stay for a while, then grab her and run when the time was right.

As I approached the fence I heard children's voices; the kids were outside, playing. Everyone looked at me as I entered, making my way to the office where Mom and I had once stood together. I could tell the kids were wondering who I was, and why I was there. I didn't look at anyone—just kept my head down as I made my way inside. A couple of kids ran past me, laughing.

I knocked on the door and heard a familiar voice say "Come in." I carefully opened the door and walked inside the office.

"Oh, it's you again," the woman behind the desk said. "It's been a while. Where is your mom?" she asked.

I didn't answer. I just couldn't bring myself to tell a stranger what had happened to Mom, so I just jumped right to the point.

"I am here to join my sister," I said.

"Interesting. Why now, after all this time?"

I was surprised that she was asking me all of these personal questions, about things I really didn't want to talk about. Wasn't it enough that I said I wanted to be here? Besides, they must have had a file about our lives since Alyona joined, and we were related.

I looked down at my feet, trying to come up with something to say. It was obvious to me that she was asking me these questions not because she needed my personal information, but more so because she must have known of my plans not to stick around; she must have seen it. Maybe I was too obvious. My face was getting red; I was scared I might blow this up.

I knew I had no choice but to tell her what had happened to Mom.

It was very rare to see a kid willing to enter such a place as an orphanage. Even kids who qualified wouldn't ever dare to show up at one. Most of the kids were either caught from the streets or dropped off by their parents, who were unable to care for them.

One time I saw a five-year-old girl begging on the streets. Afterward I saw her join her mother, who was waiting for her to give her every cent. The girl looked pretty bad; she needed some new clothes and a good meal. She looked worse than we did by a landslide. I never forgot that little girl. I couldn't imagine being in her shoes, like a slave to her mother, who was taking every penny the girl made to spend on booze. The woman looked like she drank way too much; she reminded me of my aunt's husband.

I took a deep breath and braced myself. This was it.

"Our mother passed away about a year ago," I said. "She took her own life. I have no one left to take care of me." I looked up at her. "My aunt has a disability and can't take care of me either. My sister is all I've got left, and I want to be with her." I said, wiping the tears off my face.

These were words I didn't think I would hear myself say out loud, and when I did, it was like I'd opened a Pandora's box—like I was going through hell all over again.

"Your sister is doing very well with us," the woman continued. "She is a special little girl. I don't blame you for missing her." The director handed me a tissue.

I wiped the tears off my face, feeling embarrassed for having a weak moment, and changed to a happier subject.

"I can't wait to see her! When can I see her?" I asked. I was getting pretty excited by this point, thinking I was about to see Alyona. I couldn't wait to hug her as soon as she ran into my arms. I couldn't wait to see how much she had grown, and what her interests were—her favorite toy, the friends she'd made, how she was treated, everything. I wanted to know everything she was into; after all, an entire year had gone by. We had so much to catch up on!

"It's not going to be that easy. If you're serious about coming to live here, you will have to wait three days before you can see her."

"Why?" I asked.

"We don't know what illnesses you might have, so we will need to isolate you and clean you up. When it's safe for you to be around other children, we will bring her in, okay?"

"Okay," I said.

What does "isolated" mean? I wondered, as the lady got up from her desk and asked me to follow her. We walked to a room just around the corner, which the woman unlocked, asking me to go inside.

"Someone else will be coming in to help you get cleaned up, okay?"

I didn't say anything—just went over to sit on the bed I knew was for me.

"It'll be lunchtime soon. I'm sure you're hungry?" the woman asked, handing me a blanket from one of the shelves.

I nodded.

"Thank you," I said, as I took the blanket, doing my best to keep my strong face on—although deep down inside, I couldn't help but feel scared to be facing this new life I'd signed up for, in an orphanage.

Here I was, doing something I'd told myself I would never do. I just so hoped I would be able to keep my hair!

The woman walked away, locking the door behind her so that I couldn't leave. I could hear her heels clicking against the cement floors as she made her way back to the office.

I got up and wandered around the room, checking it out, hoping I'd be able to see Alyona out the large window, but no such luck. There was no sign of her anywhere. I rested on the bed and allowed the tears to run down my face.

I couldn't help but cry again. I was missing Mom. I was already missing my life on the streets, and I was scared to be here, in this place where I'd never thought I'd end up. Eventually, I managed to fall asleep and forget all of my troubles, just for a little while.

I was woken up by an older lady with gray hair, and a bit on the heavier side. She seemed like a nice lady.

"Wake up—it's lunchtime!" she said cheerfully. She placed a tray on the table and looked at me. I was still lying there, not moving. I was so depressed, I really didn't care to eat or talk or give a damn about anything, other than getting Alyona and running away from here, this place with locked doors and constant surveillance.

"Tomorrow is a big day for you," the lady said. "We're going to clean you all up and make you pretty again, like I'm sure you are," she said, trying to make me feel better.

"Okay," I said. It was like I had some sort of disease. The lady had gloves on, as well as nose mask and something over her head—like she didn't want to get whatever it was I might have. This made me feel like I had more than just lice—like I was seriously ill or something. Turns out it was just for her own safety, so she wouldn't catch anything, or infect any of the other kids on the other side, who were already clean and cleared.

She was right. The next day turned out to be a big—and

horrible—day, as I lost all of my hair. I was officially one of them—one of the hairless orphaned girls I had seen on the streets, always praying that would never be me.

They had to shave my head because I was too infested with lice, and not just head lice. I also had clothing lice, thanks to a homeless man Mom had taken in years ago. She took him in one night when it was freezing cold outside; he would have frozen to death if he hadn't had someplace warm, so Mom helped him out, allowing him to sleep on the floor. He was gone the next morning, but it was too late—we were infected.

I couldn't believe we had so many pests in our home; aside from lice, our place was crawling with other bugs that lived inside the couch, making it smell weird. After once falling asleep on it by accident, I woke up to them crawling on me, biting me, eating me alive. It was so scary, I'll never forget it, especially the fact that Mom somehow managed to sleep on that couch all night. Then again, most of the time she was drunk as a skunk. We also had bugs that lived inside the empty kitchen cabinets. I couldn't even open them because the bugs would start falling out, scattering all over the place while I tried to catch and kill as many as I could. It was disgusting, and horrifying.

I sat there quietly crying while my long brown hair fell on the floor, clump by clump. When it was all over, I felt like the last piece of dignity I'd had left was stripped away. I had no idea I would have to pay such a price. I couldn't stand to look at myself in the mirror. I was so happy when they gave me a hat to wear; it made me feel more like myself, hiding my hairless head.

Next, I was told to take a shower. They gave me some soap, a sponge, and shampoo.

"Wash everything really well, okay?" the gray-haired lady said, showing me the small triangular tub and turning on the water. "How does that feel?" she asked, trying to get the temperature just right for me.

"Good," I said, testing the water with my hand.

"All right, it's all yours," she said. She put some clothes on a chair by the tub. "These should fit you. After you're all done, put these clean clothes on, and put your old clothes in this bag." She closed the door behind her and I was left alone to shower.

Truth be told, the shower felt amazing. It had been years since I'd taken a real shower. After everything I'd been through, it helped my body to feel relaxed and calm, like I could stay in this tub forever.

Chapter 35

Rules and Routine

Finally, the long three days of isolation were over. I was going to see Alyona, like the older lady had promised! At last I was no longer contagious, and I'd been declared completely bug-free, which was actually pretty nice. I could finally sleep without itching all over, which had been so annoying.

I got up and got dressed, putting on the oversized clothes I'd been given: a pair of pants that looked like the kind boys wore, and a long-sleeved shirt. I looked just like a little boy. I pulled the winter hat on my head and sat on the edge of the bed, waiting for the door to open and Alyona to walk inside.

I heard footsteps, and moments later the door opened and I saw Alyona standing there, with the older lady.

"It's okay, honey—go ahead," she said to Alyona, who, to my surprise, was very hesitant to come over and give me a hug. She looked shy and maybe even scared, like she didn't want to see me.

"It's okay; it's me, Ludmila—your sister," I said, as I approached her to give her a hug.

She didn't move, just hid in the lady's skirt, holding on to her hand tightly.

"It's me, Ludmila," I said again, hoping she would look at me instead of hiding behind the lady. It was like she'd forgotten who I was.

This was not something I'd seen coming. Although a year had gone by, not once had I forgotten her. I wondered if I had changed a lot; maybe my new hairdo had made me unrecognizable? It was outrageously hurtful. It felt like someone had just ripped a bandage off of my somewhat-glued-together heart, tearing it to pieces again, leaving me once more with an open, bleeding wound.

I was really angry, so when it came time for me to join all the other kids, I was even more focused on my plan. I couldn't wait for us to run away, but especially, I wanted to take Alyona away from them. For the first time in my life, I felt jealous. She was *my* sister—my blood, not theirs! I couldn't wait for us to leave this place. Maybe once we returned to the city and walked around, she would remember me again—remember that I was her big sister who loved her very much, and had missed her terribly.

"This is your bed," the gray-haired lady said. She seemed to always be on duty, but I didn't mind. She was kind, and didn't look at me like I was a worthless orphan. When she made the bed, I noticed she placed a piece of waterproof cloth under the sheets. I was glad, as I wasn't sure whether I'd wet the bed again. So far, so good, though.

"Your sister sleeps right over there," the lady said.

I took a moment to look around the room. It was like the other rooms in the orphanage where I stayed in isolation, except this one had more furniture and plenty of windows, making it nice and bright. There were at least thirty beds, all of which were smaller than normal—just big enough for a kid. Each bed had a white paper star with a kid's name typed on it, attached to the headboard.

"Why are there names on each bed?" I asked.

"So that new kids who arrive can learn each other's names," the lady said, as she made up another bed, taking the sheets off with a large yellow ring.

"Oh," I said, looking around some more.

"Come over here," she said. "I'll show you where you'll keep your clothes from now on."

She walked over to the end of the room and opened a closet door where several cubbies were stacked. Each cubby had a name tag on it, just like the beds, and clothes were neatly stacked inside.

"This is your cubby," the lady said. "We'll get you some more clothes, too, okay?"

I nodded.

"Now, this room serves as a dining room," the lady said, showing me where I was going to sit during meals. The room had a large desk in the middle where someone could sit and watch us—not a caregiver, like this lady, but more like a teacher, she explained. There were several tables lined up perfectly, creating a square, the large desk in the center. Everyone sitting at the tables would face this desk.

"You will sit here," the lady said, handing me a star made of white paper, and two more, for the bed and the closet. I wrote down my first name in all capital letters on a piece of scrap paper—LUDMILA—and she helped me type it on all three stars.

"In the morning, breakfast will be served around eight a.m.," she continued. "Prior to that, everyone will be getting ready for the day, helping the little ones to get ready, too."

The lady walked into the bathroom, where metal potty-training buckets were placed for the little kids, like my sister. Although my aunt had potty-trained her some years ago, she still had to use a bucket, as there was only one toilet—and, well, little kids can't hold it that long. After all, there were about thirty of us, or more.

"First, all the older kids—and that includes you—will help the little ones go to the bathroom properly, followed by a shower, if needed, and then you'll help them brush their teeth." The lady pointed at the toothpaste everyone shared, and the toothbrushes, once more labeled with each child's name.

"Here you go—don't forget to write your name on it, or someone else might take it."

I took the Sharpie from her hand and wrote my name again, slowly.

"Now, as for the rest of the day," the lady said, clapping her hands together, "after the little ones are ready, you older kids will be able to take care of yourselves. Once that's all set, you older kids will help the little ones make their beds nicely, and then get them dressed for the day."

"Okay," I replied. So far, so good. I was keeping tabs on all the rules around here.

"The cooks will arrive to set the tables and bring the food, so you won't have to worry about that, but afterward, everyone takes turns cleaning and wiping off the tables. The cooks will come to collect the dishes. Here, I will show you the chart." The lady walked over to the corner, where there were lots of books.

"See this up here?" she said, pointing to some sort of schedule hanging on the wall. "This is how it's done. Here, write down your name in the blank spot right here," the lady said.

I did it a little faster this time.

"Don't worry; you'll know when it's your turn. The other kids will make sure of that," the lady said, laughing. "After breakfast, it's playtime outside. Everyone goes out to the playscape to play and get some fresh air."

"Okay," I said again, listening intently.

"After an hour or two you can come back inside, but not before then," the lady continued. "Lunch is at one p.m. Before lunch, kids keep themselves occupied, either outdoors or inside, reading, drawing, or sewing," she said. She walked over to the book section and showed me where colored pencils and white paper were stored, for drawing.

"You haven't met Irina Gregorievna yet," the lady continued.

"She'll be coming in after the weekend." She told me that Irina taught the girls how to properly eat, speak, and sew. She was the big boss around here, and she decided where kids went after their temporary placement here. Some kids were not as intellectual as others, and others had an easier time following orders than others. All of this contributed to her decision-making regarding where they would go next.

"One last thing," the lady said, as she walked over to another room I hadn't even noticed was there. "This is the older girls' room," she said as she opened the door. There were three beds inside, along with a couple of dressers and a small table. It looked like any room you'd find in a normal house—like whoever lived in this room ranked above everyone else.

"Stay on Irina's good side, and you'll be fine," the lady said, checking the clock. "Oh my, it's almost time for lunch! The kids are about to come back inside. Get ready to meet everyone!" She was so enthusiastic. The only thing I cared about, though, was seeing Alyona, who was outdoors with the other kids.

"Can I pick my sister as the little kid I take care of?" I asked. At least that way we'd get to spend more time together. Maybe it would help her to remember me.

"Sure; just talk to Irina Gregorievna on Monday. Shouldn't be a problem. Anything you need, just go to her and ask, okay?"

"Okay," I said as I sat down at the table that had my name tag on it.

"Good luck, Ludmila. I hope you make some friends!" she said, smiling. "Now it's the boys' turn," the lady said as she rushed out of the room and disappeared down the hallway.

The boys lived upstairs, above the girls. The older lady was taking care of them, too, going back and forth between the two floors. I wondered what the rest of the place looked like as I sat there, trying not to panic. I didn't like introducing myself, or talking much, for that matter; I just wanted to keep to myself, and be with my sister, that's it. Instead I had to pretend as if I liked other people—that I was a good girl. What a joke!

I was so glad this was just temporary. Now that I knew everything there was to know about this place, I could start to devise my plan. I decided we'd take off during recess hour and head directly to my aunt's place. *No one will know till it's too late*, I thought.

Suddenly I heard voices and footsteps in the hallway. The herd was back. *Here we go.*

I kept an eye out for Alyona, anxious to check up on her and make sure she was okay.

She was fine; in fact, she seemed very happy, like she liked it here—a lot. I just hoped she'd want to go back home with me, too, because I wasn't about to leave her behind. I was taking her with me whether she wanted to go or not.

I watched all the kids come inside, take turns washing their hands, and then taking their seats. Everyone was ready to eat, including me. The food was pretty good here; the street kids were right: They fed us well. Just like normal people, we ate three hot homemade meals a day! After we ate, I noticed that everyone went into the bedroom and started to get into their beds, which confused me. *It's not time for bed yet*, I thought.

The gray-haired lady reappeared, cheerfully announcing that it was naptime. "It's just for an hour—let's go, everybody!" I, along with some of the other kids, didn't want to nap. *Who sleeps in the middle of the day?* I thought, as I helped Alyona to undress and get into bed.

As I lay there, I thought about the older girls who all sat together on the other side of the dining room. They were trouble. They ruled every kid around here. I saw the way they treated the other kids, bossing them around, saying mean things and laughing. They were the mean girls—orphans who weren't nice at all. I couldn't wait to take off before I got into any trouble. It was only a matter of time before the mean girls told me to do something, or said something I didn't like. No matter what, I felt strongly I would never see them again once Alyona and I were safely back with our aunt. At least we still had each other. I hadn't yet told Alyona about what happened to Mom. It just never felt like the right time, or even that she'd understand, since she was only five.

The rest of the day played out just like the lady had said. After naptime, everyone got a snack and went outside to resume whatever game they'd been playing earlier. I kept to myself, watching Alyona play with the younger kids. Most of the kids kept their distance from me, too, as they didn't yet know me, other than the fact that I was new here. I stood out, and I got stared at here and there, but other than that, I was left at peace. Fine with me.

Before we all went back in for the night, I took a walk around the entire place to see which way would be best for our escape route. I found the perfect spot, surrounded by bushes and trees. No one would be able to see past this underbrush when we took off.

I helped collect all the dirty spoons and plates and placed them in the correct bins: dishes in one, spoons and plastic cups in the other. Other kids helped wipe down the tables and sweep up the floors. I asked Alyona if she wanted to draw together, and she agreed happily. It was fun to finally spend some one-on-one time with her in a way I never had before; this was our first time drawing together! I don't recall what we drew that day, just how nice it felt to be with family, to be with Alyona. After dinner was finished and everything was cleaned up, we were free to do as we wanted. We were allowed to either stay inside and play, or go outside for an hour before it got dark out (although every morning after breakfast, and again after the post-lunch nap, we *had* to go outside, as that was mandatory).

Later, lying in bed, I tried so damn hard to fall asleep. Seven p.m. was way too early for me.

Who goes to bed this early? I thought, drifting back to city life in my imagination. It was around this time that I would just be starting my night shift of begging. I could picture it: the music, the smell of food, the crowded streets, and enough money in my pocket to buy a cigarette. I really wished I could have one right about now. I was craving a cig so bad, I was ready to run away just to get a hit.

Finally, I dozed off, imagining our perfect escape and me smoking a whole cigarette.

I couldn't wait to be free again, with Alyona, just like the old days.

Chapter 36

The Perfect Escape

A couple of weeks had passed, and I was ready to get the hell out of Dodge.

By now I had observed all the kids to see where they played, and watched the caregivers, to see where they stood watch, and where they didn't. I needed to make sure no one would see us take off.

As I sat on the playground watching the kids play on the monkey bars and the swings, I thought how amazing it was that more kids didn't run away. The craziest part was that there was no locked gate—just an opening where the fence ended on each side. Although it covered the entire perimeter of the orphanage, this gap meant that just feet away was freedom; all you had to do was walk through. As far as I knew, no one other than the people who worked here had ever done so, at least not that I had seen since my arrival.

But that was about to change.

I saw Alyona playing in the sandbox and went over to play with her. She was by herself, so I could spend some time with her while the other kids were busy playing other games. I hadn't spent much time getting to know anyone; to me, this was all temporary—and besides, I wouldn't trust a soul after what I'd had to go through a couple of weeks ago, when I was robbed of my cash and new toy.

That Monday, shortly after I'd arrived and joined the pack, all hairless and clean, I met Irina Gregorievna, the woman the nice caregiver had told me about. Let me tell you, I felt like I was on *Candid Camera*. This Irina Gregorievna turned out to be the same woman who had taken my money and the Tamagotchi toy!

When I saw her sitting there behind the desk after recess, my heart dropped. I froze right there in the hallway, not sure what to do or what to think. I took Alyona's hand and walked slowly inside, terrified. I could feel my palms sweating. *What the fuck?* This couldn't get any worse. What was this crazy-ass lady doing here?

She saw me entering with Alyona, and with that voice I knew all too well, called me over. She was dressed like a teacher, wearing reading glasses that made her eyes look even bigger, giving me the chills. She looked exactly the same except for the glasses.

I held my breath as I approached her desk and stood there with my hands folded and my head down. I was sure she was going to recognize me and apologize for what she'd done. Nope, she didn't. Instead, she played it like she'd never seen me before, which made me even more terrified and suspicious.

What part did this woman play in robbing street kids out there while working with them at the same time? I remember feeling like this was all some sort of setup. Though mostly I remember thinking how messed up all of this was. Maybe it was because I had a boy's haircut and looked different? Maybe she saw so many kids that she didn't recognize me? Either way, all I knew was that she was a shady lady who'd done a number on me, and not in a good way. I had no idea what I was really dealing with here, and that made me nervous. I couldn't figure this lady out.

"My name is Irina Gregorievna," she said. It was her for sure; I knew it the second she spoke, even from a distance. I remembered the exact quality of her voice. I don't think anyone would ever be able to forget her.

I knew she was expecting me to pretend like I'd never seen her before, and introduce myself properly, so I did. I played her game.

"My name is Ludmila. I'm new here. That's my sister Alyona over there." I pointed to Alyona, who was doodling at the table by the books.

"Welcome to the family!" she said, smiling. "Have you met the older girls in that room over there?" she said, pointing to the room where the mean girls lived.

"Not really. I've just seen them around," I said politely.

"Well, I would like you to meet them. Come on—I will introduce you to them. They are great girls; they set a good example for the rest of the kids around here, especially the new arrivals."

Oh great, I thought, as I prepared myself to put on a nice face.

She got up and led me toward the room where these girls always seemed to be; they barely ever came out. They never did many chores, either, just disappeared right after each meal, back to their secret room where no one else dared enter. She knocked on the door and announced she was coming inside.

There they were, lying in their beds and listening to music, which none of the rest of us were allowed to do, reading magazines that clearly didn't come from here.

The next thing I saw came as the final blow; all I could do was see red, like a bull who is seriously pissed off and ready to charge. One of the girls had my Tamagotchi! It was identical to mine—yellow with red buttons, and a scratch on the screen from when I'd dropped it, taking everything out of my pockets that time, when it all went down.

I couldn't believe my eyes. This was just too much to swallow! I wanted to run over to her and take my toy back, telling her—and this crazy woman—to shove it. Who the hell *was* this woman, and why did these girls fly over to her the moment they saw her, as if she was their mother or something? They were all excited, smiling and embracing her, as the crazy Irina Gregorievna did the same.

This entire thing is fucked up, I thought. I was seriously ready to go—now!

"Here, do you want to play with this?"

One of the girls was handing me *my* toy to play with. I politely declined. There was no way I was going to take anything from any of them. Again, I felt like I was being set up or something here. What in the world was I missing?

"If you ever have any trouble, you come to these girls and talk to them," Irina said as we left the room. "They will help you out, okay?" She closed the door after telling the girls that dinner was about to be served. It was like they were being displayed on a silver platter; funnily enough, I could tell how hard it was for them to play nice. I was glad we were done playing this weird game, as I was hungry and ready to eat.

"Okay, everybody, wash your hands and take a seat," Irina announced.

I washed my hands and went to sit at my table. I recall the dinner was pretty tasty that night: chicken thighs and wings, served with mashed potatoes and gravy—absolutely delicious. It made my stomach very happy, as potatoes were one of my favorite foods.

I was pretty content overall, despite my fury.

The only thing holding me together and focused, however, was our escape out of here. It was the only thing that made me breathe easier, and feel lighter. I knew this game was about to end, and I would be free once more. I would never have to see Irina's monstrous face again.

* * *

The following morning I was dressed and ready to run. Like usual, all the kids ran to the playground to compete over who got to swing or use the monkey bars first. I played dumb, taking longer than normal to help Alyona tie her shoes.

At this point, I was trusted. No one suspected a damn thing. I had made sure to follow the rules and do everything I was asked. I said the right things; I smiled a lot. I pretended to like everyone and everything, as if this was the best thing that had ever happened to me. I felt confident we were in the clear to take off.

Today was the day. I wasn't going to waste any more time. I was ready. It was now or never, and I couldn't deal with never.

I took Alyona's hand and told her we were going to see Mom. "Don't you want to go see your mama?" I said.

I felt horrible lying to her, but knew it was the only thing that would motivate her to leave with me. She had asked about Mom a lot since I'd been there, and all I could come up with each time was to say that she was at home, waiting for us. It was a horrible thing to do; I felt kind of sick telling her that, but I had no choice. We had to pull this off successfully so that we could go back to living the way we used to—together!

That morning, she went for it, and before long, we were running through the woods to catch the bus before it was too late. I knew the schedule, and our window was closing. I will never forget how scared I was. There was nothing but trees stretching for miles, and not a soul around, except for the distant echoes of birds and the cracking of sticks under our feet as we ran as fast as we could. I felt like a deer being hunted—as if at any moment, they would see us, and it would be all over.

Truthfully, I was in shock that we'd been able to get this far without anyone catching us. Even knowing there were many kids and just one caregiver per floor, I was still amazed that no one had spotted us. Now, however, despite this relief, I was realizing how much I'd messed up. Everything had seemed easier and safer in my head.

"I don't want to do this anymore," Alyona said. She started crying. She was tired of running, and I could tell she was feeling scared about leaving with me. "Bring me back, Ludmila!" she pleaded.

I didn't. I just told her we had to keep going, as Mom was waiting, excited to see us when we got home.

She wasn't convinced, but at least she started to move again.

Once we got on the bus, she started to like the idea more and more. She asked me all the way home how much longer until she saw Mom, which only broke my heart even more. How in the world was I going to tell her? I held in my tears, as I was about to crack, myself. All of this seeing Mom only reminded me that she gone, never to be with us ever again.

We safely made it back to our old neighborhood, but found out that my aunt had moved about a week earlier. Luckily one of the neighbors who was friends with my aunt told me where to find her, giving me directions.

I remember I was so relieved to know we wouldn't have to live in the "flames house" where Mom had died. Just being near the place made my hair stand up, giving me chills all over.

"Let's get out of here," I said as we made our way to the new place.

On our way there, I stopped to get Alyona a snack. She was getting cranky from traveling all day, so I got her a Chupa Chups lollipop with a twenty-five-cent coin I'd found on the bus. There was enough to buy a couple of cigarettes, too; I'd been dying for a smoke! Alyona was satisfied with her candy and I was satisfied with my nicotine buzz. I felt relaxed, not as tense as I'd felt just moments before.

Finally we made it to my aunt's new place. I knew most of the cities around here pretty well, so finding the neighborhood wasn't hard, but finding the right house proved to be a bitch! Luckily a woman was heading to the area where my aunt supposedly lived, so I asked if she knew my aunt and could point us in the right direction. She was kind enough to do so. After entering through a tight opening between a fence and a house, we found ourselves inside a courtyard where several houses stood. I knocked on the door the woman had pointed at, hoping my aunt was home.

She was.

"Alyona!" she yelled with excitement. "Ludmila! My girls—come on in!" She opened the door wide and I caught a waft of smelly air coming from what I later saw was a bucket, as there was no bathroom around here. The first room was very small, serving as a mudroom where my aunt stored her shoes, coats, hat, and gloves. There was also an umbrella and a small, worn-out rug with holes in it. As we walked inside the main room, the first thing I noticed was the large hole in the roof. The sky was visible, and the one window in the entire place was small and covered in plastic, to keep the wind from getting inside. I saw the two familiar beds, the old kitchen table we'd had since we'd moved in with my aunt years ago, and a few other belongings I recognized.

One of the beds was against the wall with the broken window, while the other bed was on the opposite side, next to the table. I noticed my aunt had placed the photo of Mom on the middle of the table, resting against some books. Seeing it filled me with joy. It was like she was alive for a moment—like she'd never gone anywhere.

I stared at the photo while my aunt entertained Alyona. She could tell I needed a moment, and she also knew Alyona wasn't aware that our mother had died. When Alyona asked where Mom was, and when she was coming back, my aunt replied, "She went on vacation—a nice long vacation!"

I knew this wouldn't be the last time she would ask about Mom.

I studied my mother's face. I never wanted to forget what she looked like. I knew my aunt wouldn't give me the photo if I asked, and part of me felt it was better that way. It was safe here with my aunt, and wouldn't get lost.

I noticed the large monster stove made of stone in the corner, barely holding together.

"Just like the old place," I said, looking at the stovetop portion, which seemed a bit smaller than the last one. *Not a beast, like the one we'd had years ago*, I thought.

My aunt had some boiled potatoes and cucumbers and tomatoes for dinner that night, just like the old days. It felt so good to be back; even though it wasn't all nice and pretty, I didn't care. I was just happy to be back where we belonged, to resume life with Alyona the best we could.

Some hours had passed, and the day turned into night.

"Well, little one, it's time for bed," my aunt said, smiling as she took Alyona's hand to get her ready for bed. I could tell she was overtired and ready, as it was way past the bedtime she'd gotten used to at the orphanage.

When Alyona had fallen asleep, my aunt and I talked about my adventure at the orphanage, and my run-in with the same woman who had ripped me off.

"Seriously?" my aunt asked. I could tell even she was freaked out. "You know, they might come looking for her," she said, looking at Alyona, soundly asleep. "She was there for a long time; I can't imagine they wouldn't come for her. If they do, you will have to go with them." My aunt looked somber. "I'm sorry, Ludmila, but I can't take care of you—never mind both of you. Look at me; look at this place. If they come looking for you here, they won't even allow me to visit you and Alyona later, if you do go back."

I'll admit, I was pretty disappointed. It was like my aunt didn't want us around—like we were a huge burden. It's not like she would be going out to work every day to earn money.

"But it would be just like the old times," I said eagerly, "We could go out and work to bring home money, so you could go to the market." After all, this had worked in the past.

"All right, all right, let's see what happens," she said, rolling herself a cigarette. She used tobacco from old cigarette butts, wrapping it in newspaper and lighting it up.

"You still smoke?" she asked, looking at me as if to say *You better quit that shit—you're too young*.

"Yeah, I do," I said, with a guilty voice.

I was lying next to Alyona on what I realized was a mattress made of clothes, inside the bed frame. I did my best to get comfortable, and covered myself entirely so I wouldn't find myself itching to death from mosquitoes in the morning. Making sure Alyona was also covered, I went to sleep with the familiar smell of smoke and food in the air.

This place wasn't as nice as the last place, but I didn't care. I was just happy to be free, and reunited with Alyona. All the pretending and planning had paid off—my perfect escape had worked like a charm, and I fell asleep feeling like a champion once more.

Chapter 37

Time Is Up

Thinking we were in the clear, I took Alyona to the city the next day, hoping she would remember more about our times together, and therefore remember me more, too! She was still shy around me. I couldn't stand the feeling of knowing my own sister didn't trust me as much as she did the adults at the orphanage.

We'd slept with our clothes on the night before, so all we had to do was get out of bed and go, which we did while my aunt was still sleeping. It was still dark outside as we walked to the city. There was a slight drizzle coming down, but it was nice, like getting my face washed, as it was early September.

I glanced over at Alyona. She seemed sad, like this was not what she wanted to be doing. She hadn't seemed all that comfortable the night before, either.

"We're going to the city," I said, holding her hand and keeping pace with her. "We're going to your favorite place with the clown, okay? The one you love?" I said, smiling, hoping Alyona would get excited to visit the McDonald's. Street kids hung out there often, as nobody ever asked us to leave. They had a playground for kids, which was pretty cool. It was the only place we had had to play where we wouldn't get in trouble, as most places were off limits.

I think Alyona liked this place mostly because someone had given her a milkshake once, as they were leaving the restaurant. Sometimes people didn't trust us kids with money, so they would get us food instead. I got to try a pastry once, with strawberry filling; it was really good! Since then Alyona had liked to go to this McDonald's, or at least, she used to, so I figured this was the right way to go. I had to ease her into it; after all, it had been more than a year since she'd been out in the real world.

"You remember this place?" I asked as we approached the restaurant. "Look, there's the clown!" I said, hoping to cheer her up.

"The clown!" Alyona yelled, pointing at the statue of a red-and-yellow smiling clown. She got excited, and started walking faster and faster toward the playground, excited to play. I was so glad she had remembered something—anything! It was like I'd gotten my sister back!

As usual the playground had been overtaken by street kids. Normal people and their little ones scattered the moment we showed up. It was like a reunion; so many familiar faces! Part of me felt like I was on vacation. It was like I could do whatever I wanted once more, like I could do this. I felt so much better having Alyona by my side.

I sat there watching Alyona play with some of the other kids. She was having a great time. I was glad she was finally smiling. I did a little begging while people came in and out of the place, to have some money for cigarettes. I planned to start slow with Alyona, to ease her into working again. I had a feeling it wasn't going to be as easy as it used be, now that she knew what she wanted to do—which was to play and have fun. She had become accustomed to life at the orphanage, and I knew some of her habits were going to be hard to break.

I saw a car pull in, just like all of the other cars that were pulling in. I didn't think much of it at first—until I saw who got out of the car.

We were busted.

I saw all of the other kids running away, screaming, "Run! Run!"

I couldn't run. I had Alyona, clueless, on the playground. She looked up and saw one of the orphanage caregivers, along with the director, Irina Gregorievna, walking toward us.

Someone sold us out, I thought. I couldn't believe they had found us so fast!

Irina Gregorievna was now standing right in front of me, and I wasn't eager to hear what she was about to say.

"So this is what you want for your sister," she said. "This is the kind of life you want for her?" The director looked so disappointed.

At this point Alyona ran right over to them, like they were her parents. I couldn't have stopped her if I'd tried.

The caregiver took Alyona inside the car while the director stood there, looking at me. "Well, do you have anything to say for yourself?" she asked.

"No. She is my sister, and you have no right to take her from me!" I was crying now, afraid about what was going to happen to me.

"You know, Ludmila, if this is the life you want, go for it. We won't stop you. But your sister is coming back with us. She doesn't deserve this sham of a life you call living; she's just an innocent little girl. She needs care and attention. Don't you get it?" The director leaned in closer. "What you did was very selfish, Ludmila. You didn't think about what Alyona needs; instead, you only thought about yourself."

With that, she walked away and got into the car, leaving me there to chew on what she had just said. I waved good-bye to Alyona, doing my best to hold back the tears as I watched the car drive off.

I will never forget that moment of striking realization.

I had given up the possibility of having a normal life long ago, but that was before I knew anything about orphanages. Now I was caught in the middle, considering my options. *Maybe it's too late for me, but not for Alyona*, I thought. Maybe she would get a chance to have a normal life, the kind led by people who had jobs, and money. I felt horrible, finally understanding for the first time what the director was saying. I had chosen to take off with Alyona because of selfish reasons. I had taken her away from a safe, caring place, from all of her friends—from a life she had grown used to. When I was little, that was all I'd wanted—safety and care.

I stood there watching the lights on the cars driving by. For the first time in my life, I didn't know what to do. I had no plan, and I found myself wondering about my life.

As I walked back to my aunt's place, part of me felt like maybe I should go back to the orphanage and give it a try—for real this time. Who knew what might happen if I actually tried? So far, all I'd known was life on the streets, begging for money. I knew this game very well, but I also felt like I'd hit a dead end. I couldn't see anything exciting about it anymore. I was getting older, and I knew there was no way in hell I was going to sell my body for money like other older girls did.

I decided I might want to try something else, and see where that took me. Maybe in the orphanage I would get a chance to learn something about myself that I didn't know yet; maybe there was more to me than just this lifestyle. The only thing waiting for me on the streets was trouble, and I didn't trust myself to stay away from it. Most of the time I felt angry and depressed. I was so damn lost. Everything I'd worked for up to this point felt like a distant memory. Everything was so different now. I could barely recognize myself or my life anymore.

I got back to my aunt's and told her what had happened.

She wasn't surprised, and said that it would be a good idea if I went back too. "You know, my daughters learned so much from being in an orphanage," she said. "I supported your plan when you left home the first time, but now, Ludmila, things are different. We don't live in the nice house we used to, and I have a hard time staying afloat as it is. My leg has really been acting up lately. I'm in a lot of pain most of the time.

"In the orphanage, they'll be able to provide you with what I can't, you know? Like my girls—they are proper young ladies now. They got educated, and now they have a chance to have a better life. I didn't want this life for them, Ludmila; that's why I sent them away when they were about your age. Nothing good would have come of them if they had stayed."

She had a worried look on her face, and I knew exactly what she meant.

"I know," I said. "I was thinking about it myself—going back, I mean. I really want to try this time." I looked up at the hole in the roof. It had started raining, and some of the rain was coming through.

"Grab that bucket over there," my aunt said. I did, and placed it under the leak.

"So when do you think you will go back?" she asked.

I looked at the photo of Mom, and then back at my aunt.

"Tomorrow," I said.

I knew my mother wouldn't have wanted this life for me, or Alyona. I thought back to the note she'd left for us, where she'd blamed herself for our situation. Although I'd never blamed her for anything, somehow I found myself in her shoes, blaming myself for her death. *Those damn strings*, I thought, looking at her photo one more time.

Just in the past two days, from the moment we'd taken off to them taking Alyona away again, I had changed. Something inside me had shifted, and I was ready to turn over a new leaf, see what else I was capable of; after all, I wasn't all that proper. I smoked cigarettes and spit; I swore a lot, and I got into fights with other girls and boys who made me mad by talking shit. I didn't know how to read or write, except for my name, and I didn't know how to sew or draw or pretty much do anything other than what I had been doing. The only thing I'd learned was a bit of basic math, from adding up money; other than that, I didn't have a clue. I'd never gone to school. I didn't even know how to read a clock, unless it was digital.

Mom would want me to do this, I thought. She had wanted better lives for us, and maybe this was a way I could make her wish come true. Alyona and I would be together—safe, fed, and in the capable hands of educated adults.

My only concern was seeing Irina Gregorievna again—she scared the crap out of me—but I had no choice. I had to put aside everything I was used to in my old life and go back with an open mind, to make it easier on myself. I was ready to try—to really try to belong.

Chapter 38

The Book

It had been about a month since I'd returned to the orphanage. So far, it wasn't going great. Most of the kids ostracized me and called me names for running away and taking Alyona. The adults weren't much better, watching me like a hawk, giving me extra chores and preventing me from joining the others—especially Alyona—for outside activities. Since all the caregivers had taken such a liking to Alyona, none of them were very happy about what I'd done, saying, "It's time to get your shit together," and warning me never to do it again.

I spent most of my time these days flipping through books with colorful, happy pictures. I was trying to teach myself to read, easier now that one of the caregivers had taught me the alphabet. I wasn't a strong reader yet, but I remember feeling pretty excited when I could read one word, then two, then a full sentence, understanding everything I was reading. It was so much fun—a puzzle made of words, where at the end I would understand the situation described by what I was reading.

One day while all the kids were outside playing after breakfast, I stayed inside to keep reading. It had become my favorite thing to do, and a great form of escape. Having so much time on my hands made me think more often about Mom's death—how she was buried somewhere on the side of a street, near a cemetery, I had no idea where. So many days, I wished I could go and visit her grave, like other people did who had lost a loved one.

I remember Easter holidays when all the street kids would visit the cemeteries, where people left food behind for other visitors to take. Visitors came to bless their loved ones, whose names were engraved on the headstones. I remember walking around a large and beautiful cemetery with many clean and pretty graves, one after the other—some with big stones, others, small. I usually found food left on all the graves, unless someone had beaten me to it. It was like a feast day for us street kids! We were so excited to collect different-colored hard-boiled eggs, along with *paska*—a very soft egg bread, sweet and delicious, with raisins inside. There were also candies of all sorts, and sometimes even money. It was the best treasure hunt ever!

I wished my mom had a nice grave like one of those, with her name engraved, with fresh flowers and family photos.

I picked up a book I hadn't seen before, most likely left by one of the other kids. We were allowed to keep the books until we'd finished reading them. The front cover had caught my eye; it was very purple, with a large cartoon illustration of a man with long brown hair and a beard, wearing a robe. He was smiling gracefully, his hands extended to the people in the crowd, who were also reaching out for him with joy. *Who is this kind-looking man?* I thought. I was ready to think about something other than death.

I opened the book and flipped through the pages real fast, to make sure there were more pictures. There were plenty, so I was sold, eager to start reading. I started from the very beginning, and ten pages into it, I couldn't put the book down. I realized I was reading faster and faster, as if I'd always known how to read. I kept up with reading the book regularly, during the next couple of days, curious to finish the story. I remember when I reached the end I was devastated, quietly crying, so no one could hear me.

What a story! I thought, closing the book and holding it close to my heart. Jesus was such an amazing person; why would they kill him?

I couldn't stop thinking about the entire book—its amazing stories, and its horrible ending. I will never forget this moment, when I learned about Jesus and who he was. It was like, for the first time in my life, I felt inspired—like I had someone to follow. I felt like Jesus and I had a lot in common, although his story was much worse than mine. I couldn't get the image of Jesus on the cross out of my mind. *It must have been so painful, but still, he did it, for all of us.*

I wiped tears off my face, wishing I could meet Jesus. Part of me felt like I already knew him—that we had a lot to talk about—like he could teach me the way.

I changed that day. Reading about all the miracles that happened in the book gave me hope that good things existed as much as bad things, or people. Mostly, I remember feeling like I wasn't as alone anymore. His story helped me to get over myself, so to speak—to go on putting my past behind me. It was time to live, and practice what Jesus had taught me through the book. After all of the horrible things I had been through, finally, I had learned about a true, amazing, kind, and loving person, who once was here on this Earth.

I thought about my last name, the one I'd finally learned. During my stay here, the authorities and the social workers had been gathering information about me and my life through various channels. I wasn't sure how this was possible, as all of our belongings had been thrown out, never to be seen again, including important stuff like our birth certificates with our birth names. My best guess was that they had found my estranged biological father and asked him for information, or maybe it was my aunt. Either way, once they had discovered the information, I was notified. I was more than glad to learn more about myself. I finally understood what that lady at the hospital had meant when she'd asked about Alyona's last name all that time ago.

I wasn't just Ludmila; I was Apostol Ludmila Urievna, which meant Ludmila, the Apostle. I couldn't believe Jesus and I had so much in common. I felt like my last name connected us even more; when I saw that he had had twelve apostles, I almost fell over! I remember I was pretty dumbfounded and shocked, but in a good way—like I was somehow related to this story; that my fate was to live by his example.

I had never learned about God before; I'd just seen the many fancy churches in the city, with their big crosses and gold roofs. They were things of beauty, and we street kids would beg outside of them each Sunday, with great success, as people felt guilty about not giving when in God's courtyard.

While I had heard the word "Jesus," I'd never heard his story. All of this time, my entire eleven years of existence, I had missed out on this truly amazing story. *Not anymore*, I thought. Suddenly I felt like I was *supposed* to be here in this orphanage—like somehow there was something waiting for me, something good and happy! I didn't talk to anyone else about Jesus. I wanted to keep it to myself. It was very personal to me, and I didn't want to spoil what I was feeling. It was a good feeling, and the other kids had a way of making those kind of feelings go away.

I put the book neatly back on the shelf and went outside. It was time for me to let go and be a kid for once. I was ready to let go of my past and start a new chapter of my life, with Jesus by my side. No more feeling like I was in a black hole with nothing but darkness and emptiness; now I had some light. I had a dream: to witness a miracle.

Chapter 39

Christmas Festivities

It was the holiday season, and as usual, all of us kids were required to go outside for a while, to play and get some fresh air. I put on the nice warm coat I'd been given, along with some hand-me-down boots and gloves. I helped Alyona do the same, and we walked outside together. She was off at full speed to go play in the snow.

Even though it was a cold morning, I loved seeing the snow perfectly covering the landscape, including all the evergreen trees. The heavy snow made the willowy branches touch the ground. I loved going under the trees to hide from everyone else when I wanted to be alone. It was like my own little world under there. I had to be careful not to cause an avalanche of delicate, puffy snow to come down on me; I didn't want to mess up the perfect little secluded nest that Nature had made.

Most of the kids had caught Christmas fever, running around and singing Christmas songs I didn't know, yelling about how excited they were to get presents. This was my first official Christmas celebration, as we had never celebrated anything before. While I wanted to be excited, I didn't really know what I was excited about—at least, not yet. But I looked forward to finding out.

Truthfully, I was more interested in a boy who had recently arrived at the orphanage. I will never forget the feeling I got in my stomach the first time I saw him. It was like a volcano exploded inside of me. I felt so embarrassed; I started to sweat, including my palms. The boy looked at me as he walked by, probably trying to be friendly, but since I liked him, all I could do was go hide in the trees.

I remember I felt surprised; I'd never liked a boy before, and didn't even know this was how it felt. It freaked me out more than anything. I didn't want the boy to know I liked him. I didn't want to get rejected; after all, I still had my boy's haircut and wore baggy clothes, none of which included dresses. I totally looked like a boy! I couldn't stand looking like that, and couldn't wait till my hair grew back. I wasn't the only one; most of us girls had boy haircuts, except for a couple, who had semi-long hair compared to our short styles. I am pretty sure I was the only one wearing a hat all the time; I was impressed by how well the other girls were handling having barely any hair.

Everyone was playing in the snow on this morning; some kids were throwing snowballs at each other, while others were making a snowman. It was entertaining to watch, but I didn't participate. I wasn't a big fan of winter play; I'd been ready to go inside long ago. Ten minutes was all I needed, not an entire hour!

"Okay, let's go, everyone—time to go inside and get ready!" one of the caregivers announced.

Finally the long hour was over and we were headed back inside. The caregiver was one I had not seen before; maybe she was new. She had short, dark hair, long pretty nails painted in red, and dark brown eyes. She was all right, although I still liked the plump, gray-haired lady the best.

Back inside, Irina Gregorievna was waiting for all the kids to choose the costumes they were going to wear for the Christmas party. She started to open a couple boxes sitting on the floor, taking out some costumes and cautiously investigating them to make sure they were a "go."

"Here—this one looks like it will fit you, Sasha!" she said, handing it to one of the girls. Sasha grabbed the costume and ran off to try it on. I could tell she was excited; all of the kids were, hovering over the boxes, eager to see who they were going to be. One by one, all of the kids received some sort of costume: Some would dress up as Snegurochka, the wife of winter; some would be princesses, or animals, while others would be jokers or clowns—a little bit of everything.

Alyona was dressed as a baby rooster. It was actually very cute; with the rooster hat, a skirt, and a sweater that gave the appearance of feathers, she looked the part. I ended up being some sort of an eighties musician. I was given a scarf, a shirt, and pants with different-colored stripes. The pants were wider at the bottom, and the long-sleeved shirt and scarf were both red. I liked my costume; it was much less ostentatious than the rest, for which I was very thankful.

We had all gathered in our costumes at the auditorium—one big room, with a couple of smaller general rooms attached—to practice for the Christmas program, or any other activities. Some of the girls—including me—had auditioned to be in a dance routine during the actual Christmas party, coming up in a couple of days. I was thrilled to be one of six girls chosen to learn a dance for the big day, and today was our rehearsal.

I remember it perfectly. The short-haired caregiver turned on the cassette player, and Alsou came on—a Russian pop artist I really liked at the time. This particular song was one of my favorites. It had a slow rhythm, with sad lyrics, reminding me of when I used to hear it on the streets shortly after Mom died. It was my favorite song to cry to. And somehow it helped.

I remember doing our dance moves at the rehearsal, moving my hands and feet just like the caregiver had shown us. As I danced, I felt like I was dealing with Mom's death in a peaceful way for the very first time. I found myself in my own little bubble, expressing my feelings through dance—like every step and movement communicated a certain feeling about Mom, and her death.

As the music died down, I finished the dance with the other girls, holding my hands up like a ballerina, doing my best to stop the tears that seemed to come out of nowhere. I swallowed my feelings to keep strong and blend in with everyone. The last thing I wanted to do was cry. That was a weak thing to do around here, and I didn't want to give anybody ideas; I knew they'd pick on me about it. The entire orphanage was here, including the boys—a lot of people to see me cry.

To distract myself I thought about the boy I liked. I realized he wasn't here yet. I was looking forward to seeing him. He had brown hair and blue eyes, and got along with all the kids. He had a nice smile, and big ears. I liked him because he was kind, and I didn't feel threatened by him, as he was about my age.

The rehearsal came to an end, and it was time to go back and prepare for dinner. I was glad that everything had gone well, and that all the kids had had a good time. I realized I was pretty hungry after all that dancing, and was ready to eat! I was bummed that the boy I liked wasn't there, and I hadn't had a chance to see him. The worst part was, I didn't even know his name!

That night we had *kasha*, a kind of grain-like porridge when boiled in water or milk, along with *katleti* for dinner. They also gave us warm tea and a slice of bread with condensed milk spread on it. I had never tried condensed milk before, and was instantly hooked, just like the rest of the kids were. I remember we all wished they would spread more of this stuff on the bread, it was so damn good.

The next few days went by super-fast, and before long it was time to get all dressed up and head to the auditorium for the Christmas party. Some of the kids had to fix their costumes slightly to make them fit right, while others had to switch their costumes outright, if they didn't fit at all. This was hard to watch. Even though some of the kids didn't want to trade, they had no choice but to go from being a princess to a squirrel. I felt so bad; I could tell they were disappointed, but the show must go on, and they had no choice but to be okay with it.

Normally there was no music of any kind around here, but today music was blaring loudly from the auditorium. I made my way upstairs along with the other kids and joined everyone who'd already gathered upstairs. All the kids looked festive, making the entire room look like one big party!

I saw Alyona dancing away; some of the other kids around her didn't pick up the moves as fast as she did. She was a pro! *What a cutie she is*, I thought, watching my little sister moving happily on the dance floor. A camera crew was there recording Alyona; even they were impressed! Occasionally crews from local news outlets attended our events, although we were not allowed to speak with them. I didn't know why, but it did cross my mind that maybe they didn't want us to say something bad or wrong on TV. After all, this was a live event, and we'd been told to be on our best behavior, especially toward the guests, many of whom were strangers to us.

The Christmas tree was tall and beautifully decorated with pretty ornaments and lights. I noticed the large glowing star at the very top, which made the entire tree look radiant. There were some adults at the party I had never seen before; come to find out they were American missionaries, here to give us presents. Stacks of decorated shoeboxes full of gifts were piled up to the ceiling—one box per kid meant at least forty boxes! They were so fun to look at, all decorated with different colors and patterns, some slightly bigger or shinier than others. I was intrigued. I had never gotten a real present before; this was going to be good!

"Welcome, everybody!" I heard the director say, as everyone

scattered to take their seats. "We have a lot of fun activities for you all tonight, including a dance number that some of our girls will be performing!"

Everyone applauded.

"We also have some very special guests here with us. They've come from very far away to share these generous gifts with you all." She pointed to the five strangers, sitting at the front. They got up and smiled, waving to everyone before they sat back down. Of course we all applauded even longer this time, to let them know how thankful we were for their gifts.

The director continued to tell us about everything that was planned for the night, and moments later it was our turn to go up and perform our dance. We had a few minutes to change into our green tank tops and skirts, all different types but made of denim. I was nervous, but also excited to be doing something I really loved. It felt good to be included. I felt like I was slowly becoming more like the rest of the kids here. I was trusted now, and doing well. I did what I was supposed to do; even on the bad days, when the craving for a cigarette felt almost impossible to deny, I didn't run away. I held myself strong, no matter what.

I sat there watching one of the boys recite a Christmas poem from memory. It was a long poem, and I was impressed he could remember it all. He finished the poem and everyone clapped, excited because it was the last hurrah, and time for presents!

"This concludes our Christmas party, children. We will now call you up by rows to receive your gifts," the director said. "Please go back to your rooms once you've received yours."

She directed the kids at the front to line up for their gifts. I will never forget how much joy and happiness vibrated from all the kids; I had never seen anything like it before—like this was the best thing that had ever happened to them! They were all sitting there, whispering to one another, pointing to the box they had their hearts set on, hoping it would be the one they received. I have to say I was pretty excited myself; I really didn't care which box I got—I was just curious to know what was inside!

When my row was called, I joined the other kids to walk up and receive our boxes. We all ran back to our rooms as fast as we could to open the gifts—a rush, for sure. I'd never felt anything like it before. Who knew Christmas presents could have such a strong effect? It was like I went from being eleven years old back to being five, I was that eager to get my hands inside that box!

When I got back to our room, all the kids had already opened their boxes and were walking around to see what the others had gotten. There was some trading going on, kids exchanging their presents and candy with others.

I saw Alyona by her bed, going through her box of gifts, so I went over to her to open mine and finally see what was inside.

"What do you got there?" I asked. I had never seen Alyona this happy before.

"Look!" she said, showing me a small stuffed animal that looked like a bear. It was beige and felt extra soft.

"Wow!" I said.

She was holding the teddy bear as if it were a baby. I could tell she loved her new toy.

"Want to help me with my box?" I asked. I knew she wouldn't mind opening another mystery box full of stuff. She looked at me with glowing eyes, and sat down next to me, ready to help. She ripped off the wrapping paper so fast I was impressed.

"Go ahead, open it," I said.

Alyona opened the box and together we went through all the presents inside. I remember there were some cool pencils decorated with characters from American cartoons, known to Americans as Rugrats.

There were erasers that fit on top of the pencils with little funny faces and purple or green hair that stood up. It gave us something to laugh about! Other goodies included a pencil sharpener, different-colored gel pens, a small tube of toothpaste, and a toothbrush. There was all sorts of candy, like licorice, candy canes, and chocolates. Last but not least, a stuffed animal, which seemed to be everyone's favorite. I don't recall what kind of animal I got, but I do remember giving it to Alyona. Of all the things inside, she liked this the most, playing with our two stuffed animals like they were best friends.

I had also gotten a small notebook with lined pages and a blue plastic cover. It was cool to get stuff all the way from America! I was very happy with everything I got. It was very helpful to have a new toothbrush and some tasty toothpaste. The art supplies also came in very handy; now when we would all draw and color together, everyone would finally have their own pencils and pens to color with—no more waiting for a specific color!

It had been tough to stand around and wait for our gifts—kids lost interest fast—but now everyone was quiet and focused, glued to their spots on the floor. All you could hear was the crinkling of candy wrappers and pencils pressing against the paper as we drew and colored, going through our boxes to find the pen we wanted, or the eraser to get rid of an unwanted line. Everyone was so happy to have their gifts.

This was definitely the most exciting time of the year! All the other days at the orphanage involved the same activities, day after day, over and over, as if stuck on repeat. I didn't really mind, though, as I was used to the daily routine. Slowly but surely, I was becoming more like the other kids—nothing to worry about except having fun. I had managed to make some friends along the way. Us girls loved gossiping about what boys we liked and why. The other girls seemed to change their minds weekly about who they liked, but not me.

I still liked that same boy, even though he was most likely clueless that I liked him. I never had the guts to approach him; I just didn't know what that would mean, so I stayed clear. Just seeing him was enough. It gave me that exhilarated feeling I needed once in a while; after all, girls will be girls. I was becoming very interested in being a girl, not the tomboy I once was.

I opened my notebook and wrote down my secret—that I liked a boy, and he was cute.

Chapter 40

Summer Camp

Summer was finally here. The air was warm and the skies, bright blue, with perfect puffy white clouds passing by. The birds were singing happily, and so were the kids, excited to be outdoors all day, playing. It was tough in the winter, as there was no plowing of any sort; this made it hard to use the entire place to run around. Plus, all the monkey bars and swings were too cold to touch for very long. Now, everything had been transformed from white to green, allowing us plenty of space to run around in and plenty of grass to lie on.

I spread a blanket on a sunny patch of grass and lay down on my stomach to read a book. I kept my eye out for the boy I liked, to see if he was coming outside to play. Sure enough, there he was, with his buddies, heading to an outdoor table to play some cards. That's what the boys did most of the time. They didn't do much girl chasing; if anything, the unwritten rules were that the girls would approach them—which was never going to happen on my part. Still, it was nice to see him.

I opened my notebook to go over the list of belongings I needed to bring with me to summer camp. It was a church camp somewhere far away in the mountains, and I had gotten a chance to go. I don't know why; I think it was mostly because I participated every week at Sunday services, held at the orphanage, learning about God and singing gospel hymns. I remember we were learning "He's Got the Whole World in His Hands" at the time. It was easy to remember, and fun to sing! There were four women there each week who spoke a language I didn't understand—turned out to be English—and a fifth lady who spoke Russian. She helped us understand what they were saying. "We're going to learn to sing it in English this time!" she said. *Cool!* I thought. I was about to learn a new language! I will never forget it. We would raise our hands as if embracing the whole world as we sang the song in English, one phrase at a time.

I enjoyed the activities as well. Most of the time we would do a fun art project, like making sheep out of sticks and puffy white cotton balls. We would use glitter glue and sparkles to make them pretty. The kids loved Sundays; they were lots of fun, as we always did something we had never tried before.

I checked off every item on my list that I'd already packed into my bag and closed my notebook, satisfied that everything checked out. Happily, I went back to reading my book, but soon realized I didn't have the patience for it. I was too excited about going to camp!

I had never been to camp before, and from what the missionaries had told us through the translator, it sounded like nothing but fun! I was beside myself with anticipation; I felt like I couldn't possibly wait another day. The thought of being away from here was exciting enough on its own!

"I'll miss you," I said under my breath as I glanced at the boy. I wished he was going, too, but only one other kid had been chosen from our orphanage, and he was not on the list. I had no idea how they picked who got to go; I was just grateful I was one of them. Alyona was going to stay behind, as she was too young, but I was okay with that. I knew she was in good hands.

* * *

A week later, I was on the bus with some other kids, the missionaries, and a few other people who spoke Russian, driving to the camp. I didn't recognize many faces; I assumed these kids were not orphans, as they seemed normal, with long, shiny clean hair and the best of clothes. We were the last stop. It was nice to be surrounded with normal people; it was so much fun! We all sang, clapped our hands, and celebrated God. It was about a three-hour drive, but it felt much shorter; as they say, time flies when you're having fun! As we got closer, we found ourselves driving on a dirt road, passing through a beautiful landscape of mountain ranges, trees, and moss covering the valley like a giant green carpet. It was amazingly gorgeous, like we were in a jungle somewhere.

The bus came to a halt and one of the translators announced that we had arrived. I put my bag over my shoulder and stood up to get off the bus. When I got outside I saw there were many people here already, kids and adults alike. Almost everyone was heading over to the bus to greet us.

"Welcome, everybody!" one of the women said. "We are all so happy you could make it here to celebrate God with us! My friends here will help you all get settled," she said, pointing to a group of older kids standing next to her. "Please ask them any questions you may have, okay?"

I realized I didn't know anyone else here, except for the other kid from my orphanage who'd been chosen. We didn't know each other at all, other than the fact we came from the same place. I didn't even know his name, though later I heard people calling him Misha.

I remember I just felt happy to be around normal adults and kids; it was like a dream come true to be part of real living, the way normal people did. This is going to be so much fun, I thought, as I waited to be escorted.

"What's your name?" one of the helpers asked kindly. She was older than me. She had a beautiful smile, with the whitest and most perfectly straight teeth I'd ever seen.

"My name is Ludmila," I said politely. I was pretty shy around people I didn't know.

"I'm Kristina," she said. She had beautiful black hair that went all the way down her back. It made me miss my long hair all the more. I felt like I was about five years old standing next to her. She looked like a proper young lady! *Maybe I'll be like her someday*, I thought longingly.

"Have you ever been here before?" Kristina asked.

"No, this is my first time," I replied, wondering if she knew I was from an orphanage. I found it surprising that she was treating me like the other normal people here. Everyone was so kind, and seemed so happy.

"Well, let's get started," she said. "I have a lot to show you."

We walked up to an area where green tents were set up, one next to the other.

"This is where everyone sleeps," she said. "This tent is yours, right here." She opened the flaps on one of the tents and invited me inside. There were two cots, one on each side, with a bench in between to hold our belongings. I remember thinking, Wait—I have to sleep outside? I was freaked out, especially because we'd been warned to be careful of the snakes that were around, and that we had to go right to the infirmary if we were bitten. That was not a pleasing announcement.

I didn't say anything, just listened to what I was being told. Kristina showed me where everything was, including the restrooms, the shower, the infirmary, and the dining area. There was an outdoor shower, but at least the restrooms had real toilets, putting me more at ease.

We walked back to the tent I was sharing with another girl, who hadn't arrived yet, and then parted ways. I put my bag on the bench next to my cot and went outside to join the crowd, already singing and clapping. I hadn't realized till then how much I loved singing, especially about God, and good, positive things. Happy miracle songs were right up my alley, bringing me a feeling I had never felt before—grace.

The next couple of weeks went by too fast. I didn't want my time at camp to end. I loved being here! We did a lot of cool stuff, like hiking in the mountains, where the view was breathtaking. I couldn't believe my eyes; I literally had to close my mouth after it dropped open. It was the first time in my life I realized that the world is full of amazing, beautiful places; it made me feel special to stand there, where not many people got to stand.

Every day held some sort of adventure: There were fun team games, like badminton and volleyball, which I really enjoyed! We helped prepare the food by peeling potatoes, shredding carrots, and cutting bread. Everyone was happy to help; in fact, this was the happiest crowd I had ever encountered—almost too much sometimes, at least for me—but overall, I was happy, too. I was thrilled to be somewhere else for a change, somewhere that was not in the orphanage.

Sleeping proved difficult, however. I slept with one eye open, paranoid that something from the outdoors was going to get in, and I kid you not, I was so happy I did, because one night I felt something in my cot, and sure enough, it was a snake! I screamed so loud I woke up the entire camp, but I couldn't help it; this snake was huge! It was green, and crawling toward me, sticking its tongue out, looking at me with its big black eyes. The girl who was sleeping across from me was also freaking out at this point, screaming "Get away from me! Get away!"

I backed up and got closer to the exit, hoping someone was going to come and help. I saw a tall man approaching our tent. "It's inside!"

I yelled. Somehow he managed to scare away the large snake, telling us to go back to sleep, like it was nothing, not a big deal at all.

I remember thinking, *You're kidding, right? There's no way I'm getting back in that cot!* All I could see was that huge green snake with its tongue out.

"What if it comes back?" I asked my tent mate.

She was sitting up in her cot, like me, too scared to sleep.

"I know—I'm afraid of that myself," she said. "Let's just stay up and play some cards, okay?" She turned on the lantern and got a deck of cards out of her bag. "Do you know how to play War?" she asked.

"I do," I said excitedly. I knew it was a long game, and that we had a couple more hours to kill before the others would start to wake up.

The girl dealt out the deck between the two of us, and two hours later, we were still going strong when the bell for the kitchen staff rang, telling them it was time to get up.

"Wow, it's time already?" the girl said. We peeked outside to see daylight had arrived.

"Good game!" I said, smiling.

"High five!" she said happily. We were both glad to be alive, and snake-free.

* * *

Sadly, the last day of camp came all too soon. As the bus pulled away, I got a sad feeling inside. I was going to miss this camp—minus the snake, of course! Slowly we drove past all the beauty once more, and before long we were on the main road back to the orphanage, where the boy and I were going to be dropped off.

"Did you like camp?" one of the American missionaries asked me, through a translator.

"Yes, it was awesome! I had so much fun here!" I said, smiling at all of the missionaries.

They smiled back, nodding and chatting back and forth with the translator, saying things in English that I didn't understand.

"*Spasibo*," I said, knowing they knew that word. I looked out the bus window and happily watched the city I once begged in pass us by as we drove back. I saw some familiar faces still at it, begging for money to survive. I realized how different my life was now, and it dawned on me that I could never go back there, to that life.

I made the right choice, I thought, as we turned a corner and the city slowly disappeared.

Chapter 41

Strange Things

Orphanage life was good. I no longer missed street life, and my craving for cigarettes had finally passed. I was happy to be with my sister and to have good food to eat. Even better, I didn't have to beg or do sexual favors to get it. Taking a hot shower was also nice, along with having clean clothes to wear; they felt so good, like my skin could breathe. I was getting along with everyone; well, almost everyone. I couldn't get along with the mean girls next door. I stayed away from them, as all they did was make fun of the other kids and make them feel terrible about themselves.

Not all of the children at the orphanage were healthy. Some had fetal alcohol syndrome; others were less physically affected, but had more mental problems. Some were just socially awkward and didn't have much in common with the other kids—like me, pretty much. I just tried to play my cards right, to keep off their radar. I was a loner, and didn't do well in groups. There were always some sort of rules to follow, always someone in charge bossing the other kids around. It was insane. I didn't see the point whatsoever, so I mostly kept to myself, observing while keeping my mouth shut.

I did feel terrible for those kids; it wasn't right for them to be picked on. I would try to help them instead, making my point in different ways, other than shouting and picking fights. I didn't want to get in trouble. Those girls hated me for it; they knew exactly what I was trying to prove.

I also got along with all the caregivers, including the mysterious Irina Gregorievna. While I was still very curious about her, I kept my poker face on all the time.

I liked my life; I had everything I needed, and Alyona was happy, so there was nothing to complain about—until one night when I was moved from my bed to another one by the large window. Thus began yet another terrifying experience in my life, one I would never forget.

It started one day when I got back from playing outside. I noticed that my bed was completely gone—no mattress, sheets, pillow, or blanket—not even my name tag. *That's strange*, I thought. No one had told me I was relocating to another bed. Sometimes they did this to separate certain kids from talking or joking around too much, basically separating friends who were too noisy and moving them to sleep next to kids they didn't know as well. Except that was not the case this time, which was surprising.

When I asked the caregiver about it, she told me that another child was arriving later on, and would take my old bed. My new one was by the window, which I was okay with at first; it was a normal-size bed with springs, unlike most of the other beds that were made out of wood, and pretty hard to sleep on.

That night I went to bed like any other night, except sometime in the middle of the night I awoke to screams coming from outside. I remember thinking *What the hell? Is someone being killed out there?* It was horrible. I kept hearing a young woman's voice pleading for someone to help her. "Please, somebody—help me, please!" she yelled.

I kept my eyes closed; I was scared, not for me, but for this woman. Something was terribly wrong. It was like someone was chasing her and she was trying to get away, yelling and screaming desperately for help. I remember thinking it was happening close by, like if I could see outside through the pitch-black night, I would be able to see this woman running from whoever was chasing her. I was crying, picturing the terrible end that was possible, and I hoped that this young lady got away from the monster, whoever it was.

The screams finally stopped after what felt like forever, and I realized I could still hear her screaming in my head. I was so terrified to look outside; I felt like the bad guy would break the glass and get me too, so I stayed low, barely breathing, keeping as quiet as I could to listen. I opened my eyes and looked around at the thirty of us kids, all sleeping, not a peep.

How could no one hear that? I thought.

I did my best to go back to sleep, but I couldn't; I was too freaked out. I stayed in the same position all night, doing my best to calm my heart down—it felt like it was skipping beats—too afraid to sleep.

The next morning, I asked Sasha if she'd heard anything last night. Sasha was about my age, and we got along well.

"No, I didn't hear a thing," Sasha said. She smiled and poked my arm in a friendly manner. "Why? Were you trying to play a trick on me or something?"

I shook my head. "Nothing? Not a thing?" I asked. I was shocked to find out she hadn't heard anything. Nor had anyone else, for that matter; no one was talking about it. I kept my mouth shut, too, thinking it was for the best.

Freaking strange, I thought, as I made my way outside to investigate. I wanted to find some sort of clue to prove it wasn't just my imagination.

Sure enough, I found some large men's footprints, and some blood spots here and there, but nothing obvious. I had to look for it to really notice the blood. *It was real*, I thought, as I kept walking around the area where I'd heard the young woman screaming for help. I had a bad feeling in my stomach. *What if she was dead?*

About a week later, another strange thing happened. I was being moved to live in the room with the mean girls! The funny part was that anyone else would have been honored and excited to be with these girls, but I was so not into it. I even asked for someone else to take my place, but apparently there was no way to do that, for whatever reason. I felt like I was being set up—again. Those girls knew I didn't like them, and I knew they hated me; man, they sure knew how to throw a mean look. I would have to shake it off like an animal that had just made it, running for its life so it wouldn't become the lion's breakfast.

"I hear you're moving in with us," Svetlana said.

She was the worst of them all. I was certain she was the boss of the other two girls.

"I just found out; it's crazy, right?" I said, playing it cool, like I wasn't scared at all to be inside their lair.

"Yeah, well, I guess you proved yourself worthy by being caring and mature around here, so they're putting you with us as a thank-you," Svetlana continued. "You know—so you don't have to be around all those little kids anymore?"

"Oh, of course, I get it," I replied, doing my best to seem happy about the whole thing. "Well, I guess I'll see you there," I said, as if I was excited.

"Yeah, well, so you know, it just happens to be your turn to clean the bedroom this weekend, as we girls have been doing it for a long time. You don't mind, do you?" she said, looking at me like she totally had me.

I played dumb, saying I didn't mind, and in fact, looked forward to it.

What a joke, I thought, as I walked away to check up on Alyona. It was like things were getting worse and worse around here! So much for liking my life; even the boy I liked was gone, moved to another orphanage like so many other faces that had come and gone.

* * *

"You missed a spot, right here," one of the mean girls said as she spot-checked my cleaning job later that weekend.

I couldn't believe these bitches; I wanted to punch them all in the face. Instead I played dumb again, saying, "Oh, no problem—I'll get that."

I got up on the chair and wiped down the walls close to the ceiling.

"Is that better?" I said, making a concerned face, pretending I was following their orders, totally oblivious to what they were really doing. These girls bullied me to the point where I felt threatened to sleep in the same room with them. They were mean, bad to the bone; they had no kindness in them except for kissing up to Irina Gregorievna, who was clueless about their cruel behavior. I was disgusted when I saw her smile at them, and tell them how great they were. I couldn't believe it!

I was not a narc, so I didn't tell anyone about the hard time those girls gave me. It entertained them, messing with other kids' lives, spreading rumors about me that were not true and turning other kids against me. The worst part was that they had control over every kid—everyone except for me. I was less interested in them than I was in being my own person, dealing with my own shit. I didn't need their drama, too; that's why I stayed away from all groups and cliques.

"I heard you did a great job helping the girls clean the bedroom!" Irina Gregorievna said one day, sitting at her desk like a queen. She was so creepy. I wished I could tell her how I really felt. Every time I looked at her, all I could see was her taking away what was mine—like I had no say. It was getting harder to keep a happy face when I was around her. I was getting fed up.

"I'm glad I could help," I said, smiling and pretending once more that there was nothing better than hearing those words come out of her mouth.

"I'm proud of you, Ludmila," Irina Gregorievna said.

I could hear the satisfaction in her voice, thinking she had me under her control.

I was getting impatient. I wanted to tell them all what was up. It was like being back home all those years ago, when all the kids picked on me and called me names—except back then, I could at least get away. Here, I had to take it, without reacting at all, like I was a damn zombie or a robot.

I was ready for a change. The winter sucked. Christmas was long past; most of the candy and treats were all gone, and the kids weren't as happy as they'd been before the holidays. They'd gone back to arguing, fighting and acting out. I was so fed up! I felt like the walls were closing in on me again, like I could barely hear my own thoughts in my head; everyone was so damn loud!

I thought about the summer, and how I would get to go to camp again. It made me feel a bit better—slightly less claustrophobic, and a little more like myself. I looked forward to taking a break from here and avoiding all the drama, as the camp was way bigger than this place, where everyone felt too damn close.

Chapter 42

Another Summer Vacation

Finally the time had come: I was getting ready for camp once more! I remember feeling an excitement I hadn't felt in a while, especially after the window incident.

I packed my bag with the best clothes I had that actually fit me, and went to the bathroom to grab my toothbrush and toothpaste. I still had some left over from the Christmas gifts we'd received this past winter, just like the year before. I had traded some of my stuff for toothpaste and notebooks, more useful than some of the toys and pencils I'd gotten. *This will last me the entire summer*, I thought, as I stuffed my second tube of traded toothpaste and toothbrush in my bag.

"Is everyone ready to go?" my favorite caregiver asked as she walked into the room to make sure we'd packed properly. "The bus is coming within an hour for pickup. Come on, girls—less chatting and more packing! I know you're all very excited, but you need to pack first, okay?" she said, smiling.

I could tell she was excited for us. This trip wasn't like the last one I went on; it wasn't a church camp, and we were all going! The entire orphanage—and not just for two weeks, but for the entire summer! We were coming back the last week of August, and it was only the first of June. I remember I couldn't believe it; it was so amazing to know that I was going somewhere beautiful, by the sea. I'd never been to the sea before, just the lake. This was going to be something completely new!

This is going to be so awesome, I thought as I closed my notebook. I'd packed everything on my list, and I was ready to go on our fun camp vacation.

"Can you believe it? I still can't!" Sasha said, with the biggest grin on her face. She was a cool, down-to-earth, caring girl. Her looks were a bit off, but her great personality made up for it. I liked Sasha; she was a good friend.

"I know; me neither!" I said, smiling. "I hear there are going to be kids from many other orphanages there, too, from all over."

"Yeah, I can't wait—there are going to be lots of cute boys!" Sasha said, giggling.

I laughed as we grabbed our bags and made our way to the bus.

Soon we were driving toward the sea. All of the kids were singing, playing tic-tac-toe and other games they had invented while on the bus. The camp was about two or three hours away, and we were all getting restless after an hour and a half on the bus. There were no stops on the way, as there was too much risk of someone taking off.

"I'm going to close my eyes for a while—is that cool?" I asked Sasha, who was talking to someone across the aisle.

"Of course! I'll wake you up when we get there if you're still sleeping," she said. "It's going to be so much fun!"

I smiled and closed my eyes, resting my head against the window. *I hope Alyona is doing well*, I thought. She was on a different bus with the younger kids.

"Wake up, sleepyhead! I can't believe you slept the whole time!" Sasha said.

"Wow—are we here already?" I asked.

"Yeah, look!" she said, pointing out the window.

I looked outside and saw several other buses in front of us, as well as more behind.

"Wow," I said, shocked. I had never seen that many buses before, or that many kids! Some buses were all the way at the front with the doors open and kids jumping out with their bags and smiling faces.

I looked at Sasha. I could tell she was way too hyped up. I realized that I'd better catch up and get excited too! I shouldn't have slept; I felt dazed, and my bag felt heavy as we walked off the bus, one by one, to follow someone to the area we'd be staying for the summer.

"Everyone from this bus, please come this way!" I heard someone say. Our group took off to settle in to our new quarters.

That day, I somehow ended up staying with girls who were not from an orphanage, which was a big surprise. I didn't even know there were going to be normal people here. There were three of them, and every one of them looked shiny and new, with pretty clothes that actually fit, long beautiful hair, and even jewelry on their hands, ears, and feet! I could tell they were not orphans; they had real lives, with real parents, and they most certainly were going to real school.

I knew I was in trouble. I could already feel that these girls were beyond me, and we were not going to get along. Maybe they didn't have enough beds or something, so they had stuck me in with these girls with whom I had nothing in common.

It didn't really matter, as I was barely there except to sleep. They were about my age, but seemed older, with the makeup and clothes they wore. I didn't talk to them much, but we got along all right. I didn't give them any trouble, and they left me alone too.

This camp was way better than the last; it was total kid heaven, with delicious meals and fun activities. I will never forget the feeling of constant excitement from the moment I woke up until I went to bed at night.

Going down to the sea was my favorite. We'd swim in the sea for the entire morning after breakfast. I couldn't believe how endlessly big the sea was, how transparent and clear. I was very surprised when I tasted some of the salt water, definitely different than a lake. No one cared that the water was cold, either; we would just run in as fast as we could and swim underwater to see the bottom, pretending we were mermaids.

Every night, we had a dance after dinner, with a DJ playing good music all the kids liked. My favorite song was "Don't Speak," by No Doubt. Everyone would get so into this song, even though we had no idea what she was saying. I loved the dances; the kids from all the orphanages gathered to dance and show off, wearing their best outfits to impress that special someone.

I will never forget the boy I liked that summer. He had blond hair and kind blue eyes, and he'd smile at me once in a while when I saw him around the camp. I thought he did that because he knew I liked him. When I approached him at one of the dances to ask him to slow-dance with me, he didn't say a word; he just took off. I ran after him, but he was a fast runner, long gone.

That's weird, I thought, walking back to the dance. I didn't understand. Was there something on my face? I didn't bother him after that, just kept my distance, and it worked. One night at the dance he asked me to slow-dance with him! I remember I felt so shy, which was a surprise to me, since I liked him. I understood how he felt when I'd approached him that time, but as uncomfortable as we both were, we did manage to have one slow dance together—my first official slow dance with a boy! We didn't end up "going out," like other kids did; we were both younger, and felt it was enough to dance together, and sometimes talk.

I remember the boy was kind, and didn't make fun of my short hair like other boys did back at the orphanage. Luckily, it had grown longer, and was ready for a cut that would make me look like a girl again, or at least, more like one. He made me feel good about myself, and I was happy to know a kind boy who actually liked me for who I was.

Man, life was good—too good, like I was dreaming. This was the best summer of my life! I couldn't believe every day was nothing but fun, and no chores; it was insane! I felt like a queen, and never wanted to leave. It was everything I had ever wanted: perfect weather, endless summer dances, contests, festivities of all sorts. It was never boring, with something to do or somewhere to go every day! Plus I had a boy who liked me, which made me feel pretty damn good—like I was worthy, and not as ugly as I thought I was.

Every day I would go visit Alyona to see how she was doing. She was in a different section with all the younger kids. They had a different daily routine and an earlier bedtime; nevertheless, Alyona was very happy. She didn't mind if she didn't see me at all; she was too busy having a great time with the other kids. She would wave and come running to give me a hug, but not every time, as she was too busy enjoying herself, playing tag with the other kids. It was priceless. I couldn't believe this was our lives—that we had it so good!

Our orphanage won a prize for putting on the best play that summer. It was so much fun to compete against the other orphanages, making costumes, rehearsing our lines, being someone else for a short while. I don't particularly recall what the plays were about or what we all dressed up as—just that it was awesome, fun, and exciting to have a chance to win!

We were due back at the orphanage in about a week, and I could tell that no one wanted to leave. We all wished we could stay at the camp forever, but everything comes to an end eventually. Everyone did their best to make the most of our last week there, and do as much as possible before going back to where everything felt like we were on repeat, and not in a good way.

As the buses pulled away one by one that last day, all the kids waved to the friends they had made over the summer. Some of the kids were crying, they were so sad to leave. As we drove down the curvy road, I looked back at the camp and said good-bye in my head. I was so happy to have been at this amazing camp. No snakes, real rooms with real beds, and even though we didn't sing gospel songs together, I did before I went to bed. I even got to dance with a boy! I felt proud of myself; stepping out of my comfort zone was a scary thing, but I'd done it. And damn, it felt good.

Chapter 43

Bombshell News

Shortly after returning from camp, my happiness groove came to a halt when the director pulled me into her office to tell me that Alyona and I were going to be moved to another orphanage.

"Ludmila, I know this is hard for you to hear, but you knew this day would come," she said, opening a folder with papers inside.

I didn't say anything—just stood there, doing my best to process the news.

"It's hard when you've been with us for so long. I understand that you've made this place your home, and I am sorry," she said, then went silent, reading something in the folder.

"When? When do we go?" I asked.

"Well, here's the thing, Ludmila: Because your sister is much younger, she will be going to a different orphanage, for younger children, while you will go to the one near the church you used to attend sometimes—it's literally within walking distance," she said, smiling, as if that was supposed to make me feel better. "The good news is that in a couple of years, Alyona will be eight, and they will bring her to the orphanage where you will be staying." She closed the folder and put it aside, with a look that said *And that's not the worst part*.

She took off her glasses and placed them on the desk.

"You and Alyona will be leaving next week. We finally have all of your paperwork in order, Alyona's, too. It's time." She made a sad face, like she cared, which I really think she did.

There were only a few caregivers here, and during the past couple of years that I'd lived here with them, I'd begun to feel like they were my family. After all, they did care for us; they fed us, and helped us with our laundry; they taught us manners, and how to read, helping us grow into decent human beings rather than rough street kids. We were much more now, and all thanks to them, playing the role of a mother, or a grandmother. Most of us didn't have any parents or siblings to look after us, and in my case, getting all the right attention and care, I couldn't help but feel like we were close, like family.

I was heartbroken. I couldn't believe we were leaving within the week; it could be as soon as tomorrow! It all depended on when the beds became available. Two years was a long time to be away from Alyona. I was pretty angry that they were separating us, but I also knew there was little I could do. I just hoped Alyona would have a better time with this than me. She was almost six—still plenty young enough to adjust to her new home.

I, on the other hand, had mixed feelings. Part of me wanted to go so that I wouldn't have to stay in the room with the mean girls anymore; that was a plus. The orphanage I was going to wasn't in a faraway place in the middle of nowhere, so that was another plus. Some kids who were slow or had mental health problems were sent to orphanages that were far away, in the middle of nowhere, while healthier kids were sent to better, more popular orphanages, like Kerch, where kids had the chance to graduate from the orphanage school and go to college on a scholarship. That place had so many sponsors, it wasn't even funny; only the brightest kids would be placed there.

I was glad I was going somewhere that was familiar, where I would get to reunite with Alyona someday, but I couldn't get rid of this sinking feeling inside. I was really nervous about having to start all over again. Here, I was on top, trusted and liked; at the new orphanage, I would be on the very bottom, disliked, not trusted, treated like a five-year-old, to make sure I wouldn't run away. I'd have to try hard not to get into fights with other kids who I knew would be testing me.

I felt like I couldn't go through it all over again, just when I was finally starting to feel like I belonged here. I had no idea I would have such strong feelings of wanting to stay; I hadn't realized I'd gotten so close to strangers who were just doing their jobs, taking care of us. I felt like a fool. *What the hell was I thinking?* But how could I not? If I hadn't established trust and relationships here, I never would have gotten anywhere.

It's just that I never thought I would have to pay such a high price. I'd gotten too comfortable. I'd forgotten that things would change, like they always did.

This is a lesson, I told myself. *I can never let myself get this comfortable again.* It was too painful, like leaving a family home. I would never get to see them again.

I felt all of my goodness slowly drain away; everything positive I had stored somewhere inside of me was leaking out fast, and before long, I was right back where I'd started, when I first arrived at the orphanage—angry, depressed, and ready to return to the streets. I was so damn mad, I wanted to do something stupid just to prove to everyone how much pain I was feeling, how betrayed I felt. I couldn't help it! I didn't want to leave. I wanted to stay here, together with Alyona.

I went outside to get some fresh air. It had been a while since I'd gone through such a big change in my life, and I was out of shape. I sat outside, the trees around me, and did my best to hope it was all going to work out.

I can always run away, I thought, as I went back inside to spend some time with Alyona.

Chapter 44

Arrival

The gray-haired caregiver—the one I really liked, and would greatly miss—was taking me to my new orphanage. The director had already taken Alyona to the other orphanage, for younger kids. It had been so hard to say good-bye for the next two years. If I had a way to visit her, I could, and one of the church ladies had told me she would take me to visit Alyona so I could be reassured she was doing fine. I was looking forward to that day already. Alyona didn't seem to mind, as I knew she wouldn't; she was too young to care about the things I did. Her needs were met, and would continue to be in the new orphanage. I wasn't worried about her as much as I was worried about myself, not being able to see her for so long. I just really hoped the nice lady from church would come through with her promise.

We got out of the taxi van and started walking toward the orphanage. Children who were being moved would take the taxi van so that none of us could take off, which would have been pretty easy to do on a trolley. I put my bag over my shoulder and prepared myself as best I could. I had no idea what to expect here. Was it big, or small, like the one I'd come from? What were the kids like? What were the bedrooms like, the rules, the boundaries? I was freaking out; every part of me wanted to tell the gray-haired caregiver to take me back.

I really didn't want to go in, mostly because I was scared I wouldn't fit in. I didn't know what to do other than expect the worst—it was much safer that way.

At least one good thing had come out of this: I didn't have to deal with Irina Gregorievna any longer.

"You haven't said a word the entire way here," said the caregiver, looking at me.

There was nothing to say. This was how it was, and that's all there was to it.

I glanced at the caregiver, cracking a smile the best I could, knowing my face painted a different picture.

"You'll be all right, you know?" she said, placing her hand on my shoulder and then hugging me as we walked down the sidewalk. "There are a lot of kids your age here. You'll make lots of friends, and will have plenty of opportunities to prove yourself."

I smiled, hoping she was right.

As we kept walking I realized we were passing a place where I used to hang out back in the day, begging for money. It was the nice train station with a clock tower and several trains coming and going. There were lots of people here all day long, just like now as we walked by. I couldn't believe how many memories flashed through my mind; who knew all these years later that I would be walking by this place, knowing how to read, write my name, and be proper, for the most part.

I saw several gypsies walking around in groups as their kids ran out to do the work. I didn't like those guys—not after I'd met two of them at the place where Mom died, and I'd seen the flames.

Apparently, Mom's friend, the one who'd let us live at his house, was a gypsy. He had two sisters who came by one day to visit Mom and tell her they didn't want us living there, and how they were next in line for the house.

"We are his sisters—his blood. We deserve to live here first," they'd said.

I remember this because I'd shown up just when they were talking to Mom. I will never forget how I felt—the same feeling I had when I'd seen the house on fire.

I looked in front of me and then at the caregiver, to snap myself back to the here and now.

"You all right? You look like you just saw a ghost," she said, looking worried.

"No, I'm fine," I lied, and kept walking.

"Well, here we are!" the caregiver announced as she pointed to a large two-story building with big windows.

We had officially arrived.

I was surprised to see there was no fence—at least on this side of the place.

We walked up the steps and the caregiver helped me to open one of the giant doors.

"Go ahead, Ludmila," she said, following me in.

We walked up a couple more steps and into a small room with a chair and table that had a telephone on it. There was a woman sitting on the chair, looking like she was expecting us.

"Hello," the caregiver said. "I'm here to drop off Apostol Ludmila Urievna, twelve years old, going into the second grade."

"Yes, we've been waiting for your arrival!" the lady said, smiling.

"Here is her paperwork," the caregiver said, handing over a white folder. The lady took it and flipped through the contents.

"Everything is in order here. You are good to go," the woman said.

"Good luck, Ludmila," the gray-haired caregiver said. "Remember to listen to what they say, and you'll do fine, okay?" She gave me a hug and a kiss good-bye on my forehead.

I hugged her back, and couldn't help the tears that slid down my face. I was really going to miss her. I watched as she looked at me one last time with a kind smile and disappeared behind the giant door.

I was all alone with strangers now. I hugged my bag to my chest like a scared child would grab a pillow, and followed the lady. We walked up two flights of stairs and stopped on the second floor. There were two doors on each side.

"This room is for the boys, and this is the room where you will be," the lady said as she opened the door to the girls' room.

We walked inside a large living space with nice light coming through the big windows, making the room look happy, not gloomy. There was a large rug over hardwood floors, and some plants. I noticed they had a television, and several wooden chairs. There was a sturdy table with playing cards and puzzles on it, and some toys on the floor.

So far, so good, I thought.

Moments later an older lady came out to meet us from the other room. She was in her sixties, plump, with thin red hair. She was wearing earrings and red lipstick, and I noticed that after I shook her hand, mine smelled like fish.

"Okay, she's all yours," the first lady said as she waved good-bye to me and disappeared.

"All right, Ludmila, this is going to be your new home now, okay?" the red-haired woman said. "My name is Larisa Petrovna, but everyone calls me Ms. Petrovna. Now, come this way," she said, smiling, as she led the way into the other room. "Right here is the bathroom, and this door is for the shower, or laundry."

Ms. Petrovna showed me the bathroom that had two bathroom stalls, with real toilets. There was also a large metal sink that looked older than the lady. The faucet made a song as it dripped. The shower was right next door, with two small sinks, a mirror, a bench, and a shallow tub made of stone. I remember wondering why they'd painted everything sky blue—the tub, the walls, the floors, even the radiator.

Ms. Petrovna showed me the bedroom where the girls slept. I remember thinking, *Where are all the kids?* No one was around except us. The bedroom was also nice and bright, with big windows, which I really liked. The walls were painted white, which was typical, and there were at least fifteen beds, some on each side. Between each bed was a nightstand with a drawer and a cabinet.

"This is your bed," Ms. Petrovna said, pointing at one of the beds toward the middle, on the window side. "You will be sharing this nightstand with the girl next to you." She opened the drawer and the cabinet to show me. "Half of it is yours, and as you can see, the other half belongs to the other girl," she said, pointing to the other half to make sure I understood.

We walked over to one of the wardrobes and Ms. Petrovna opened the door. "This is where all of the uniforms and dresses go after school," she said. "You will receive a uniform to wear for school; that's where everyone is right now," she added, smiling.

She showed me another wardrobe with an empty shelf where I would keep my daily clothes. "Make sure you keep everything nicely folded and clean, okay?" She pointed at all of the perfectly folded clothes on each shelf. I nodded in agreement and followed her. Next, she showed me the shoe rack where I would find a spot to keep my shoes. I looked at all the different shoes, some stylish, some worn-out, others brand-new—a strange mix.

"All of your dirty laundry goes in here; I've made a place for you," Ms. Petrovna said as she opened one of the closet doors. Several small cloth bags were hanging inside, with names on each bag. The caregiver handed me an empty clean cloth bag, and I placed it on the hook she indicated. As always, I wrote my name on everything, and then we made our way to the kitchen, which was on the other side of the building, in the basement.

The cafeteria was part of the kitchen, with several long tables and metal chairs. It could seat at least a hundred people! It smelled really good, like they were making bread.

"Everyone gets three meals per day, as well as a snack around eleven a.m.," Ms. Petrovna said as we walked out of the kitchen. *I could use a snack right about now*, I thought as we left the cafeteria. Next, she showed me where everyone took real showers, as there was no hot water here other than on the weekends.

I took some time to organize my belongings as she watched my every move. I felt like a thief or a prisoner; I was uncomfortable being followed around everywhere I went, even though I understood that new arrivals were always watched constantly. I was going to have to go through this period until I earned their trust, just like at the other orphanage.

I put my notebook and pens and pencils in the drawer on my side of the nightstand, and my toothbrush and toothpaste in the bottom cabinet, and closed the door.

"Great job," she said. I could tell that Ms. Petrovna was satisfied with me thus far, a good sign. She was not a mean, complicated woman, and she sure as hell wasn't Irina Gregorievna. I didn't feel as sketchy being here at this orphanage, with Ms. Petrovna showing me the ropes.

"Do you have any questions?" she asked, looking at me.

"No," I said, even though I did. I just didn't know where to start.

Chapter 45

School

I remember the next day was the most difficult for me. There were so many new rules and ways that they did things here, driving me up the wall! I really hoped I wouldn't blow this. I had to stay on my best behavior; after all, I had just arrived—fresh meat.

A different caregiver showed up in the room to wake everyone up to get ready.

"Good morning, everybody!" she said loudly. "Time to get up! Let's go, let's go!" She was walking around the room, making sure everyone was up.

This caregiver was older, in her fifties or sixties, with short gray hair. She was very well dressed and was wearing jewelry. She looked tough—like she wouldn't take crap from anyone. Part of me was scared of her; I had never been in front of someone this strict and serious before.

"That's Mrs. Alexeevna," said the girl who slept next to me. She looked a couple of years younger than me, with short, curly, blondish hair and green eyes. She had good teeth, too, which was a rare thing to see in orphans.

"Thank you for letting me know," I said. "I am Ludmila." I smiled to let her know I had no beef with her, and that we could potentially be good friends.

"I am Katya," she said quietly as we rushed to make our beds.

I made sure my covers were smooth and perfect. I puffed up my pillow and placed it nicely on the bed, watching the other kids to make sure I was doing everything right. All the kids kept their distance from me, which was normal; I did the same. It would take some time to get to know everyone before we would talk and share stories, although it looked like Katya was an exception—the first person to speak to me without an agenda.

I'd been given a small towel to use for washing up, so I grabbed it and followed the kids to the bathroom. Everyone was washing up like it was nothing! I walked out of there so fast, thinking *There's no way I'm going to take a shower or wash up in front of everyone.* I didn't feel comfortable doing that; I wanted to keep my private parts to myself. I decided to wait till everyone was done and go in last. Big mistake. I lost a lot of time, and fell behind in getting dressed and joining the line of kids to go eat breakfast before school. The other kids were mad at me. Their faces said it all.

Way to go, Ludmila, I thought as I went to join the group.

Mrs. Alexeevna saw that I'd learned my lesson. I was so grateful that she didn't yell or punish me. I was sure I was not the first—and wouldn't be the last—to learn this harsh lesson. It was not easy to be naked in front of other girls, but if they had gotten used to it, then I would, too, even though it was so hard for me to believe I would be doing such a thing one day.

"You'll get used to it," Mrs. Alexeevna said when I finally joined the other kids, lined up in twos to head for the cafeteria. "After breakfast we'll find you some school clothes."

Mrs. Alexeevna walked to the front of the line where we stood in pairs, telling us to wait quietly while she went to get the boys next door. When the boys joined us in the big living area, we walked to the cafeteria and stood by the entrance, waiting for our group to be called. There was a lot of noise inside; between chairs being pulled out, plates clattering, and the kids' voices, I couldn't believe how loud it was in there. Seemed like the walls down here echoed, making everything twice as noisy. Finally we were called and everyone followed Mrs. Alexeevna to our section, where we sat down to eat.

I sat in an empty seat and waited till everyone else had started eating. I wasn't all that crazy about their food; it was a lot worse than what we'd had at the other orphanage. It was some sort of grain with milk and sugar. I'd had it before at the other place, but it was delicious—buttery and milky and sweet. This stuff tasted watered down, barely sweet, and definitely no butter.

I put it aside and ate the bread and drank the tea instead. At least the bread tasted like it was supposed to, and although the tea was not as strong as I liked, it was good, as they put some milk in it. *Milk tea*, I thought, as I took another warm sip.

"You gonna eat that?" one of the boys sitting next to me asked.

"No," I replied.

"Can I have it?"

"Go ahead—I'm not eating it," I said, pushing the plate toward him.

He gobbled that stuff down like there was no tomorrow. I couldn't believe it.

I was a picky eater; even when I was extremely hungry, I still wouldn't eat something I didn't like. I just didn't see the point. I hoped the food would improve, as this was only the first day.

After breakfast I was given some school clothes: a nice white blouse with a jean skirt. I was so happy that everything actually fit me right. I looked in the mirror and felt like I was looking at someone else. My hair was finally cut so it was mostly one length, coming down to my ears. I finally looked like a girl! I will never forget putting on an undershirt before the blouse and noticing that my body was changing. I was taller, and my figure was changing, including my chest. I was becoming a teenager; without even realizing it, I'd been growing up.

I recognized that wearing this uniform and the nice shoes with heels made me feel like a lady. I couldn't believe how much I'd changed in such a short amount of time. I remember those days when I'd wished I was going to school, wearing a nice uniform, looking nice. All these years later, here I was, looking pretty, on my way to school, to learn! I treated those school clothes like they were holy, always hanging up my blouse and keeping my jean skirt super clean.

The school building was just a few steps away, on the same property as the orphanage. The building was the same color and style as the one we lived in, except for the inside. I followed everyone up the stairs and into the building. We got to the third floor and walked inside the first classroom on the right. For the first time in my life I saw a classroom, and school desks. There was a large green chalkboard stretching all the way to the end of the wall, with something written in cursive on it. I didn't understand, as I didn't know how to read cursive well.

I noticed a lot of crafts from art class placed around the room, which I was very excited about, too.

"Come, sit down here," I heard a voice say. It was Katya, the girl who slept next to me.

I walked over to the desk and sat in the empty chair next to her.

"It's okay; don't be nervous. You will do fine," she said, as she took out a notebook.

I looked around and noticed that all the kids were getting out their notebooks and writing utensils, except me.

I remember feeling so nervous—like I had just joined the army or something. I was so scared to fail at school, and not having any supplies like the other kids made me feel even worse.

Shouldn't I be prepared? I thought, as I admired the other kids' notebooks, pencils, pens, and books. I looked forward to getting those things too, like a real student!

"Good morning, everyone," a woman said, as she made her way to the desk at the front of the room.

"Good morning, Ludmila Andreevna," the kids replied.

Wow, we have the same name, I thought.

I'd never met anyone before who shared my name—except my aunt, of course, but she was family, so that didn't really count.

Concentrate, Ludmila—don't wander off. This is important, I thought, glancing up toward the front of the room.

The woman seemed kind. She had blue eyes, and red hair that came down to her shoulders. She was dressed like us, except her white blouse was a bit different, and she wore a black skirt with black tights and heels. I could tell the kids weren't afraid of her as much as they were of Mrs. Alexeevna. They all seemed much more relaxed and talkative.

"I hear we have someone new joining us," Ludmila Andreevna said as she looked at me with a smile. "Come here," she said kindly, gesturing for me to join her by her desk, which I did. "Everybody, this is . . ." She paused, asking me to introduce myself to the class. I looked at all the twenty or more kids who were now staring at me.

"My name is Ludmila," I said, as loudly as I could.

"Welcome, Ludmila!" all the kids yelled, doing what the lady expected.

The teacher gave me a new notebook like all the other kids had, and a blue pen and a pencil.

"Only use blue pen for tests, and practice with the pencil," she said.

I nodded. I was so happy to get my own notebook!

My new teacher asked me to share Katya's textbook, until I got my very own.

"Thank you," I said as I went back to my seat and prepared myself to learn.

"I will help you if I can, okay?" Katya said.

It was like she could read my mind. I was so thankful I had someone kind as a friend just two days into being here. She was more like me than anyone else I had ever met before; she was a helper, and I, too, liked helping if I could.

The teacher went up to the board and pointed to the alphabet poster hanging on the wall. I heard a loud buzzing sound, the same sound I had heard all those years ago when I'd snuck up to the school.

"All right, everyone, class is now in session," the teacher said.

She went around and introduced herself to a couple of other new kids. (Later on I learned that some kids came to school here because they had problems and couldn't fit in at the normal school.)

"Today we will be learning how to write in cursive," she said, pointing to different letters on the poster. "I would like you all to copy each letter on each line of your notebooks, but make sure you skip one line to practice on. When you're all done, bring your notebooks up to me."

I was so excited to learn! This was it; this was what I had been waiting for all my life!

I eagerly opened my notebook and very carefully, doing the best I could, copied the letters one by one, practicing my cursive. Some letters were easier to write than others, so when I went up to the teacher after I'd finished, she circled the letters she wanted me to keep practicing. She told me I was doing a good job, and it totally made my day; I was in school, learning! Better late than never.

The following week I got another notebook to practice writing cursive. There were combinations of letters to practice as well as whole words; it was awesome!

I remember many kids would complain about homework and

school, but I was happy as a clam. I actually looked forward to school! I was so excited to see my grades, to see how well I was doing. I loved all the subjects in school. We had writing and grammar, math, art, gym, and dance aerobics. I was doing well in all areas, which made me feel like a complete person! I was finally going to school; even though it wasn't like normal schools, I didn't care. I was learning so much, things I never knew!

The other orphanage didn't have school, but at least they had taught us how to read. I was surprised to see so many kids having a hard time. I realized that learning came differently to each person. Some kids required more one-on-one time, while others were done pretty fast. We were allowed to go outside to play while the caregiver finished helping the kids who needed more time with their homework during the afternoon. Just like the other orphanage, we had to take naps, after which we were to go outside to play, and then back to the school building to get our homework done.

I loved finishing all of my homework early. I knew that if I did, I would get a little bit of extra time to investigate and roam around before the caregiver came back out with the rest of the kids. Once she came out, we couldn't wander off the property. She was there to keep a close eye on us kids.

I wasn't the only one who took advantage of the unsupervised time; other kids did the same. I learned that some kids smoked cigarettes, and that was their window of opportunity. I was ready to do the same. I liked smoking, and decided to start up again, as I knew it would help me feel better and more relaxed to be here.

I wasn't really used to all the kids yet, and hadn't made many friends, except for Katya, even though we weren't *real* friends yet. I wasn't eager to try, as I didn't trust anyone very much, if at all. Even Katya, whom I liked, was also being observed. I had a tough time trusting a single soul, and that was a hard thing to live with.

Even though I loved school, I still missed the other orphanage a lot. I felt like maybe I belonged there more than I belonged here. The kids weren't kind; they were all focused on themselves, ready to get someone else in trouble to be favored more. I got busted by one of the girls who saw me coming back through the hole in the fence, on the other side of the property. She told on me, which really sucked, as I was scolded and treated like shit.

I didn't know how much of this I could take before I did something stupid, like the other kids did here—fighting till one of them won and got the respect they wanted by defeating the other kid. It was like Fight Club, except girls fought boys, too (although I don't think they ever won). All problems were handled through fighting and swearing; it seemed to be the only way, as just talking about it, or doing nothing, only made things worse. At this point I was getting picked on by kids I didn't even know, from different classes at school or groups at the orphanage. It was like news traveled fast, and suddenly all the attention was on you, the next target—unfortunately, a game I knew all too well.

I missed the family I had made back at the other orphanage, where I felt close to the caregivers. It felt more intimate and comfortable there, as it was much smaller, and with way less kids. There wasn't as much competition as there was here, where many of the kids were older, scarier, meaner, and more unpredictable. I didn't like that a bit. I felt like I was swimming with sharks now instead of mostly dolphins. This place was making me feel even more motivated to maybe try to get away and go back to my old orphanage, where I was known. Plus, the food there was way better!

I missed Alyona a lot, too. She was the only one who *knew* me, and who I once was.

It was like I didn't know who I was at all anymore. Going from one place to another, losing so much in my life, had caused me to question everything, including this place, where no one had any clue as to who I was, and what I had been through.

Chapter 46

Escape—Part Two

I got very tired of trying to belong. Even though I did my best to fit in, it just didn't seem to work. It was like the kids here were all about the drama and gossip, some worse than others.

I remember I got into a physical fight for the first time because one of the girls just wouldn't leave me alone, always saying mean remarks and giving me dirty looks. One day I just exploded. I couldn't take it anymore! I hated it here. The only thing I enjoyed was school, but that didn't help me to belong; instead, it made me even more of a target. The kids hated me for being good at school.

About two weeks into living at the new orphanage, I decided to run away, back to my old orphanage. The kids there were not corrupted like they were here; there was no competition or fighting, no eighteen-year-olds to be afraid of. (Some of the older boys scared me; they reminded me of Victor, and I really didn't want to go through anything like that again.)

Somehow I managed to pack all of my belongings in a couple of plastic bags. I will never forget how I managed to walk right by that room with a telephone, where there was always someone keeping watch, sitting in that chair. I was so scared. If I got caught, I would never have the opportunity to escape again, as I would be watched like a hawk, twenty-four/seven. I don't know what I was thinking, but somehow I believed that if I ran away successfully and reached my old orphanage, I would never have to come back here—like they would be proud of me for coming back to them, as if somehow they had all missed me as much as I'd missed them.

I walked right by the room where a woman was sitting, talking to couple of kids. They happened to be standing right in front of her, giving me a chance to take off.

Moments later I was outside the orphanage property, on my way to catch a trolley. I knew all the neighborhoods around here as well as a tour guide, and was familiar with almost all of the trolley routes.

About an hour later I was walking down the road, getting closer and closer to the old orphanage. I walked in and made my way to the director's office to tell her that I didn't like the new place, and I'd decided to come back here. I knocked on the door and heard her say "Enter." I opened the door slowly, as if to surprise her, but when she saw me, she didn't seem happy to see me at all.

"What are you doing here, Ludmila?" she asked, looking worried, as she knew exactly what I'd done.

"I want to come back here," I said. "I really love it here, and the other place is just not for me."

"Ludmila, you know we can't take you back, right?" she said. "That's not how it works. You know that."

"Why not?" I asked. "I won't cause any trouble, and I'll help out with whatever you need." I was hoping she'd appreciate what I had to say and allow me to stay.

"I am sorry, Ludmila, but you can't stay," she said, as she approached the telephone to do the unthinkable—call the new orphanage to let them know I was here.

I was very upset. I had so hoped that my old orphanage would take me back—that I could return to the awesome life I had built here—but it wasn't to be. I was naive to even think such a thing might be possible. I felt so stupid. Part of me had always known I wouldn't be taken back, but the other part still hoped I might be. That side always seemed to win: I saw what I wanted, and that was it—I would find a way to get it done.

The director personally brought me back to the new place, and on the way there, while walking the last stretch, she got me an ice-cream sandwich, which I thought was very kind of her. It made me feel like she did care about me; after all, she was trying to make me feel better.

I was scared shitless to go back through those doors and face Ms. Petrovna and Mrs. Alexeevna.

"You ready?" the director asked, as I finished the last of my ice-cream sandwich, putting the wrapper in one of my shirt pockets. I was wearing black pants and a hoodie—my "I feel angry" outfit, more tomboy than girly. I placed the two bags over my shoulder and walked inside with the director of my old orphanage in front of me. I saw some kids from my class standing around, along with other groups, looking at me as if to say *You're in big trouble, and we are here to watch.*

I kept my head down, prepared to take the hit and get yelled at by the staff, who weren't nice very often, as someone was always getting into trouble.

I was relieved when I saw Ms. Petrovna, the red-haired lady who smelled of fish, coming toward us.

"Welcome back," she said with a chuckle. "That was pretty stupid, you know?"

I didn't say anything, just kept looking down.

I was so happy it wasn't Mrs. Alexeevna, who most likely would have scorned me much more, all to prove the point that what I had done was very wrong. She was so darn strict, and I knew the day would come when I would have to face her too.

The director from my old place asked me to promise her I wouldn't run away again, which I somehow did, although I'm pretty sure I didn't really believe it.

Moments later she was gone, back to the other orphanage, where other kids relied on her to keep helping them like she had once helped me.

I realized that now I would be treated even worse, and I also knew I would be starting from scratch all over again. At least I hadn't lost much, other than my freedom, as I now had to stay glued to Ms. Petrovna all day long.

At this point, I really regretted running away. It dawned on me that while the kids here didn't respect me, the caregivers did. They thought I was a good kid with potential, and I'd been trusted. Now I was about to learn just how much I'd messed up, as Mrs. Alexeevna took away some of the pretty dresses she'd given to me, and gave them to another girl about my size.

"You don't deserve these dresses," she said, looking at me in a way she'd never looked at me before, disappointed.

I was just glad it was over. She was strict and tough as nails, but for now, the worst was over, and I could slowly move on from this failed attempt of mine.

I walked to my bed, as it was the weekend, and we were allowed to hang out in the room. I took out all the birthday cards I'd been given by the kids at my old orphanage. While we'd never had real birthday celebrations, we all knew whose birthday was coming up, so we would make each other birthday cards. I looked at all the drawings and wishes, and reflected back on the old days, when things had been much simpler. As I sat there, I thought about the fact that I was not a kid anymore—that there were more expectations of me now, more responsibility. I had to find a way to fit in here. *No more running away just because the kids were picking on me.*

I promised myself I'd never run away from my problems again.

Instead, I'd face them, even if it meant fighting. I needed to get my foot in the game, and at the same time, stay on the good side of the caregivers. Time to renovate myself. I had a big choice to make—either be a wimp, or gather myself to stand up and fight, even if it was the tallest and oldest girl with big platform shoes on that looked like they'd hurt a lot if she kicked me with them. I didn't care; I had to get past everyone thinking I was weak.

Before long, everyone was talking about me and my bravery, as no one else dared to stand up against this tall, strong older girl with the platform shoes. For whatever reason she didn't like me, so I decided to confront her after she was talking shit about me. I will never forget feeling like my life was about to end when I got close up to this girl and told her what was up. I was talking to her waist, mostly, doing my best to keep my head up to look at her. I remember she was mad, but she didn't do anything; she just said "Hmmm," and walked away as if she was proud of me for what I'd just done.

I was confused. *What? I'm still alive?* I couldn't believe she'd just walked away.

Then again, it was like ripping someone's head off in a battle for respect. Finally, I'd earned some. Not many kids messed with me after that. I was finally left at peace—most of the time.

I was glad to put my history behind me and start fresh again. After all, Alyona was going to come here one day, and I needed to be here for her as well.

Chapter 47

Fall Brings Blisters

It was now November, and all the leaves had finally fallen down to rest. I loved fall because the leaves changed colors; they looked out of this world, bursting with red, yellow, and orange colors.

By now, though, all the leaves were brown and the trees, entirely naked. Winter wasn't far off. Our group was told to take the leaves and dump them in a giant pile where everyone else had dumped theirs. It was a joint effort of all the kids who lived here, including the little first graders.

Our block was by the school entrance. This area had a thick carpet of heavy, wet leaves that proved very hard to move. We were all given rakes, shovels, and a large plastic tarp to carry away the leaves. Since we didn't have any gloves, everyone would walk around with blisters on their hands, including me. My blisters were really bad, and very painful. I had never done anything like this before, so I was having a good time, raking and working hard, when I realized my hands were hurting.

I went to the nurse's office to get bandaged up. "Try to keep your hands clean," the nurse said. I hated being in the nurse's office. Nothing good ever happened to me here, plus, I didn't like the smell. It made me feel like I was in a hospital or something.

As I walked back outside I saw my shadow standing there, ready to walk me back to the rest of our group. I was pretty used to being followed by one caregiver or another, always watched to make sure I didn't take off again. I just couldn't wait to be on the other side of the fence, with some freedom and privacy to myself.

As we walked I thought about Alyona and when I would go visit her, like the church lady had promised. I still hadn't heard from her. I was hoping she would come visit me and explain when we would go; it was the only happy thing I had going.

I wondered what Christmas was going to be like here; would it be as fun as it had been at my old orphanage? It was only a month away, and I found myself looking forward to the once-a-year event where everyone was happy. This time of year always brought out more happiness in people, and I loved being around that atmosphere.

When we'd finished cleaning up the property, all the kids ran to play in the giant pile of leaves. I sat and watched as the first graders disappeared into the pile, laughing and having a great time. There were at least twenty kids taking advantage, using it like a trampoline, jumping and doing tricks.

I wasn't big on playing, really; I enjoyed some games here and there, but mostly I just longed for some freedom. I wanted to get away and have a smoke. I wasn't happy and I was in pain, with my blisters. Smoking always made me feel better, and helped me to tolerate my life.

By now I knew all the kids who smoked, and I planned on talking to them one day when I was set free and no longer had to have a shadow following my every move, like a prison guard in jail.

I checked my blisters to see how they were doing. They hadn't popped yet.

"You too?" I heard a familiar voice say.

It was Katya, who was also working very hard to clear the land. She showed me her hands, which were just as bad as mine.

"Yeah, there are going to be a lot of visits to the nurse's office," she said, giggling.

I liked Katya. She was more mature and less wild and crazy than some; she didn't smoke cigarettes, but I didn't mind. I was glad we were talking and getting to know each other. It was like the long period of kids giving me the cold shoulder was over, and I was finally bonding with Katya, even though she was so much younger than me. She was the type of friend I needed, and little by little I was able to let some of my heavy fences down to make a friend, which meant I had to find a way to trust her.

Katya and I ended up becoming good friends, sharing our life stories, talking about the boys we thought were cute, and how easy or hard the homework was. We helped each other with whatever we could, and always had each other's back—until one day out of the blue I learned she was getting adopted by an American family. She was amazed. Come to find out, she had a baby brother who'd been adopted; he remembered his sister, so his American family came back to adopt her, along with another sister who was older, and lived in another orphanage.

I will never forget how she changed after learning this news. She went from being nice to being a complete snob—like she was too good for me, or anyone else. She stayed at the orphanage for another week or so, until she was gone forever, on her way to America. Our friendship didn't last after she found out she was getting adopted. All the kids were at her feet, kissing up to her in hopes she would give them something.

I remember she got an entire wardrobe of brand-new clothes from America, and she had snacks and fruits and candy, too. The kids couldn't help themselves; they made her their queen for a week. I couldn't believe it; it was such a disgusting thing to see. I mean, didn't she know they were all just pretending to like her? Maybe she didn't care, and I guess I couldn't blame her; after all, she'd just found out she would be living happily ever after in America.

The Americans were nice. I don't remember what they looked like, but I do remember that they purchased candy for our class, and fruit, like bananas. It was awesome! The entire adoption stirred up a lot of feelings. I remember some kids were wishing they were getting adopted.

I, on the other hand, didn't care. I had one thing on my mind—to reunite with my sister. That's as far as my mind went.

I remember it was extra quiet for a while as the kids dealt with losing one of their own so unexpectedly. I was feeling it, too, a different vibe now. Some girls were crying, missing Katya; others were happy that she was gone, as all the jealousy stopped and things got back to normal.

I remember seeing the empty bed and feeling a bit sad myself. Who knew any of us would feel this way?

I certainly hadn't expected it.

Chapter 48

Christmas Is Here!

Finally, Christmas was here! Winter had given us plenty of snow and some brisk, cold weather, just perfect for making a long ice strip to slide on.

Man, I will never forget how much it hurt when you fell down! I was bruised all over, and so were the other kids, trying to compete against the older boys who could slide the entire way without falling. A whole bunch of us kids gathered around, watching and cheering as the next kid gave it a try. Some kids had luck; others would fall halfway through, while some didn't even make it off the track. It was so entertaining! I will always remember those fun times where we were all just kids for a while, forgetting about our horrible pasts, and leaving our shields and armor behind for a bit.

Christmas was my favorite time of year; to me it represented how everyone should always feel, happy and excited to play, live, and enjoy life the best way we could with what we had.

The gym was turned into the gathering place for Christmas celebrations. I remember walking inside and seeing the Christmas tree. I almost fell over it—it was the most enormous, beautifully decorated tree I'd ever seen! Some of the kids were helping to put on the lights and ornaments. Several of the kids had Christmas costumes on, just like at the other orphanage, and the makeup that went along with the costumes looked professional. I was impressed. I didn't care to wear a costume this year, and was happy I wasn't required to wear one.

All the caregivers and employees were there, too, cheering and singing Christmas songs with the little ones as they walked around in a circle, holding hands. There were games, raffles with prizes, and lots of Christmas joy! Someone dressed up as Santa Claus and was giving out presents to the little kids, like toys and books. This was the only time of year I got to see so many smiles in one place!

After the celebration, we got to watch real dancers from a traditional dancing school perform for us. I remember thinking "I am going to steal that move!" They were no older than any of us, but looked like they'd danced longer than they had been alive. I had never seen anything like it before, professional dancing with costumes and all! It was so much fun to watch. I was so inspired, I even performed better at aerobics class after seeing this performance.

The older kids didn't get presents like we had at the other orphanage; instead, we got to go see a real play at the theater, and were given a small bag of individually wrapped candies of all sorts, from caramel and chocolate to fruit flavors. In fact, for the entire month of December, we went to see plays in different theaters and were handed bags of candy, over and over. It was awesome! I remember no one would eat their dinner during this time; so much food was wasted because the kids were stuffed with candy. Just like at the other orphanage, we all traded our candy for the flavors we liked best, with those who were willing to trade. I was among the group of kids who ate their candy right away and then had to watch other, more squirrelly kids who saved theirs for later. Total torture! So many of us were mad, saying things like "Hurry up and eat it already! Christmas is over!" I was amazed that some kids were capable of making their candy last so long.

That winter we were also given a whole bunch of clothes that people from church had donated. We were all so excited to see what was in the bags that we might like, and better yet, that might fit us! I will never forget the shoes I got, that had heels. They were not like any other pair I'd had; these were brand-new, pretty much, and much more stylish. One of the other girls really wanted them, so she took the shoes and tried to squeeze her foot into one, but it wasn't budging, so Mrs. Alexeevna told her to pass them to me to try. Oh, the look on her face! I thought she was going to jump me right there.

I took them from her and put them on. They fit like a glove, which only made the girl angrier. It was impossible to stay on anyone's good side around here; what was I supposed to do—not take the nice shoes I adored? Things like this really tended to put a wedge between kids, who often had to watch other kids wearing something they wished they had. It was terrible, but that's just how it was; if it fit, it was yours, and if it didn't, you had to pass it along.

I loved my new shoes. They were the best pair I had ever owned!

Chapter 49

Summer Camp, Here We Come!

After the last day of school, everyone was getting ready to go to camp for the entire summer. I was just as excited as the rest of the kids, running around, showing friends what clothes we were bringing to impress the boys. I was most excited to see the blue sea again. It was my favorite part of camp; I wouldn't get out for hours! I was also looking forward to seeing new faces and meeting new friends who didn't know me or my bed-wetting problem.

It was like the moment I had come to live at this orphanage, my bed-wetting issues had returned to haunt me again. It was so hard to be older and still wetting the bed like a two-year-old. I was thirteen now, officially a teenager, so this didn't look good on me at all. I so wished it would just go away. Luckily, during summers at camp, I barely had any accidents—which was a good thing, as I had no idea how often the sheets would be changed there. At least it was warm out now, which helped; my issue was at its worst during the winter months.

A couple of days later we were all loaded up and riding to the camp on big buses. This year we were going to a different camp, still by the water. As usual all of us kids were crazy with adrenaline, excited to see the camp and all the kids from other orphanages. It was one way kids with siblings could visit with their brothers or sisters, as most of the orphanages were going to be participating. Unfortunately, the kids from my sister's orphanage weren't coming, but I didn't care; I only had one more year to wait until Alyona joined me at my orphanage.

When we got to the camp everyone got off the bus and lined up in pairs in their groups, with their caregivers. We walked to the two-story buildings where our orphanage was going to stay and ran inside, claiming our bedrooms with the friends we wanted to stay with for the summer. I ended up on the first floor with some of my classmates, all of whom were decent outside of class, so I was more than glad we were all roommates for the summer!

There were four beds in the room, with access through glass doors to a nice porch. I remember thinking that if I ever wanted to sneak out, this was going to be very easy.

I picked a bed by the wall near the entrance, as it felt cozier there, far away from the windows. (After the incident back at the other orphanage, I could never sleep next to a window again.) Everyone was unpacking and talking about what it was going to be like here. I agreed with the others: This was going to be a kick-ass summer! We had much more freedom to roam around and hang out after breakfast, which was a feast; actually, every meal was amazing. I couldn't believe it! I was stuffed and satisfied every day. The sea was just a short walk away, so close that those on the second floor could see it. Just like last time, the water was crystal clear, and as blue as ever. I remember we all screamed bloody murder as we ran into the water like crazy people, so excited to be here and swim in this beautiful sea the entire summer long! It was like going from hell to heaven; everything changed completely. We were now in an environment where there was no school, and our job was to have fun, and enjoy every last bit of what the camp had to offer.

I would wander along the beach with some friends, looking for empty beer bottles to turn in for some change. There was a city nearby where you could redeem bottles for a little money. The more bottles we found, the more money we made, so it was like a race, really. All the kids were doing the same thing, trying to eat as fast as they could to get a head start. Amber bottles were worth more than clear bottles, and the same applied to nice, dark green beer bottles. Those were the ones we really watched out for; after all, who wouldn't want to make the most money possible!

I will never forget how much fun it was to compete with the other kids, racing to the same bottle. The one who grabbed it first got to claim it.

This caused a lot of arguments.

"I saw it first!" a kid would yell. "No, I saw it first!" another would say, trying to pull the bottle from the other kid's hands.

I remember some of the kids would get so mad, as they couldn't race to the bottles fast enough. One time a girl from my orphanage fought for a bottle she had seen first, but didn't get to first. It would get wild sometimes, though in the end, everyone got enough bottles to earn a little cash, and we would go on our merry way, laughing ourselves silly. There were normal folks there, too, enjoying their summer, and we knew they must have thought we were crazy, fighting over simple beer bottles.

I turned in plenty of those bottles that summer, using the money I earned for some cigarettes.

I was back to smoking regularly now. A whole bunch of us smokers would hide somewhere and huddle together, passing along the match to light our cigarettes. Some kids had fancy cigarettes, like Pall Mall or Parliament, while others had cheaper kinds, without filters. Those were the ones I got; I was able to purchase an entire pack instead of just a few. I didn't mind the non-filter, as Vanya had taught me how to smoke them years ago. I loved feeling the buzz; it was really great, especially after eating.

After the sun went down and it was getting dark, all the girls got ready for the nightly dance. Great music that we were all into was blaring. It was awesome! All of us girls would get ready together, putting on our short skirts and our mini tank tops that showed our bellies. I didn't have any makeup, but the girls who did were busy making themselves up to look like Barbies.

I always wore something that was comfortable to dance in, as all night long I danced like it was my job! I loved dancing, and by now I was pretty good at it. The kids considered me one of the best dancers here, aside from an older blonde girl, and a boy who was also an incredible dancer. I found him intriguing, as he was black, with a perfect white smile and big brown eyes. He was the second black person I had ever seen, aside from the nice man who had told me to never stop dancing all those years ago. Except of course this boy was our age, young and handsome.

All of the girls were drooling over this boy, and he sure knew it. I remember one time he came up to me and grabbed my hips and my hand to slow-dance with me. I was shocked, and totally off my guard, but I did it; I danced in his slow style, swaying with a lot of moves as we danced, making many girls unhappy. They couldn't help but glare as we kept dancing. I remember feeling like I was special for a moment, like him dancing with me helped me gain something within myself, something called confidence. Not that it stuck for long, but in those minutes I was on top of the world, and that felt good for a change.

I ended up "dating" him for about two days, until he decided to moon all the girls. I was, like, Yeah, it's over, and he was on to the next girl in line. I realized he was a total player, and I didn't want to be with someone like that. It didn't make me feel good, or special, like I did when we danced, which was the whole point. I think we held hands a couple of times, but that was it.

During those couple of days, though, I changed. I was suddenly more confident in myself, and less afraid to talk to boys I liked. It was like suddenly, I didn't feel so ugly, or unworthy. Instead I felt like I was pretty, and that I deserved someone who would treat me right. Someone I could trust, believing that he wouldn't let me down like this boy did. I didn't spend much time dwelling on it; the summer was plenty young, and I had a lot of time to meet other boys, or make some good friends.

While at camp that summer, I saw several girls making out with guys, and heard all about how some of them were sleeping together and having sex. They were no older than me. I couldn't believe it. I remember thinking, *Is this normal?* I felt like what they were doing was wrong—not that I said anything to them. I just made sure to be around kids who were not into that sort of thing. The "easy" girls always had boys with them who only cared about one thing. I realized that many girls planned to lose their virginity this summer.

Just like at last year's camp, a talent show was held where each orphanage got to showcase their most talented campers. I remember the older blonde girl who was really good at dancing performed a piece that was fantastic! I ended up learning a lot of cool moves from watching her. Other kids recited long poems, and some sang with beautiful voices. It was a great time; at the end everyone clapped to determine who had won, and the winner was announced by a man dressed up in a suit. He had introduced all of the contestants throughout the night. Everyone went nuts, clapping and whistling and yelling congrats to the girl who won—the dancer with the long blonde hair. I was happy she won, as she was my favorite.

Everything was going great until a rumor started to spread that there was a strange creepy guy living in one of the abandoned buildings right next to ours. I remember everyone was pretty freaked out, including me. We were all afraid that he was up to no good.

I ended up seeing him once at the square where our dances were held. I'd gone early that night so I could smoke real quick behind the building. Suddenly I noticed this guy walking past me, holding something in his hand. I got this creepy feeling inside, so I watched to make sure he'd really left, and wasn't going to sneak up on me or something. Luckily a couple of boys were coming my way, and they were also watching this guy.

I got my matches out of my shoe and lit a cigarette.

"What's with that guy?" one of the boys asked.

"I don't know," I said, keeping an eye out to make sure he wasn't coming back.

"I think he had a knife in his hand," the other boy said.

"I know—I thought so, too," I said. "He walked right past me." I was freaked out; I could have been his victim.

We all stood there, smoking our cigarettes, wondering if that was the guy everyone had been talking about. We saw him again that night, walking back and forth some distance away, possibly with a knife in his hands.

Every night after that, we made sure all the doors were locked so the creepy guy couldn't get inside. Everyone was on high alert, afraid to get kidnapped or killed.

Recently there had been an incident in one of the buildings where he had climbed up the metal frame and onto one of the balconies. One of the girls had decided to sleep there that night; it was very hot out, and the balcony was much cooler, as there was a natural breeze. We didn't have anything inside to keep us cool, like a fan. From what I heard, she woke up to the guy standing over her with a knife. Luckily, the girl wasn't hurt in any way, as she screamed loud enough to scare him off. I don't think he had expected her to wake up. What if she hadn't?

I couldn't get the ugly thought out of my mind, and neither could the other girls.

No one saw him again after that incident. For the rest of the summer everyone was ordered to walk in pairs for safety, and no one was allowed to go in or near the empty building where everyone thought the guy was hiding. I was glad we were leaving within the week. Some firefighters inspected the empty building and didn't find anyone, although they did say it looked like someone had lived there at some point, as they found food wrappers and items that belonged to some of the campers, like girl's underwear, bras, and some pornographic pictures.

I heard all of this by listening through the wall to some of the caregivers who were discussing all of this with each other, just as freaked out as we were. Some of these caregivers had kids and grandkids of their own, and they couldn't shake the feeling either that this could happen to one of their own loved ones. I was so glad Alyona was not here, and that she was safely away from all this craziness.

Slowly, I snuck away from the wall without them hearing me listening in. I made my way to the hidden smoking area to release some of my stress. It dawned on me that in reality, there was no such thing as a safe place; anything was possible, regardless of how safe we might feel.

I lit up one of my unfiltered cigarettes and took a nice, long, drag. This incident had brought back some memories I had forgotten all about until now, and smoking felt pretty damn good right now.

Chapter 50

Music School

The time had come, and everyone was back to school once more. It took us a couple of weeks to snap ourselves out of vacation mode. Part of us was still back at the camp, swimming in the clear, crystal-blue water, enjoying the perfect weather and a nice breeze.

Now it was time to think, time to make the bed perfectly, time to get back to chores and crappy food. I remember dreaming about the feasts we'd had at the camp, wishing I'd eaten all of the good food I was too full to finish back at camp.

I was doing very well in school, and because of this, Mrs. Alexeevna picked me, along with another girl and a boy, to go to a music school. At first, I didn't want to do it; I wasn't even asked, just told that I had an opportunity, and I shouldn't complain. None of us wanted to go, but we had no choice but to give it a try. I was pretty impressed that we were allowed to go to the music school by ourselves after the first couple of times. We would take the trolley and then walk a little way to get there. The music school was a place I'd walked by many times back in the day; in fact, this was the part of the city where I'd worked the most. It was such a strange experience; I couldn't believe I was now a student at a music school rather than begging for money on the streets.

We went directly to the second floor where our music teacher was waiting for us. He was an old man with big ears who looked like he was mad all the time, even though he wasn't; he was just serious, and very much into his music. All of us were going to learn how to play the accordion. When he played for us for the first time, it sounded great; I was dumbfounded. How could he play both sides at the same time, and make real music? He played us the songs we were going to learn and later perform for the judges as our final exam, to see if we could move to the next level of difficulty.

Truthfully none of us wanted to learn, but we did, starting with learning to play each note on the accordion, and then slowly picking up the tune. Somehow we got an accordion in the orphanage to make sure we practiced, which was pretty sad. I remember while all the kids were playing and having fun, I had to sit there and practice playing notes over and over. We all took turns practicing, slowly getting better at it.

I even started messing around to see if I could really have some fun and play the song I was obsessed with after watching *Titanic* for the first time. Everyone was sobbing at the end of this movie, including the boys. We were all heartbroken when the *Titanic* sank. I remember some kids came up and listened to my version of the song, which sounded just like the movie soundtrack. From then on, I had more fun when I practiced, with the kids trying to guess what song I was playing.

All of us did a great job passing our midterms to move up a level. I was so glad I passed! I'll never forget the fear and pressure I felt. I didn't want to fail! We would stand around, waiting for our turn, hearing someone inside either whizzing through, no problem, or stopping and restarting, because they were so nervous. My heart was racing, and I felt like I was going to throw up. My mouth was dry and I was sweating.

"Apostol Ludmila Urievna," a lady called out.

It was my turn, and I felt sure I was going to fail.

I went into the room, sat down, and did everything I was supposed to do. I made sure my legs were properly spaced, and my elbow properly held up. I placed my fingers on the appropriate starting keys and looked at the three women and one man sitting across from me, ready to listen.

"Are you ready?" one of them asked.

"Yes," I answered, looking down at the keys.

I started to play the polka, and I didn't mess up; I couldn't believe it! After I was done playing, I bowed and walked out quietly, closing the door behind me, still in total disbelief that it was all over. Just like that, I was in the clear.

I did it! I exclaimed in my head. I had passed my first real exam!

This was the most exhilarating moment of my life! Especially because there were normal kids here, too, taking their exams and freaking out just as much as we were. I felt kind of normal for a moment there, like I was capable of normal-people things, even though I was not living a normal life.

I've done the unthinkable! I thought. I had had no idea I was capable of playing an instrument like normal folk, but here I was, with normal kids who went to normal school, passing, while some of them failed. I wondered how I'd gotten so lucky, forgetting for a moment that I'd practiced my ass off.

The boy who'd started with us didn't last, giving up sometime in the second semester. It was just the two of us now, myself and Tanya.

It was interesting to watch how everything changed for the two of us. It was like the caregivers now thought of us as champions, giving us extra food if some of the kids from normal households were not around. (Many of these students were picked up early by their parents, before dinner.)

It was difficult for most of us orphan kids to be mixed in with kids who had parents, families, a house, and whatever they desired. These students came to our school because they lacked the academic skills, although sometimes you couldn't even tell the difference. They looked totally normal, aside from their better clothes, fancy shoes, and basically better everything compared to us orphans. I didn't care; if anything, it was nice to have some kids around who introduced something new to the environment of our closed-off, hand-me-down of a world here. It was cool to see the latest and greatest.

There was no better feeling inside than the moment I realized I was no longer a nobody around here. I was going to music school, doing well in all of my classes, and behaving accordingly. Because of this, I got to have nicer clothes, and warmer coats and boots, as we were representing not just ourselves, but our orphanage as well. I was so grateful to finally belong, to finally be trusted and given responsibility to watch over other kids who came to the orphanage and decided to run away, as I had done. Finally, I was no longer fresh meat; I was treated as one of their own.

Life was good. I was looking forward to Christmas again, as this year we were going to go to Kiev to attend the biggest Christmas event of the year, where celebrities were scheduled to perform. I don't know how our orphanage staff had managed to get us invitations. None of us could believe it! It was all we could talk about; we were so excited to go somewhere none of us would have gotten a chance to go otherwise. What a perfect Christmas surprise; this was going to be epic!

I was beside myself. Never in my life would I have imagined I would be experiencing such events as an orphan.

Chapter 51

Hospitalized

Everything was going according to plan. I was even going out with a boy from seventh grade. Andrei was about a year older than me, and always smiled at me when he walked by. I smiled back, not thinking much of it, and shortly afterward, he asked me to be his girlfriend. I accepted.

I remember I was so excited; I couldn't believe it! I never thought this day would come. Our relationship was nothing more than talking, and once in a while I kissed him on the cheek, letting him know I was not ready for anything more serious, which I knew he would want at some point. I told myself I would think about it once we got there.

It was the beginning of December, and everyone was relieved to be done raking leaves and picking up garbage. Now it was time to get in the mood for the holidays, as we all knew what was coming! It was going to be perfect—plenty of candy for the train ride to Kiev. Like the previous year, the gym was decorated with Christmas decorations, including a giant Christmas tree, all lit up and sparkling.

The first holiday celebration was finally at hand, and all the kids gathered in the gym once more to watch the younger kids putting on a program. My favorite part was imagining Alyona in the crowd of little kids at her orphanage, dancing with Santa Claus and Mrs. Claus and other fictional characters.

I couldn't wait till September when I would get to see her next. The church lady had finally come through, taking me to see her before we'd left for camp for the summer. I almost didn't recognize her; she looked so much bigger and taller. She was growing up so fast. I wondered what her Christmases were like, and if she received gifts and toys. I wondered how she was doing, how well she was treated; from what I'd heard since my last visit, she was doing well, but I still felt like she would do better being here with me! It was all I wanted—my one true wish.

After the Christmas party, it was time for the rest of our holiday festivities, when we got to go and watch a play in the city and were given candy. Like always, all the kids stuffed themselves with candy and no one showed up to eat dinner, making all of the caregivers angry with us. There was nothing they could do but watch us eat the worst possible thing for us.

I realized I wasn't really eating any of my candy. I felt dizzy and weak, and very cold. I went to the nurse to tell her I wasn't feeling well, so she told me to stay in bed and cover myself with lots of blankets. She gave me some vitamins that were orange and tasted good when I crunched them down. I felt worse and worse by the day, but I pretended I wasn't as sick as I felt because I really wanted to make the Kiev trip.

My friends were kind to me, bringing up my dinner, which I told them to eat instead, as I wasn't hungry. Truth be told, I could barely stand the headache that made my forehead throb with pain. My eyes hurt from all the lights, and I was shaking, burning up with fever. One of my friends was so scared she went and told a caregiver I was really sick.

Luckily it was Ms. Petrovna who came up, the red-haired caregiver I really liked. I had to ask her to help me to the bathroom as I couldn't walk by myself; I was shaking so hard from the chills, like I was going to burst.

"Okay, I'm calling the hospital," Ms. Petrovna said. She touched my forehead and explained to me that I had an extremely high fever and had to go to the hospital immediately.

At this point I didn't care what happened to me; I was in so much pain, I was just ready to be done with it. I'd never felt anything like this before. Not even when my kidneys would seize back in the day; that was painful, sure, but this was constant agony!

About half an hour later, I saw a man and a woman walk into the bedroom.

"Let's take your temperature first," said the woman, dressed in white. They both wore gloves and had face masks covering their mouths. They tried to take my temperature, but my fever was so bad, it was beyond the numbers on the thermometer.

"She needs to go to the hospital immediately!" the man said, a worried look on his face

I could tell they were panicking.

"Why did you wait so long to call us? She could die!" the woman dressed in white said. She grabbed one side of the sheet while the man grabbed the other, and they carried me out to the ambulance parked right outside.

I don't remember much after that. I was so sick I passed out. Later, when I woke up in the hospital bed, I saw a nurse walk into the room.

"I'm glad you made it," she said, smiling as she checked my forehead to see if I still had a fever. She gave me a shot in my butt cheek and told me what was going on.

"You have kidney disease. Did you used to sleep or sit on cement a lot?"

I nodded, wondering how she knew that.

"Your kidneys need to stay protected, so no more sitting on any cold surfaces, okay?!" she said. She changed my bathroom bucket in a small closet-like area; there was no real toilets here, which I thought was strange.

"When will I be discharged?" I asked, trying my best to speak up. I was still pretty weak, but I wanted to know if I would make it to Kiev.

"You just get better first, okay? Then we'll talk about that," she said.

I remember I would cheat and bring my temperature down by shaking the thermometer, hoping to get out sooner. I hated being here alone, with crappy food—worse than at the orphanage—and there was nothing to do but lie in bed all day; no books, no music, no visitors, other than the nurse coming to stick a needle in me. I couldn't wait to get out of there.

I will never forget the day I was finally discharged, just a couple of days before the trip to Kiev. I was ordered to take all of the medicine I'd been given, and to wear a wool scarf around my waist to keep my kidneys warm and happy.

I was so glad to be leaving. I hated hospitals. They just gave me a bad feeling; nothing good ever happened there. It was literally like hell. There was nothing to do but think, so I did a lot of that, going back to a painful memory lane. I missed my mom so much. I missed Alyona, too, and imagined what our reunion would look like, as it was fast approaching. I couldn't wait to hug the crap out of Alyona, and tell her how much I'd missed my little sister. After all this time, we would finally reunite in the first week of September, which was only nine months away now, not an entire two years.

One thing at a time, Ludmila, I thought, as I patiently waited for one of the caregivers to come and get me. It wasn't always who we would expect, that much I knew from what other kids who had been hospitalized in the past had told me. Like them, I did a lot of window-watching every day, just like the old days, except I was looking out for a familiar face that would indicate I was really going to get the hell out of Dodge, finally escape this shit show of a place.

I really felt worse than a dog when it came to how we were treated:

no toilet, no real food, not even a hot meal. All I got was some nasty watery porridge that was tasteless. I think I lost about ten pounds while I was in the hospital. Everyone who came back from one always looked like they needed some serious food in their tiny bodies. We were all already as skinny as can be, but after discharge we looked like dying little zombies. Right now I was looking like one myself, as I could barely walk from being dizzy. I hadn't really eaten in three weeks.

Finally the caregiver came to get me, and we went back to the orphanage. Some of my friends had gathered outside the main doors to greet me. As the taxi van pulled in and I got out, I heard all of the familiar voices I had missed so much.

Kristina was there to give me a hug. We had ended up becoming good friends at camp this past summer.

"I am glad you made it, Ludmila! This trip to Kiev wouldn't have been the same without you!" she said, smiling.

I could tell she really meant it. "Me too!" I said, smiling myself as we ran inside with the rest of the girls, who were also there for support.

"Thank you, Petya," I said, as one of my classmates helped me bring my belongings upstairs to the second floor. I was so happy to jump right back in where we had left off. And to top everything, I still had a shitload of candy left!

Of course I was even more excited to have my first cigarette after three weeks of hell.

I always felt much better and more relaxed when I smoked. Normally I did my best not to think too much about things, but when I did, it took a while to shake off the feelings that came up along the way. Dwelling on my mother and sister so much during my hospital stay had really brought me back to emotions I never wanted to feel, ever again. Nor did I want to go over all that had ever happened to me, which of course I had done, as I had had way too much time on my hands. It had taken a real toll on me, and all I knew to do was to smoke one or more cigarettes to bury it all back down, where it belonged.

I was glad when one of the boys shared his smoke with me.

"You excited about Kiev?" I asked the boy. He was about my age, but in a higher grade, same as my boyfriend Andrei, whom I hadn't seen yet since I'd been back.

"No, not really," he said passing me the cigarette. "You?"

"Yeah, I'm so excited!" I replied. "I got discharged early from the hospital so I could go," I added, exhaling and passing it back to him.

"The train ride should be fun," he said. "Here, you can have the rest," he said. "I gotta go." He handed the cigarette to me, a good portion of it left, and went on his way.

I have to say, having a boyfriend came with perks. The boys treated me well, and I was never picked on, as Andrei would kick their ass. He wasn't the tallest boy around, but he was nevertheless a badass, and reminded me of my long-ago friend Vanya, who could also take care of himself. I liked knowing that I was protected.

I stood by the tree I liked to climb on and rested against the trunk to finish my smoke, keeping an eye out for anyone I didn't want to see me smoking. It was good to be back, back where I was used to being.

* * *

Taking the train was as easy as one-two-three, as the station was just a short walk away from the orphanage. As usual, we all stood waiting in pairs, group by group; we looked like the military during formation, waiting to be told what to do. It felt surreal sometimes when I was in the city; who knew that all these years later I would find myself in the same shoes as those kids I had seen on the streets long ago, paired up and walking to the circus.

Our train pulled in and the doors swung open.

"Okay, everyone, let's go—one pair at a time, please," Mrs. Alexeevna said. The other caregivers did the same with their groups, spread across the platform. I remember there was a set of bunk beds on each side of the railcar, with a table in the middle by the window. I took the lower bunk, as I didn't want to have to climb up and down, and put my backpack under the bunk. I'd filled it with my belongings, like my medicine, some school books, and a bottle of water.

It took two days for us to get to Kiev by train. During the trip, most of us were glued to the windows, watching what we passed by. The first day, I remember seeing nothing other than a couple of houses here and there, tiny little homes with tiny windows glowing yellow from the distance. Everything looked the same for miles and miles, until the next day when we were finally getting closer to Kiev.

I took my medicine again, as it was time, and then replaced everything I'd taken out back into my backpack.

"I think we're here!" one of my roommates exclaimed.

It was Kristina; she was my age, and one of my really good friends. We were on the same level with everything, including boys. In school we were midway between second and third grade, so there were a lot of younger kids. Kristina and I were the oldest students in our class and over time, we had become good friends; we had a lot in common, including smoking.

"I'm so excited!" I said.

We screamed with joy as we looked out the window to see big tall buildings and lots of people walking everywhere. The streets were decorated with Christmas lights and banners, wishing everyone a happy holiday. There were shopping centers with big windows where a beautifully decorated Christmas tree was displayed.

As the train slowly came to a halt, we fell back into our bunks from the force of the train stopping.

"Let's go!" Tanya, my other good friend, exclaimed. She was younger, but very mature for her age.

"I can't believe we're here!" said Kristina, squealing with excitement.

We walked outside to gather in pairs once more, and then made our way to the bus that was taking us to the building where the Christmas event would take place later that evening. It was a short ride, and as we all walked off the bus, I remember still feeling amazed that this was happening, that I'd gotten to go on this trip, so soon after being in the hospital.

A couple of people took pictures of us kids as we got off the bus.

"Gather together, everyone," the photographer said as he held the camera and snapped our picture. I smiled without showing my teeth, happy our picture was being taken. *I wonder if we'll all get a copy*, I thought. I would have loved to have a picture of this amazing moment in my life.

We were told to wait inside a nice restaurant that had been reserved for us orphans, just feet away from where we had gotten off the bus. As we entered, I noticed that everything was set up fancy, with crisp white tablecloths and paper napkins. I remember wondering why there were two forks and two spoons for each person. We'd been told to behave and not touch anything other than our glasses, filled with water.

Awkward, I thought, as I sat there with the rest of the kids, wondering why we had been brought here if we couldn't touch anything.

"The seats are pretty comfy," Kristina said, laughing, pretending like she was a fancy rich person. It was hilarious. We were getting antsy, as nearly an entire hour had passed.

At last, we were on our way to take our seats and watch the show we had traveled so far to witness! The inside of the venue was huge; it felt like at least a million people were gathered there. I'd never seen so many people in one place!

I will never forget the feeling I had when the famous young singer came onstage to sing. I had seen her on many banners before, but couldn't believe I was seeing her with my own two eyes! There were several other famous pop stars as well, but I didn't know any of them; they were singing in Ukrainian, and I only knew Russian. We were from Crimea, where Russian was the main language. I'd never heard much Ukrainian before; it is somewhat similar, but not enough for me to understand every word.

At the end of the show I couldn't help but wonder how all of these pop stars got to be so famous, especially the seven-year-old girl who was so young and yet so talented. *What did it take?* I wondered as I ran to catch up with Kristina and chat about the show. It really was something!

Our train ride back felt longer than the trip to Kiev. I was pretty tired and burned out from all the excitement of the past three days. I lay down on my bunk and got my goodie bag out to have some candy, as I didn't want any of the dinner we were given on the train. It didn't look good at all. I did take my medicine, though, and checked to make sure the scarf hadn't shifted and my kidneys were still protected. I really didn't want to end up back in the hell hospital. I was told it was very important that I took the medicine without skipping any doses, as well as protected my fragile kidneys from the cold. As long as I followed through, I would be in the clear.

"You want to play some cards?" Kristina asked, taking out a deck to put on the table. It was going to be a long ride back, and we had plenty of time to burn.

"Yeah, let's do it," I said.

I took the deck to shuffle the cards and dealt them out into two stacks, as we were about to play a game of War. I shared some of my candy with Kristina, which made her happy.

"I wish they fed us better," Kristina said, as she inhaled the couple of pieces of candy I had given her.

"I know. I really thought we were going to eat some fancy meal at that restaurant where we waited. I know there was food there; I smelled it," I said, placing the card down, as it was my turn.

"I know, I did too—so weird," she said, putting a card down and taking them both, as mine was lower, a ten, and she had a king.

"Still it was pretty cool wasn't it?" I asked.

"Right? Who knew we orphans would ever experience such an event and actually see famous people!" Kristina said, looking outside to see what progress we had made traveling thus far. "Still just snow, and nothing else," she said as we started a new game.

Chapter 52

You Gotta Be Kidding Me

Spring was finally here, and my sister was due to arrive at my orphanage any day now, to be with me. Many excited faces were eagerly awaiting the arrival of brothers and sisters who would be joining them after some time. Some of the kids hadn't seen their younger siblings for more than five years! I considered myself lucky that I hadn't had to wait that long. I was so happy at the thought of finally reuniting with Alyona, I couldn't wait to hug her and kiss her and show her around. I was going to be the best sister I could be for her here.

The last day of arrivals came and many kids were reuniting with their siblings—except for me. Alyona never showed up. This made me nervous. *Why isn't she here?* I wondered.

I'd been told for sure that she was coming here; it was her time, as she had turned eight in December. Luckily one of my friends, Svetlana, had a younger sister at the same orphanage as Alyona, and she was going to visit her. I asked her to check on Alyona's whereabouts; maybe I was mistaken and she wasn't due to come to my orphanage yet. "I'll ask, but no promises," she said.

I prayed that Svetlana would learn something; I had to know what had happened. *Maybe she's sick*, I thought, looking at the photograph I'd been given by the people at church, taken of Alyona and me during church festivities. She looked so happy, and we both looked so young. I remember looking at my hair in the picture and thinking how happy I was to have long hair again. (It wasn't really that long, just coming down to my shoulders, but to me that was long compared to what I'd had before.)

"Hey, Ludmila, Svetlana is back from the orphanage," Kristina said, coming back into the room to grab me. I'd asked her to keep an eye out for Svetlana's return.

I ran downstairs, to the other side of the building where Svetlana lived as fast as I could, and ran up the three flights of stairs to speak with her. Moments later she showed up, and I could tell that whatever Svetlana had to tell me wasn't good.

"So—what happened?!" I asked.

My heart was pounding. I didn't know what to think—just hoping that whatever she had to tell me wouldn't break my heart. I really didn't know if I could handle that.

Somehow I just felt it; something deep down inside warned me that it might be worse than I expected. It turned out that what she had to say did paralyze me. It broke my heart—the one I'd worked so hard to glue back together—into millions of tiny pieces, once again.

"Ludmila, your sister was adopted last year," she said. "I am so sorry."

She didn't know what else to do, or say. I wouldn't have either, if I'd been her. This was any kid's nightmare, never to see their siblings again. I could tell she was having a tough time; her face said it all. She gave me an empathetic look and quietly left the room.

I stood there, not sure what to do first; scream—punch a wall—cry? All of the above?

I ran back to our room to talk to Ms. Petrovna, who was working that day. Maybe she knew something. By the time I got back I was crying uncontrollably and couldn't find the words to speak.

I couldn't believe it. I couldn't believe that no one had told me about this—no one! It was like they had just stolen my sister from me—the only family I had left on this Earth, and now she too was gone!

Ms. Petrovna was nowhere in sight, so I went to the shower room and sat down on the floor by the closet, where no one would see me cry. I felt so alone, all over again, and more so than ever before, because now I really *was* alone. I had no one left. I felt like all of my scars gushed open—all the shit I had worked so hard on keeping down all these years was catching up with me. I felt sick to my stomach. It felt like I was having a *Matrix* overload or something. I think the proper term is a severe panic attack.

In the days to come, I remember feeling like a black hole was slowly swallowing me, little by little every day. Every morning, I had less and less motivation to get out of bed.

Everyone noticed I wasn't my usual self, and worried because I wasn't eating much and didn't partake in activities with my friends like I used to. Even my music teacher asked me what had happened. Crying all over again, I told him what had happened to my little sister.

It felt like I had no purpose anymore; she had been my purpose my life. I'd been so patiently waiting for her to join me, always thinking I would see her again, only to find out I never would. I would never see Alyona again. To make things worse, we didn't get to go to summer camp that year; not enough donations had come in to allow us to go. No one was happy to hear the news, not even the staff.

That summer, a new woman started to work in our section. Her name was Nadia, and she looked after the fifth-grade kids in the next room. I remember she was the youngest of all the caregivers, with thick, healthy black hair and kind blue eyes. She had a set of perfect white teeth and some light makeup that made her eyes look even bluer. She was nice to everyone, and we all liked her right away.

I was still messed up, wondering how I was going to get myself out of the black hole that was sucking me in stronger every day, without my permission. It was like I just didn't have it in me to go on and fight anymore—like it didn't matter if I was alive or dead. I couldn't get out of this depression, just sinking deeper and deeper, wondering what my future held, or if I would even have a future. I was certain I was becoming someone else. I didn't recognize myself anymore, just the pain and the dark stormy clouds following my every thought and every feeling.

It was now early November, and most of the leaves had finally found their resting place down on the ground. Like every year, it was time to rake some serious leaves, although this time around I looked forward to my blisters. I felt like I needed to feel pain, as nothing else seemed to be working. I had started to cut myself a little to feel better, too; some days it helped, and others, not so much. My friends were very supportive; even the girls I normally fought with were being nice, hoping I would return and be more like myself again. It was like if one of us was off, all of us felt off, except that no one could do much about it, not even me.

While lying in bed one Saturday, admiring my blisters, Nadia walked into the bedroom and sat on my bed beside me. She was the only caregiver here that we could call by her first name. Somehow it mattered to us; somehow calling her by her first name brought us all closer to her, like little ducklings looking for that safe wing of their mama. She felt safe, light, easygoing and kind; even when she had to tell us to do something, she did so without yelling or making us feel less than.

As she sat on my bed, I sat up a little, to be more respectful, as I knew she was about to tell me something.

"Do you know Jesus?" she asked.

"Yes, I've read about him," I replied. It was like I had forgotten all about him ever since I arrived at this orphanage. I'd had to change and become a different version of myself in order to survive.

"Do you believe in Jesus?" she asked.

"What do you mean?" I asked, confused.

"Do you believe in his miracles?" Nadia asked.

"Oh, of course; he was an amazing man," I said.

"Well, you know that if you truly believe, all you need to do is pray one time, with faith, knowing your prayer will be answered, and it will be!" she said, smiling.

"That's amazing!" I said, doing something I hadn't done in a while—smile.

We ended up talking for a while that day. We talked about the extraordinary things that Jesus had done for those who truly believed—how they had received what they had asked for. It was like suddenly I had a way out; suddenly there was hope once more for Alyona and me. After all, it was my wish to witness a miracle. Suddenly, all of my feelings about God and Jesus flooded into my mind, and I felt like I weighed less. I didn't feel as paralyzed. I reminisced about the first time I had ever learned about Jesus, and how my last name was Apostol, like one of his twelve disciples.

How could I have forgotten? I thought as I lay there in bed, somehow different, and somehow filled with hope.

That night, I decided to pray one time to Jesus, and ask him to please, please help me to get adopted, so that I could find Alyona and reunite with her. At the time I thought that getting adopted by Americans would help me to find Alyona. I didn't see any other option left.

When the lights were out, I got ready to pray. I closed my eyes and held my hands together in the praying position I knew it was proper when talking to God. As I imagined Jesus just like I had seen in the books, I started to talk.

"Dear Jesus, I pray to you this one time only, as I believe in you and your miracles with all my heart. I ask you to please help me to get adopted by an American family, so that I may find Alyona."

At that point I felt tears running down my face, and for a split second, I once more felt what I hadn't in a long time—God's grace. I was really pouring my heart and soul into this one-time desperate prayer, so that God would know how much I meant every word. If anyone knew, God did; no one could lie to him. I had been through so much that was bad and shitty, I had no trouble believing in God's power, and in his incredible ability to perform miracles.

At this moment, I prayed just for that—my own miracle in life. Not just any miracle, but my own personal one, straight from God himself.

"Thank you, Jesus—thank you for answering my prayer. Amen."

I wiped the tears off my face and slowly drifted off to sleep, knowing that God had heard my every word.

It didn't even dawn on me that my own life would change, too. All I saw was Alyona's face, and her missing me, some thousands of miles away. I prayed that she was all right, and had a good family who really loved and cared for her. I looked forward to seeing her again, even if it took years. It was better than never seeing her again. I could wait; if anything, I had plenty of time on my hands.

I fell asleep that night, confident that my single desperate prayer had been heard, and that my day would come.

Chapter 53

Americans Coming to Town

The following year went by pretty fast. I continued to live my life, getting good grades, going to music school, and doing my best. I felt reawakened. I was happier now that I had Jesus in my heart once more.

I would pull out the book I'd gotten years ago at Bible camp and sing my favorite songs, teaching them to any of the kids who were interested. I remember one time we got a whole bunch of stuffed animals donated to us, so we ended up putting all of our new gifts in a circle and walking around it, singing grateful songs. We knew to thank Jesus for our gifts.

Everyone seemed to be doing better at the orphanage: The kids were kinder to one another, sharing their toys instead of fighting and arguing. The word of Jesus spread like wildfire, and kids from other sections started to gather around to hear Nadia tell stories about Jesus. Kids would walk away smiling, different somehow, just like I'd been changed when I first learned about Jesus years ago at my first orphanage—except this time, I was talking about it. I didn't hold anything inside this time.

We made thank-you cards for Nadia, telling her how much we loved her, and how happy we were that she worked here. She understood us and how we felt more than anyone else who worked here. It was like she could see into our souls. Everyone got along with her, and looked forward to the next time she was on duty.

Unfortunately, the staff at the orphanage wanted us to go to the Catholic church every Sunday. One of the Catholic caregivers took the younger kids in her care to service each week.

Sometime that spring, Nadia was fired for speaking the word of Jesus. It was like the other caregivers didn't want her to be talking to us about Jesus, I was very angry when she was let go. Many of us were upset, and we made a pact to always keep talking about Jesus and sing the songs we'd learned.

At Easter time, shortly after Nadia was fired, we were all forced to go to a Catholic church to attend a nighttime Easter vigil service. The church was lit only by the prayer candles everyone was holding. I didn't feel the usual spark I used to feel when I talked about Jesus. For some odd reason, I felt heavy and sad when I was inside a Catholic church. There was too much sadness, and no celebration at all. There were a lot of people crying, praying, and asking for forgiveness as the priest walked around, blessing everyone. He carried a fancy container with incense, and the smell of it made me sick to my stomach. It was attached to a chain so the priest could swing it around. I don't know why, but the priest scared me as much as the church did.

I fell asleep on the floor, unable to stay up all night, holding a candle. I was so glad when it was all over so I could go outside and get some fresh air. It was like I could breathe and be myself again. That was the last time I ever went to a Catholic church. I am pretty sure I smelled of the oils the priest was blessing us with for weeks, reminding me of that night. Honestly, I was grateful I didn't throw up inside holy ground, as the smell from the oils made me pretty nauseous.

* * *

About a month later, we all heard that some Americans were coming to our orphanage to adopt somebody. I remember the hair on the back of my neck stood up—like part of me knew they were coming for me, while the other part did its best to keep calm and not get crazy or carried away just yet.

Several other children were being groomed and prepared to show off to the Americans. I remember the kids were talking about it, wishing it would be them. It was many children's dream to have a home and a family, as most of us had no one left. Our parents were either in jail with no parental rights, or worse, dead. Some of the parents were still alive, but they were severe alcoholics and addicts who couldn't even care for themselves. I remember I didn't talk to anyone about the Americans; I kept my feelings to myself.

The next day, while at school, all the kids who were eligible for adoption, from the youngest to the oldest, were taken to the director's office, where the Americans were waiting. I remember my class was next after several other classes had gone. The administrator came to our room and called several kids' names, asking them to line up at the door. My name wasn't called, along with a couple other kids in the room who weren't orphans; they had parents, and just attended our school.

One by one the kids from my class came back, glowing, hoping they would be picked.

Everyone had returned to class and we were all busy, writing down what the teacher was dictating in our notebooks. It was a test day, to see how well we knew how to spell words with silent letters. Everything was quiet except for the sound of our pens on the paper.

Suddenly, the door cracked open, and the administrator was back. She called out my name and told me to come with her. All the kids stared as I closed my notebook and walked to the door.

On the way I tried to come up with some excuse to get out of going with her. I knew she must have been bringing me into the director's office to be shown to the Americans.

I was so scared.

Just the day before, I'd gotten busted with a couple of other kids for smoking cigarettes, by the damn director herself! It was the most horrible feeling when she walked behind the little enclosure where I was standing with a cigarette in my mouth, releasing smoke. Man, she was so mad!

She told us to meet her in her office, along with the caregivers who were supposed to be watching us. We were so severely scolded, I thought my ears would fall off. I couldn't believe the words coming out of her mouth! She was swearing, yelling and hitting her desk with her fist. She made us feel so small; we wished we'd never been born.

The worst part was that our punishment included cleaning out the enclosure where we smoked. Kids would shit there rather than make a trip to the bathroom. I remember it was so bad that we had to stand at the very edge of the walls so as not to step in it, and the smell was horrific. Cleaning that area was dreadful. I will never forget how all three of us who'd gotten busted were gagging from the smell as we shoveled it all up and then poured buckets of hot water over the area. I didn't even mind having to take a cold shower afterward—I just wanted to wash all of the nasty, disgusting smells off of me.

Now, just a day later, it was too soon to go back to see the director. *This is going to be bad*, I thought. I was certain the moment the director saw me, she would say bad things about me to the Americans and send me back to my classroom, ashamed.

I pulled my hair over my face so that when we got inside, no one could really see me. The administrator opened the door and told me to go inside. I hesitantly walked in with my hair in my face and my head down, getting ready for another scolding.

To my surprise, none of that happened. Instead, the director smiled when she saw me and started to say nice things about me, things she'd never said to me before. I just stood there, completely dumbfounded, but at the same time, very relieved.

"This is Ludmila. She is older, but she's one of our brightest kids," she said to the pretty young woman sitting next to the Americans.

"Take your hair off your face so we can see you," the director said, smiling at the Americans, playing her role perfectly. It was like everyone wanted to impress the Americans, even the director, which made me laugh a little inside.

I pulled my hair behind my ears and looked up, relieved I wasn't in trouble. I looked at the director and then at the American couple sitting next to the young woman. Her name was Vanessa, and she was translating what the director was saying. She kept talking about me, and how I went to music school and had excelled there, through my second year.

I stood there, smiling at the Americans, wondering where the director who'd scolded me almost to nothingness just twenty-four hours ago had gone.

About ten minutes later I was back in my classroom, changing my clothes to go to gym class, relieved that everything had gone okay. I remember I felt something inside I had never felt before, like something big was about to happen, but once again, I kept myself humble and went on my way to gym class.

The gym teacher told us to warm up and run some laps around the gym before we got into a game of volleyball, which I loved, and looked forward to playing. It had been quite some time since I'd played back at the Bible camp, three years ago. I looked forward to playing again!

As I ran, the feeling kept growing and growing. I wasn't sure what was happening, just that the feeling was very strong, nagging me, as if trying to tell me something. I will never forget it.

Just minutes later, before we'd finished our run, we heard the gym door open, and the administrator came inside.

"Apostol Ludmila Urievna, come with me, please," she announced.

I remember I kept running, thinking I was imagining it—but no, one of the boys from my class tapped me on the shoulder and said, "Ludmila, you're being called."

"Really?" I said, excited. For some reason, I felt certain that I was about to be asked by the Americans if I wanted to get adopted. I remember feeling so strange and excited, all at the same time.

"Run and get changed first," the administrator said.

I ran as fast as the wind, getting changed as fast as I could, and skipped my way back to the administrator, who was waiting for me in the lobby.

A few minutes later, we walked back into the director's office. The Americans were still there, with Vanessa, the translator.

"Ludmila, these nice Americans would like to adopt you," the director said happily. "Would you like to be adopted by them?"

I couldn't believe she'd just asked me that. My prayer had been answered. I'd been chosen to be adopted by the Americans! They wanted me! Holy crap!

That day I went out to eat with the American couple, to get to know them, and them, me. We communicated through Vanessa as I told them about my life—how I had never met my dad; how my mom had died; and that I had a younger sister who'd been adopted not long ago. I told them how I wished to find her, and to know that she was okay. More than that, I hoped to be reunited with her someday.

My future parents said they would try to find out where Alyona was—that they wanted to find her for me, just as much as I wanted it. They were very kind people, and seemed to care about my well-being right off the bat, which I thought was very nice. We went to the train station area where there was a McDonald's and went inside to eat.

I couldn't believe I was inside one of these restaurants! I'd walked by so many of them back in the day, begging for money as people came out, and today, here I was, going inside to eat with my future American parents! I got a burger and fries for dinner. I recall being so excited to try these foods that I had only gotten to smell outdoors, passing by. I had never had such food before. It wasn't a big surprise when I instantly fell in love with the French fries! I also got a shake and a small cherry pie, just like the one Alyona had gotten all those years ago when we stood outside another McDonald's on the other side of the city.

I remember Vanessa asked me if I was full, or if wanted more. "Whatever you like, we will get it for you," she said. I didn't argue, and asked for another order of fries!

Afterward we went back to the orphanage, and Vanessa told me that the Americans had had a great time, and looked forward to seeing me again tomorrow. I gave the Americans a hug and went back inside to the residence building, as school was almost over, and it was time for lunch.

I remember this as if it were yesterday—the feeling inside that made me drop to my knees. I ran to the shower room while no one was around and burst out crying and laughing, all at once. I was beside myself with happiness and joy. I was getting adopted—me! Out of all the kids, I was the last one to be shown. What were the odds?

I sat there, praying and crying as I thanked Jesus. It was exhilarating! I cannot describe how marvelous and incredible it felt to have my own miracle come true. This was the most divine feeling I had ever felt. I spent ten minutes there, alone, as several memories of my life flashed before me.

"Thank you, Jesus—thank you so much!" I said, still sobbing and taking it all in.

I heard kids' voices and got up to wipe my face and try to look presentable.

I walked out of the shower room and did my best not to act crazy happy, as I didn't want to hurt any of the other kids. Turns out, they'd already found out; the news spread like a virus. Soon everyone knew I was getting adopted, and, most importantly, that my prayer, my single desperate prayer, had been answered by Jesus.

I had a chance meeting with Nadia—the caregiver we had all loved and adored—one day at the park, just down the road from us. I don't remember how it was that I ran into her there, but there she was, walking in the park. I don't even remember how it happened that I was off the property at the time; I think maybe I was given more freedom after the director knew I was getting adopted. No one worried that I would run away.

I ran up to Nadia and we hugged each other.

"How are you, Ludmila?" she asked, happy to see me.

"I am really good!" I said, smiling. I couldn't wait to tell her all about my miracle, and how it was all thanks to her.

She started crying as I told her everything, especially the fact that she'd been a part of it right from the start, a year ago, when we'd sat together on my bed and she told me about true faith, and how those who truly believed would be heard.

Even as we talked about it, part of me still felt like it was unreal, like I was in a dream—the most amazing dream of my life! I was going to have a family! I was going to have a real chance at life, and reunite with Alyona!

I realized that Jesus had given me another chance at the life I had always wanted, where I had a mother and a father, a good stable home, my own room, and a true chance to really be somebody one day. Nothing promising was waiting for me here—only trouble and shame. Most everyone who graduates from an orphanage ends up either on drugs or involved with gangs or prostitution. There were no jobs for kids like us.

As I walked back to the orphanage after Nadia and I had said our good-byes, I thought about who I wanted to be when I was in America. I knew I couldn't continue being the way I'd been. I remember I told myself that once I was in America, I would change completely, giving up smoking, fighting, and swearing. I would become the most perfect daughter I could possibly be. I would have the kind of life I'd always wanted. All of my dreams would come true, and I would be a real person in the world!

Chapter 54

The Miracle

My new future parents came to visit with me every day, taking me out for lunch and dinner. It was awesome! I remember I ate an entire pizza all by myself; I couldn't believe I could do it, but I did. I got to have soda, too. Coca-Cola was my favorite, along with Fanta.

We were having a good time talking, with Vanessa translating what the Americans were saying as they showed me some pictures of my future home—it looked huge!—and the most adorable dog I had ever seen, small and white. *Wow, they must be rich!* I thought, noticing two cars in their driveway in one photo. I didn't know that it was normal in America to have more than one car, so each person had their own. I asked about this, and couldn't believe that one day I would also be able to drive!

I felt so cool, knowing that one day I could be like the lady I'd seen once, pulling up to a car wash located on the orphanage property. The well-dressed young woman had gotten out of the car, wearing a pair of sunglasses and a scarf over her head. I'd thought it was strange at the time, as this was the first woman driver I had ever seen.

As we sat in different restaurants, eating and talking, I got to learn more about my future relatives as the American couple showed me pictures of my soon-to-be grandparents, an aunt, an uncle, and a cousin, a girl around my age.

Every day felt more real than the day before, and soon enough, I didn't feel like I was dreaming anymore. I felt alive and excited to be heading toward my new life with my future parents. I didn't know anything about America or how to speak English, but I wasn't afraid; anything was better than staying here. I was so happy that no one could mess this up for me, or take it away. This was my fate, my destiny, my miracle.

A couple weeks later, I would visit the church near the orphanage; I had attended services here on occasion before, so I knew the congregation. I would go to a Sunday service to talk about the miracle that had happened in my life. One of the ladies in church would ask me questions about how I'd come to get adopted; she even took a picture of me holding the Bible I'd received, when the church had given them out for free. The church lady was crying as she listened to my story. Many hearts were touched that day. Another week later, I got a copy of the church newsletter article about me and my story, along with the picture she took of me. It was so amazing! So many people were inspired by my story. Those who didn't believe, believed, and those who were already believers only believed more strongly. It was like I became a celebrity of sorts, which made me feel very uncomfortable. I didn't like to be the center of attention; I liked to stay behind the curtain, not in front of it. I did my best to do my part, however, and to not act too shy.

The only ones who were unhappy about my adoption were most of the kids from the other sections. The news had spread that I was not the one the Americans were coming here to adopt; instead, it was one of the other girls they'd had in mind. According to the story, she had been told that she was the one who was going to be adopted by the Americans, who'd been shown her photo. From what I gathered, the Americans had changed their minds when they saw the girl all these years later and picked me instead. The photo they'd had of her was outdated, from when she was about eight; today, she was twelve, and the Americans now felt she was not the one they wanted.

I felt bad for that girl. I couldn't imagine how terrible she must have felt, and I remember I even apologized to her, not that it mattered; I was still hated. While I really didn't have anything to apologize for, I did it anyway. I didn't like knowing I was causing someone else pain.

Some kids were trying to play the same game with me as they had with Katya, who'd gotten adopted a while ago. I wasn't falling for it, keeping my distance from almost all of the kids who were trying to kiss up to me in hopes of getting some sort of reward.

Because I didn't want to stick out like a sore thumb, I told my future parents that I didn't want any new clothes, but that I'd much rather have a cassette player. They agreed, getting me a nice cassette player and two cassettes to listen to, that I'd chosen myself: Oksana Pochepa (a Russian pop singer known as Akula) and Ruki Vverh! (a Russian pop and techno band). I walked around everywhere with that cassette player, listening to music with a pair of headphones my future parents had also gotten for me, along with extra batteries. I would rewind the tape over and over again to repeat my favorite songs. It was quite nice to be able to mute the world outside, and all its noises. I was also given some cash, so I would get myself chocolate-covered peanuts and, of course, some cigarettes. (I planned to quit when I was with my future parents in America, but for now I was still here, so I allowed myself to smoke.)

Since I was fourteen, and technically too old to get adopted, I found out that I had to wait a couple of months before I would officially become the American couple's daughter. They told me that first they had to find the biological father I had never met, and ask him to give up all of his parental rights. Second, I had to go to court to get sworn in and agree to be adopted, since I was over the official adoption age, which was about twelve. And third, I had to wait till all the paperwork came through over the next couple of months before we could resume the rest of the adoption process. Because the Americans hadn't planned on staying that long, and their time for this visit was coming to an end, they had to fly back to America and then return some three months later, when the paperwork was complete.

I remember the Americans reassured me that they were not leaving me; they would be back to make me their daughter. I guess when the director found out I wasn't eligible, she told the Americans to choose another child instead of me, but they said no. They'd already promised to adopt me, and they didn't want another child. I was relieved to hear they weren't changing their minds and would be back in about three months to get me.

On the last day of their stay, the Americans took me out to eat, and even gave me a photograph to keep until their return. Vanessa also told me that the Americans would leave some money with her in case I needed anything while they were away. It was so unreal to be loved and cared for, even before we were officially a family. I was so happy they really liked me, and looked forward to the three months going by as fast as time could fly!

Meanwhile, I had to get a lot of tests done. My blood was drawn several times, and I received many shots to make sure I was healthy enough to travel to America when the time came. I was glad to find out my overall health was good and that I wasn't ill anymore with anything contagious or serious. I knew the only way to know this was by drawing blood—my least-favorite part—but at the same time, it reminded me that the Americans *were* coming back for me.

I was glad I hadn't gotten any fancy clothes; blending in with everyone else was the right way to go, especially as I had two more months to get through. It was hard when the other kids said things like "The Americans aren't ever coming back for you," and "You don't deserve to be adopted!" The fact that I didn't turn into a bitch—acting like I had the world at my fingertips—and also, that I ignored all the kiss-ass kids, meant that I was hated even more. They wouldn't leave me alone about it the entire summer.

I couldn't wait to start my new life and get the hell out of here. I knew the Americans were coming back. I didn't believe anything the kids had to say. My destiny was sealed with the help of Jesus himself, and no one could mess with that!

Chapter 55

Final Weeks

While waiting for my future American parents to come back and get me, I decided to pay a visit to my aunt, whom I hadn't seen in years. I wanted to tell her my news, that I was being adopted by Americans.

I finished music class early one day, and had some time before I had to be back at the orphanage. I didn't know if my aunt still lived at her last address, but figured I'd take a chance. The real reason I wanted to visit was to ask her for my mom's photo, the one she'd had years ago. It was the only photo of my mother that existed, and I wanted to take it with me to America.

I took the trolley to get there, and got off twenty minutes later at the nearby stop. I walked up the street and through the small opening between the fence and someone else's house, finding myself next to the scratched brown door that still looked the same.

I stood there for a second and gathered myself. I wasn't sure if I could go inside this place. I didn't want to get lice, or catch something worse; I really didn't want to get any more shots or have to have my hair chopped off again. I figured I would just ask my aunt to come outside to talk.

I knocked on the door a couple of times, but no one answered. I knocked again, with no reply. She wasn't around. I found a stone

I could use as chalk and wrote a message on the door, asking her to come visit me at the orphanage, as I was getting adopted by an American family and wanted to get the photo of Mom. I left, hoping it wouldn't rain; I really needed her to get my message. That photo was the only thing I wanted to take with me to America.

Sometime the following week I was summoned to the lobby. I was told I had a visitor, so I went downstairs, where I saw my aunt standing there. She looked exactly the same, except most of her hair was now gray. Other than that, she looked exactly the same.

Since we weren't that close, we didn't hug; we just talked about my leaving soon for America. I remember being furious when she told me that she'd "lost" the photo of Mom. I wasn't sure if she was lying or telling the truth, but either way, it didn't matter. I wasn't getting the photo of my mom, which broke my heart. *How the hell could she lose it?* I wondered.

Then she had the balls to give me her home address so that I could send her money from America.

"You know, Ludmila, I am so poor; it would help so much if you would do this for your family." She smiled and tried to act all victimized, waiting for me to agree.

"Sure—of course I will do that for you," I said, also cracking a smile as I looked at her convincingly. *What a bitch*, I thought. She didn't give a crap about me; not once had she come to visit me or Alyona, and yet she expected me to give her money? I couldn't believe this woman; apparently the only reason she'd come here was to give me her address and tell me she'd lost Mom's photo, a total blow. It would take some time for me to get over this; I couldn't make peace with the fact that I didn't have a single photo of Mom.

As I made my way back upstairs I went to the bathroom and flushed the slip of paper down the toilet. I didn't want anything to do with her, ever again. I'd never really liked my aunt, but now I truly couldn't stand her. I wasn't eight anymore, and I knew better. Maybe if she'd given me Mom's photo, I would have considered it, but she didn't. It made me feel like she didn't care about Mom at all, to have lost the only photo of her. I heard the toilet gurgle and seconds later, the paper with her information was where it belonged.

* * *

Once June rolled around, we were once again gathering our belongings to go to summer camp. We were told it wasn't going to be the same as the last times we'd gone to camp. We hadn't gotten as much money from our sponsors, so we could only afford to go to this cheaper camp. If it hadn't been for the fact that the orphanage buildings were being renovated, we all could have stayed put, somewhere familiar. Not even the caregivers were looking forward to going to this camp; it wasn't going to be as exciting as the last two places we'd had the pleasure of experiencing (minus the creepy knife guy).

I packed all of my stuff and went outside to sit in the sun before the bus arrived. It was such a beautiful sunny day, with a perfect breeze cooling me off. I went behind the building and lit up half a cigarette I'd saved from my last smoke. It was going to be a long ride, so I figured I'd better get my smoke in now. I heard a loud engine noise; the bus was here.

I hurried up, taking big puffs one after another to finish my cigarette, and then ran to the front of the building to get on the bus. I wanted a window seat so I could keep to myself and look outside. Everyone loaded up, filling all eight buses, the caregivers doing a head count to make sure no one was missing, as usual.

I ended up taking a nice long nap, making the ride feel much shorter. So much for looking outside. I woke up to the kids screaming as we got closer. We were about to pull up next to the rest of the other buses already there, letting kids off. I noticed there weren't as many orphanages here as at the last camps, just a couple others in addition to our group.

I remember thinking how crappy this place was; it felt like an abandoned kindergarten, with little swings and tiny monkey bars. The building was square, with a courtyard in the middle. The rooms were just like at the orphanage—big, with several beds in each instead of smaller bedrooms—but the nice part was that we could open the windows. Even so, it was so damn hot, and we didn't have any way to really cool off. We tried to stay inside, but it was worse than being outside. We all wished we had the sea like we'd had at the other camps.

To make matters worse, because we had to keep the windows open, all of the mosquitoes flew inside. There were so many of them in the bathroom we couldn't see the ceiling. Every night I made sure I slept with the covers completely over me so as not to get bitten by the army of mosquitoes, waiting to strike. I'll never forget all that buzzing, as I thought "You're not getting me, you suckers!" By the morning many of the kids would be itching bad, bitten everywhere, including their faces. By the third week, kids were walking around with open wounds from scratching their bites raw. It was awful. I got bitten too, but not as badly as some of the other kids.

Not all of it was bad; we still got to have dances every night in the courtyard, and we had decent food. We got to go wander around a little and see what was nearby. All we found was more of the same desert-like terrain, with nothing but sand and a couple of newly built apartment complexes. I remember Kristina and I looking at each other, scratching our heads. Where the hell were we? There wasn't even a place to buy cigarettes or candy or gum. There was no one around here but us, in the middle of nowhere.

We still managed to have fun, as usual flirting with the boys and trying to impress them by wearing our best clothes and getting all dolled up. I didn't have a boyfriend anymore; after Andrei and I had shared an intimate moment, he'd gone off and told all of his buddies how my boobs felt nice.

It had happened while here at camp, when he had come up to visit me in the room while everyone else was either playing outside or still finishing lunch. He came in and sat next to me on my bed. It wasn't even a big deal—he just rested his head on my chest—but that's all it took before he went crazy, saying he'd "touched" my boob. Come on! What a loser. It was all he cared about after all. I was glad I'd broken it off after that.

Later that summer, I had my eyes on another boy from a different orphanage there at camp. He was not like any of the other boys here; he had confidence, and he was cool. He wore clothes I liked and was a total badass. I knew I didn't stand a chance with him, as he preferred prettier and more mature girls, and I didn't consider myself one of them. I didn't wear makeup, nor was I a member of the older class. I was still down with the younger crew.

But lo and behold, one day I heard that he wanted to go out with me. He'd been going out with one of the girls from my orphanage, but he ended up breaking it off with her and started to pursue me instead. Camp was getting much more exciting!

I remember seeing him around all the time. He was mature, and mostly kept to himself; he didn't act stupid like the other boys, and boy, was he hot! He had big muscles and was solid like a stallion, a perfect ten. He had brown hair and dark brown eyes that were kind and sweet. I had never expected to go out with him; I'd admired him from afar before we started dating. He had a mysterious vibe about him, and I liked his calm energy.

He gave me a gift the same day we started dating: a precious little baby mouse! It was snow white with red eyes and an adorable tiny tail. I was so excited to keep this little guy. Mostly I remember it because he was the first boy to ever give me a gift. I had gotten some valentines from several admirers, including Andrei, which had also made me happy, but not like this. This felt bigger, more special, like he really liked me.

I remember we sat together by the swings, talking. He told me he'd had his eye on me for a while, but had felt like I was out of his league. I remember thinking, *You're kidding me, right?* If anything, I was out of his, so I guess we were perfect for each other!

Too bad we weren't from the same orphanage, I thought.

Not that it mattered, as my time was running out each day. I would be going to America soon enough.

Chapter 56

Surprise—We're Here!

I still had a couple of weeks left at camp before I was going to be with my American parents—plenty of time to gather my thoughts and prepare for my departure. But to my surprise, as I was walking back inside the building one day, I saw Vanessa standing there, smiling at me.

"Surprise! We're here!" she said.

For some reason their arrival hit me like a brick.

There was a red car in the camp driveway, and my future American parents got out of it and walked toward me, smiling, happy to see me.

I was very happy to see them, too—but in two weeks. This came as a big shock to me, as I didn't really get a chance to say good-bye to anyone.

Everything happened so fast. First, I had to take a shower with some special shampoo, and then put on new clothes the Americans had brought me. Next, I was told to get all of the belongings I wanted to bring with me to America, except for the little white mouse. (I'd had to give it away shortly after I'd gotten it from my new boyfriend.) I took the few photos I had with me and threw away everything else: all the cards I'd collected, the newspaper article with my story in it, and whatever else I had. I felt like I didn't want to bring my entire past with me, just a couple of memories.

Everyone I knew had gathered outside to say good-bye—at least, those who were around. Some of my good friends had gone somewhere, to explore. I remember it hit me all of the sudden: the realization that I'd never see any of these kids again. They were like my family. We all cried as we said our good-byes. I hadn't expected it to be so painful, so difficult to say good-bye.

As the red car pulled away, I waved to all of my friends as they stood there, crying and waving back. I couldn't shake the feeling that what I'd just done was a mistake—like I wasn't ready . . . I needed more time.

As the car drove further away, I felt worse and worse—sick to my stomach, asking myself, "What did I do?" I hadn't realized that saying yes was the easy part; everything else was going to be much harder. I was now with complete strangers, going to another country, leaving everything I ever knew behind.

* * *

That very day we drove back to Simferopol, where my future parents were staying. They were renting an apartment from Vanessa's parents, who lived on the same floor of the apartment building.

When we got there, we went straight to Vanessa's parents' place first, as they were looking forward to meeting me. I liked Vanessa, and her parents were also very kind. The first thing Vanessa's mom did was ask me if I wanted to get my nails painted. Of course I said yes. I ended up picking the blue nail polish. It was my favorite color—the color of the sky that reminded me of perfect summer days. Later on, she fed me some borscht with sour cream and bread, which I hadn't had in years. It was very good! She was an excellent cook. She showed me around her home, and told me I was welcome to come over to visit if I got bored being in the apartment with my adoptive parents.

Not speaking any English made it painfully difficult to communicate. At this point I really wished I'd studied harder when the tutor (hired by the Americans) was teaching me English. I just remember not wanting to do it; I was done with school, and wanted to play outside and do my thing like the rest of the kids. Luckily we'd gone to camp, so I hadn't had to keep it up for too long. I was relieved, as I always seemed to disappoint the tutor by not doing the work.

Now I understood why she'd wanted me to learn as much as I could before my future parents came for me. I had no way to communicate with them, only able to say hello and good-bye in English. I also felt lonely, without anyone to talk to about how I was feeling. I had no idea I would get this depressed, and spent every night crying.

On the ride back from camp my American parents had told me they were also adopting another girl, who would be my future adoptive sister. I'd only been half listening at the time; doing my best to keep calm, hoping I wasn't about to throw up from all the anxiety and motion sickness I was feeling. I remember Vanessa translating, telling me that the Americans had wanted to adopt a younger girl, as well, and that they had found her in the orphanage in Kerch, the best orphanage around.

The day had come to go and pick up my new sister, whose name was Marina. It took a long time to get to Kerch, where we met another translator who would help us through Marina's adoption process. She was nice, and very helpful. We drove to the orphanage in the same red car after the driver had taken us to the court, to finalize the paperwork. The process was nice and easy; all the Americans had to do was sign some papers, and then we were off to pick up Marina.

I was looking forward to meeting my future adoptive sister. I was happy that I would have someone to speak with; it was becoming unbearable, not being able to communicate with my American parents. Plus, we both were orphans, which made me feel like I was not alone on this planet.

I thought about Alyona, and how I was so much closer to knowing where she was. I missed her so much, as usual. Knowing that I could make my new little sister feel less alone made me feel less alone too. I just hoped Alyona was not alone; I hoped she didn't have big problems communicating with her family, like I did, causing me to feel like crap.

It won't be long now, I thought, as we finally arrived at our destination. We all got out of the car, including the translator, who was still with us. We walked to the front entrance of the orphanage where a little girl stood with a caregiver, waiting for us.

She was the sweetest thing, with playful brown eyes and short blonde hair, still growing back after having it cut. She looked like a little boy, as I once did. She was so excited to see her new parents arrive! She ran right up to them and gave them both a big hug, smiling away. I could tell she was shy, but she did an amazing job of holding it in, welcoming her new parents with open arms.

"Ludmila, this is your sister, Marina," the translator said.

I looked at Marina and introduced myself.

"Hey Marina, I'm Ludmila." I said, smiling, letting her know I was happy to have another younger sister.

"Hi, she said shyly, smiling back at me.

Once we had Marina, we left the orphanage to go and meet some of the translator's family, who lived nearby on the Black Sea. She wanted us to come over on our last day in Kerch to celebrate the successful adoption of Marina. We met another young girl about Marina's age that day, and a couple of adults who were very happy to see us all. They had prepared some homemade food for us to eat during our visit.

Marina and the other girl went swimming in the Black Sea while I watched them having fun in the water. I didn't want to go in myself, as it was murky and unclean, with a black slimy bottom. I didn't like that at all. Not seeing the bottom freaked me out. I liked being able to see where I was stepping.

After we had finished visiting, we went to a hotel room where we stayed overnight, as we had some more paperwork to finish the next day. I remember I still had the taste of olive salad in my mouth; it was so damn delicious, I could have eaten it all day long!

In the morning we met our translator and walked to a building where our photos were taken for our passports, one last step before heading to America. Afterward, we grabbed a bite to eat at a nice restaurant nearby. The lunch was very tasty; as usual, I ate everything on my plate, and so did Marina. Neither of us could get enough food! We had a good time together eating lunch. My new American parents thanked the translator for helping them throughout, and handed her an envelope with what I guessed was cash.

We said our good-byes to the translator and drove back to Simferopol to take care of my paperwork next, as I still had to go to court to get officially sworn in and to testify that I wanted to be adopted.

Vanessa and her parents were eagerly awaiting our arrival, to meet Marina.

We had a blast in Simferopol the last couple of weeks. I was doing a bit better with my depression, crying less and feeling less heavy and sad. Marina got her nails painted, like me, and she was just as excited as I'd been. Neither of us had ever had our nails painted before.

We spent most of our time with Vanessa and her parents. We went out to eat together, and once got to go and visit a cave! We were given jackets and socks, as it was much cooler underground. We all went down in an elevator, and after a couple of minutes, we found ourselves underground, inside a beautiful cave. It took my breath away, truly; I had never known such a thing as caves even existed! This was certainly something worth seeing. It felt like I was inside a divine sanctuary, with gorgeous natural formations of ice and sand. It was amazing, like being inside a womb.

Marina and I also ended up getting our ears pierced. I was very scared initially, but I did it. Marina and I were both so excited! We felt just like other pretty girls, with nice clothes and pretty jewelry. Marina did well with her piercing, but my ears ended up getting infected; they developed blisters, and it hurt a lot.

Marina was so sweet to help me, blowing on my wounds while a fan was also blowing on the fastest setting, to make my ears feel less like they were on fire. So much for wearing earrings! I had to take mine out just a couple of days after I'd gotten them pierced. Definitely a bummer.

Finally, the court date had arrived. Marina and I wore our pretty court dresses our adoptive mom had bought for us in America. Everything went according to plan: We got to the court; I stood in front of the judge as my adoptive parents stood on the other side with Vanessa, who was translating everything the judge said; I answered all the questions with a "yes," and my new American parents did the same. The judge rapped his gavel against the wood, and pronounced that I was now the Americans' daughter; they were officially my parents! I had never felt better. I was so happy that we were finally at this step, and that I legally belonged to my new family!

Later on that night, we went out to celebrate being a family. We went to a nice outdoor restaurant, which was absolutely stunning. The waitresses wore traditional Ukrainian costumes, and the outdoor patios looked like old-fashioned homes with hat roofs. It was so cool to see! In all my years in the city I had never seen such a place before. The food was amazing, as everything was fresh, crisp, and perfectly seasoned. Marina and I wore our pretty dresses that matched our nails, making us feel so proper and girlie. We both did our best to eat politely by cutting the chicken breast, when we really wanted to just grab it with our hands and eat it like we were used to doing. We were both scared to use our knives to cut the chicken; luckily we didn't stab ourselves, or anyone else, and the chicken remained on the plate as well!

There was music, with a live band playing traditional folk songs, and some people were dancing. I remember every once in a while I had to pinch myself. This amazing life was mine, and I was living it, right here, right now!

We ended up taking several pictures together, as it was our last night in Ukraine. It was time to go to our new home in America. I couldn't believe how fast the time had gone, and that soon, very soon, I would be on a plane, heading to another country far away.

We all cried, of course, as we said our good-byes. We really loved Vanessa and her parents; they were the nicest people I had ever met, and we were going to miss them. We knew we'd never forget their kindness and generosity, nor their smiles and laughter that would fill the room.

Chapter 57

Good-bye

The next day, the driver with the red car dropped us off at the airport to get on a plane. I wasn't sure how I felt about this, as I'd never flown before. I could tell Marina was nervous, too.

Our new parents paid the driver after he'd helped us with our luggage. Everyone grabbed their belongings and we went inside the airport, where many people were walking around, while others lined up to get on their planes. I heard a voice over the loudspeaker announcing several flights that were departing soon as we waited in line to hand over our tickets and get on the plane to fly to our new home.

Marina and I sat together, with our new parents in the row behind us.

"Put your seat belts on," the flight attendant said. She showed us how to properly lock them in place, though mine wouldn't click right, so I had to tie the belt around my waist.

Moments later, I heard the engine start and the plane started moving, faster and faster, forcing me back in my seat. I heard the wheels leave the ground and looked outside the tiny oval window. The plane was getting higher and higher, till everything looked completely different, reminding me of the times I spent on the roof, watching everything from above.

This isn't so bad, I thought. I hadn't known what to expect, but this flying business was way easier than I'd imagined.

I thought about my life, and how I was now here, on this plane, on my way to true happiness and a real chance at life. This was it; we were on our way home.

I wondered who I would become one day, living in America. All I knew was that Mom would be so proud and happy for both of us. Alyona and I had ended up okay, safe from harm, and with a real chance to live our lives, like Mom had always wanted for us. I hoped she knew that no one could ever replace her, not even my adoptive parents, for whom I cared very much. Mom had a very special place in my heart, right beside Jesus, who had helped me to get here.

I thought about all the things I was leaving behind, all the labels I would never have to see as true anymore. I was not homeless. I was not alone. I was not an orphan without a future.

And the same was true for Alyona. She was out there somewhere, waiting for me to find her. *I am coming, Alyona—I am on my way!* I thought, looking at the rays of sunlight beaming through the big puffy clouds that surrounded the plane.

Never in my wildest dreams had I ever thought this would be my destiny—that everything that had ever happened to me would lead me to this exact moment in my life. It was like everything I had gone through—losing our home, Mom, Alyona—had led me here. Every choice, every decision, every prayer, every time I held on with faith . . . it had all led me right here.

I looked out the window again, to see my country one last time. It was really fading out of view now, and I needed that one last look, one last reminder of where I'd come from.

"Good-bye, Ukraine," I said. "I will never forget you."

I looked at Marina and we both smiled. We couldn't wait to get to our new home and start our new lives in America.

As I sat there, totally and humbly dumbfounded by my own life, a thought crossed my mind.

I will write a book about my incredible journey someday.

I wanted to let everyone out there know what I had endured, and how God himself had helped me to escape the ugly reality I had otherwise faced. I was finally on the other side of the fence—I had made it—and I looked forward to writing my life story.

I turned around and looked at my new parents and gave them a smile to let them know we were good. Marina had already put her headphones on to listen to the movie that was playing on the big screen. I did the same, making sure mine fit on right.

Darn—this is in English! I thought, adjusting my headphones as I smiled at the large TV screen.

Made in the USA
Middletown, DE
01 June 2019